PENGUIN BOOKS

THE BATTLE OF KURSK

Robin Cross is a distinguished military historian whose books include *VE Day: Victory in Europe 1945* (1985) and *We'll Meet Again* with Vera Lynn (1989), both of which were bestsellers. He is also the author of *The Bombers: Strategy and Tactics* (1986) and *The US Marine Corps* (1986). He was consultant editor on the *Guinness Encyclopedia of Warfare* and was a contributor to *The World at Arms* (Reader's Digest, 1989). For Telegraph Newspapers he was series editor and contributor on the *Telegraph Second World War* (1989) and the *Telegraph Battle of Britain* (1990). He was editorial consultant and contributor to the *Telegraph Gulf War* (1991).

D1039115

The Battle of Kursk

Operation Citadel 1943

ROBIN CROSS

PENGUIN BOOKS

PENGUIN BOOKS

Published by the Penguin Group
Penguin Books Ltd, 80 Strand, London WC2R 0RL, England
Penguin Putnam Inc., 375 Hudson Street, New York, New York 10014, USA
Penguin Books Australia Ltd, Ringwood, Victoria, Australia
Penguin Books Canada Ltd, 10 Alcorn Avenue, Toronto, Ontario, Canada M4V 3B2
Penguin Books India (P) Ltd, 11 Community Centre, Panchsheel Park, New Delhi — 110 017, India
Penguin Books (NZ) Ltd, Cnr Rosedale and Airborne Roads, Albany, Auckland, New Zealand
Penguin Books (South Africa) (Pty) Ltd, 24 Sturdee Avenue, Rosebank 2196, South Africa

Penguin Books Ltd, Registered Offices: 80 Strand, London WC2R 0RL, England

www.penguin.com

First published as *Citadel: The Battle of Kursk* by BCA
by arrangement with Michael O Mara Books 1993
Published under the present title as a Classic Penguin 2002

7

Copyright © 1993 by Robin Cross
All rights reserved

The moral right of the author has been asserted

Printed in England by Cox & Wyman Ltd, Reading, Berkshire

CONTENTS

FOREWORD

Asked which was the greatest battle of the Second World War, few in the West other than students of military history would nominate Kursk, which was fought on the Eastern Front in July 1943.

Some might give pride of place to the Stalingrad campaign, which lasted from August 1942 to February 1943 and reached a climax with the encirclement and destruction by Soviet forces of the German Sixth Army. Stalingrad was the Soviet Union's first clear-cut victory of the war, and it was marked by the ringing of the Kremlin's bells. Nevertheless, in spite of the fearful mauling it had received at Stalingrad, the German Army in the East recovered and, after some savage fighting, retook Kharkov on 15 March 1943. Thereafter the Eastern Front subsided into the long period of preparation which preceded the German summer offensive and the titanic confrontation in the Kursk salient.

The build-up to *Zitadelle*, the codename for the German attack at Kursk, lasted three months. The battle lasted only two weeks, but it unleashed armoured and aerial clashes of unprecedented scale and ferocity. For the first time on the Eastern Front, the Red Army did not give way at the first impact of Hitler's elite armoured formations. Rather, it was the Germans who gave way and were then driven back to the line of the River Dnieper.

Zitadelle was the last major German offensive to be launched in the East. If the psychological advantage began to pass to the Red Army after Stalingrad, it is clear that after Kursk the Soviet forces not only seized the initiative, never to let it go, but also established an inexorably growing material advantage which the German mobile forces could no longer offset with tactical verve. They never fully recovered from the battering they had received in the summer and early autumn of 1943.

Zitadelle's long and agonizing gestation – which stretched Hitler's and Stalin's nerves to the limit – has enabled me to attempt an analysis of the two warlords' differing methods of command and how they affected the outcome of the battle. The build-up and the battle itself have been placed in the context of the strategic problems facing Hitler and Stalin in the spring and early summer of 1943. For Hitler, these problems were to exert a baleful influence over the planning of the German summer offensive. During these months the Führer finally lost his grip on events. The remainder of the war for the Germans was to be a grim holding operation doomed to end in defeat.

Finally, it has been my aim to provide a picture not just of single battle but of the war on the Eastern Front at its most critical point, and how it was seen by senior commanders and ordinary soldiers on both sides. In the Second World War no theatre was more gruelling and destructive than the Eastern Front, and nowhere was the fighting more bitter. I hope that *Zitadelle* gives the reader some insight into the scale and savagery of the war in the East and a picture of the sweeping terrain over which it was fought.

In the preparation of this book I have received help from many people. I would like to thank the staff of the Dome Library at the Imperial War Museum, particularly Mr Terry Charman and Mr James Taylor for their assistance and informed advice. For fresh insights into the fighting at Prokhorovka on 12 July 1943, and the chart of Fourth Panzer Army's tank strength throughout *Zitadelle*, I am greatly indebted to Major Kent A. Larson, who has shared the results of his research with me. Thanks are also due to Mr James Lucas for permission to quote passages from his book *Das Reich: The Military Role of the 2nd SS Division* and to Mr J.J. Fedorowicz for permission to quote a passage from *Tiger: The History of a Legendary Weapon 1942–45.*

'How many people do you think even know where Kursk is? It's a matter of profound indifference to the world whether we hold Kursk or not. . . . Why do we want to attack in the East at all this year?' Hitler's reply was: 'You're quite right. Whenever I think of this attack my stomach turns over'. I answered: 'In that case your reaction to the problem is the current one. Leave it alone!' *Correct !?*

General Heinz Guderian in conversation with Adolf Hitler, 10 May 1943

CHAPTER 1

Crisis in the South

'The Russian is finished.' Adolf Hitler, July 1942

ON 19 JULY 1940, Adolf Hitler convened the Reichstag in the Kroll Opera House in Berlin to witness the creation of twelve field marshals. At the end of a long speech he told the puppet deputies: 'In this hour, I feel it to be my duty to appeal once more to reason and to common sense in Great Britain, as much as elsewhere. I consider myself in a position to make this appeal since I am not the vanquished begging favours, but the victor speaking out in the name of reason. I see no reason why this war should go on.'

But the war did go on, and in time Hitler acquired enemies vastly more powerful than the British. On 30 January 1943, in circumstances very different to those which surrounded the triumphal gesture of July 1940, Hitler created a single new field marshal, promoting Colonel-General Friedrich Paulus, commander of the German Sixth Army encircled on the Volga in the Soviet city of Stalingrad.

No German field marshal had ever surrendered. In effect, Hitler had pressed a suicide's pistol into Paulus's hand. The new field marshal did not pull the trigger. On 31 January a young Red Army tank lieutenant, Fyodor Mikhailovich Yelchenko, stepped into Paulus's headquarters in a ruined department store. Paulus stepped out into captivity. Fifteen generals surrendered at the same time. Two days later the last German troops holding out in the northern part of Stalingrad laid down their arms.

On 6 February the journalist Alexander Werth drove into Stalingrad. The temperature was 30°C below zero. In a corner of the ruined main square, which had changed hands several times during the savage street fighting of the previous September, Werth came upon a large mound of litter:

> . . . letters, maps and books, and snapshots of German children, and of German middle-aged women with smirking self-contented faces standing on what looked like a bridge over the Rhine, and a green Catholic prayer book called *Spiritual Armour for Soldiers* and a letter from a child called Rudi writing that 'now you have taken die grosse festung Sevastapol the war will soon be ended against die verfluchten Bolschewiken, die Erzfeinde Deutschlands'.

Later, after interviewing Lieutenant Yelchenko, Werth returned to the silent, shattered streets, littered with frozen corpses and the skeletons of horses, stripped for meat by starving German soldiers. In the yard of the gutted Red Army House he passed 'an enormous, horrible cesspool, fortunately frozen solid'. Then Werth saw a human figure crouching over another cesspool,

> hastily pulling up his pants, and then slinking away into the door of a basement. But, as he passed, I caught a glimpse of the wretched face – with its mixture of suffering and idiot-like incomprehension . . . The man was perhaps already dying. In that basement into which he had already slunk there were still 200 Germans – dying of hunger and frostbite. 'We haven't had time to deal with them yet,' one of the Russians said. 'They'll be taken away tomorrow, I suppose.'

At the far end of the yard, by another cesspool, lay the corpses of a dozen Germans, yellow, emaciated and wax-like, who had died in the basement. Werth could not face entering this fetid morgue: 'What was the good? What could we do for them?'

In the Stalingrad pocket the German Army in the East, the Ostheer, had lost twenty divisions and over 200,000 men. Of the 108,000 who marched into captivity, only 5000 survived the war. Six more divisions – two of them Luftwaffe – had been destroyed outside the encirclement. Germany's allies on the Stalingrad front, the Italians, Hungarians and Romanians, had lost four armies, 450,000 men and any desire they might originally have felt to play an active role in the Russian campaign.

The German losses at Stalingrad between 10 January and 2 February 1943 pale in comparison with Soviet losses in the summer of 1941 – nearly 500,000 in the Kiev encirclement alone – but they represented the worst defeat the German Army had suffered up to that time and delivered a heavy blow to morale at home. For three days German radio broadcast an uninterrupted programme of solemn music. It was decided not to release the letters sent by the survivors from Soviet prisoner-of-war camps. They were intercepted and destroyed. Only a handful slipped through the net to sow further doubts about ultimate victory in the minds of the German public.

On 3 February 1943 the Armed Forces Report issued from Hitler's headquarters by OKW (Oberkommando der Wehrmacht, the Armed Forces High Command) attempted an epic gloss on the disaster at Stalingrad. It began:

> The Battle for Stalingrad has ended. True to its oath to its last breath, Sixth Army, under the exemplary leadership of Field Marshal Paulus, has succumbed to the overwhelming strength of the enemy and to unfavourable circumstances. The enemy's two demands for capitulation were proudly rejected. The last battle was fought under a swastika flag from the highest ruin in Stalingrad.

The official communiqué did not reflect Hitler's true feelings. He had confidently expected his newly created Field Marshal either to commit suicide or to perish gloriously at the head of his troops. At his midday briefing on 1 February he railed:

> When you think that a woman has got sufficient pride, just because someone has made a few insulting remarks, to go and lock herself in and shoot herself right off, then I've no respect for a soldier who's afraid to do that but would rather be taken prisoner . . . I can't understand how a man like Paulus wouldn't

rather die. The heroism of so many tens of thousands of men, officers and generals is cancelled out by a man like this who hasn't the character when the moment comes to do what a weakling of a woman can do . . . He could have freed himself and ascended into eternity and national immortality, but he preferred to go to Moscow.

In Moscow Josef Stalin could strike a more expansive note. On 25 January 1943, issuing the first congratulatory order of the day in the Great Patriotic War, Stalin expressed his thanks to the commanders and troops on the Southern Front and urged them on with a new rallying cry: 'Onward to defeat the German occupationists and to drive them out of our country.' A month later, on 23 February, the heroes of Stalingrad received their rewards. The honour of Hero of the Soviet Union was bestowed on 112 officers and men; forty-eight generals received the Order of Suvorov or the Order of Kutuzov; 10,000 more decorations were handed out to men of all ranks; and 700,000 received the campaign medal 'for the Defence of Stalingrad'.

Contemplating the destruction of his Sixth Army, Hitler drew morbid satisfaction from his insistence that Stalingrad be held to the last man. Information supplied on 4 February by Colonel Reinhard Gehlen* estimated that 107 Soviet divisions and brigades, and thirteen tank regiments, had been tied down in the battle for Stalingrad. Had they been released a month earlier, when Hitler had received and rejected a Soviet offer of capitulation, the entire German southern wing would have caved in under the weight of the renewed Soviet offensive launched in mid-January 1943 along the front from Orel to Rostov.

Convinced that the Red Army had seized the strategic initiative, Stalin planned a series of staggered offensives which would unroll across the entire Eastern Front. In the south the task of driving the Germans from the Ukraine, the second most important political unit in the Soviet Union after the Russian

---

* Colonel (later General) Gehlen was the intelligence officer in command of the Russian section of the Foreign Armies, East department of the OKH (Oberkommando des Heeres, the German Army High Command). After the war Gehlen performed a similar function for American intelligence.

Federal Republic, was assigned to the Bryansk, Voronezh, South-Western and Southern Fronts.*

In Moscow confidence ran high, and with it the expectation that success would entomb seventy-five German divisions in the Ukraine. There was a precedent for Stalin's strategy, but not one which was wholly encouraging. In January 1942, as the Germans fell back from Moscow, Stalin had ignored the advice of his commanders and ordered an all-out offensive along the Eastern Front from Lake Ladoga to the Black Sea. But the Red Army was spread too thinly, and too debilitated by the fighting of December 1941, to maintain its initial momentum. The Germans regrouped, resistance stiffened, and in March 1942 the offensive slithered to a halt in the mudbath of the *rasputitsa*, the spring thaw.

This time the prospects looked more inviting. The Soviet advance from Stalingrad had thrown Army Group Don, commanded by Field Marshal Erich von Manstein, back on the city of Rostov, the 'gateway' of the southern front at the mouth of the River Don. To Manstein's south, Field Marshal Ewald von Kleist's Army Group A had been forced to withdraw from the Caucasus into the Taman peninsula, on the north coast of the Black Sea, separated from the Crimea by the Kerch Strait and from Manstein's front by 300 miles. To the north, heavy Soviet pressure on the Eighth Italian and Third Romanian Armies threatened to detach Manstein's left flank from contact with Army Group B.

From Rostov to Voronezh the German front was in disarray. On 15 January 1943 General Nikolai Vatutin's South-Western Front rolled over the Eighth Italian and Third Romanian Armies between Starobelsk and Voroshilovgrad, tearing open a 200-mile gap between Army Group Don and Army Group B. By 8 February Vatutin had crossed the River Donets to the south-east of Kharkov. The tip of his advance, swinging south-east to pin the Germans

---

* The Soviet high command used the term 'front' not only to designate a zone of deployment of troops and the line of battle but also as a distinct operational organization of armed forces. Roughly equivalent to a German army group, a front consisted of some five to seven armies, with one or two tactical air armies, and special armoured and artillery formations in support. An entire front could total up to one million men and extend over a battle frontage of up to 150 miles, with a depth – if one includes the rear zones of operation – of up to 250 miles.

against the Sea of Azov, was pointing ominously towards the Dnieper crossing at Zaporozhye, the main supply centre for Army Group Don. On Vatutin's right flank General Filip Golikov's Voronezh Front was threatening Kharkov, the fourth largest city in the Soviet Union and the focus of fierce fighting in the spring of 1942. By 4 February General Pavel Rybalko's Third Tank Army had reached the Donets south of Kharkov but was then temporarily halted by the presence of Ist SS Panzer Grenadier Division Leibstandarte Adolf Hitler,* part of General Paul Hausser's I SS Panzer Corps, which had just arrived from France.

Two days later Manstein flew to meet Adolf Hitler at the Führer's headquarters near Rastenburg in East Prussia. Manstein was a master of the operational level of command and was perhaps the greatest commander of the Second World War. He had developed the Sichelsnitt (Sickle Cut) plan which secured victory in the West in 1940 and he had been the conqueror of the Crimea in 1941–2. He remained unruffled by the developing crisis on the Southern Front. Ignoring Hitler's orders that not an inch of ground be yielded, he had been conducting an elastic defence against the renewed Russian counter-offensive. He had also responded to Hitler's increasing dilatoriness in taking urgently needed decisions by reporting that, 'in default of an OKH directive by such-and-such a time or such-and-such a day, we shall act on our own discretion'.

Tall, aloof, with a prominent hooked nose, Manstein personified the pre-Nazi officer class for which Hitler harboured an almost pathological hatred. Beneath Manstein's cool and correct exterior, however, there pulsed a keen intelligence and an analytical brain which could assess a fluid situation with a speed and sharpness few could match. Provided that he could persuade Hitler to allow him to withdraw to the line of the Donets, evacuate Rostov and take up a much shorter line along the River Mius, Manstein remained confident that he could concentrate a powerful

---

* The Leibstandarte was formed in 1933 as Hitler's personal bodyguard. It served as a motorized infantry regiment during the 1939 campaign in Poland and the 1940 campaign in the West. Expanded into a motorized division in 1941, it saw further action in the Balkans and the invasion of the Soviet Union before taking part in the occupation of Vichy France. In 1942 it was designated a panzer grenadier division.

armoured striking force against the expanding Soviet counter-
offensive.

Fluidity was anathema to Hitler. His approach to defensive warfare was conditioned by his own experience on the Western Front
in the First World War. As Manstein later observed:

> His way of thinking conformed more to a mental picture of
> masses of the enemy bleeding to death before our lines than to
> the concept of a subtle fencer who knows how to make an occa-
> sional step backwards in order to lunge for the decisive thrust.

There was no subtlety in Hitler's determination to hold ground,
an obsession strengthened by the apparent success of his strategy
in the winter of 1941–2, when he had refused requests for large-
scale withdrawals and had averted the prospect of a 'Napoleonic
retreat' from Moscow. Willpower had won the day, leaving Hitler
convinced that his own will had only to be translated into faith
down to the youngest private soldier for the correctness of his
decisions to be confirmed and the success of his orders ensured.
To this was added a fixation with holding on to territory for
economic advantages which were often illusory and defied
military logic.

Manstein's requests to manoeuvre and yield ground where
necessary – indeed where there was no choice – raised the spectre
of abandoning the Donbas, the coal-mining and industrial region of
the south-eastern Ukraine, whose resources Hitler claimed were
vital to the German war effort and whose denial to the Soviet
Union was equally important. In fact, as Manstein had already
ascertained, the coal deposits in the area from which he wished to
withdraw were unsuitable both for coking and locomotives.
Manstein was only too well aware that Hitler's strategic aims,
largely conditioned by the requirements of the German war
economy, presupposed the defeat of an enemy who was now
threatening to roll up the Ostheer's southern wing and with it the
entire Eastern Front.

Manstein might have expected a rough ride from the Führer
during their four-hour conference at Rastenburg on 6 February –
interminable harangues and a refusal to budge an inch. Hitler,
however, was still unnerved by the loss of Sixth Army. At the

beginning of the meeting he admitted full responsibility for the disaster at Stalingrad, leaving Manstein with the impression that

> he was deeply affected by the tragedy, not just because it amounted to a blatant failure of his own leadership, but also because he was deeply depressed in a purely personal sense by the fate of the soldiers who, out of faith in him, had fought to the last with such courage and devotion to duty.

This contrasts sharply with Hitler's initial reaction, but the Führer was expert at tailoring his moods to fit different audiences.

Having caught Hitler in a mood of apparent vulnerability and, as the meeting continued, apparent rationality, Manstein secured permission for the surrender of the eastern Donets region as far as the Mius. It was not all plain sailing. During the meeting Hitler rallied, restating all the economic arguments for holding firm and, finally, suggesting that an unusually early thaw would halt both the Soviet offensive and the evacuation of the Don-Donets salient. Manstein refused to stake the fate of his army group on the hope of an unseasonable change in the weather. All he would promise Hitler was 'not to issue the withdrawal order until I reach my headquarters at noon next day, provided the situation report sent up that evening does not necessitate immediate action'.

Manstein now ordered the hard-pressed Army Detachment Hollidt to fall back on the Mius. First Panzer Army, which had passed northwards to safety through the corridor which Manstein had kept open to Rostov, was transferred to the threatened northern wing of Army Group Don on the middle Donets. Meanwhile, Fourth Panzer Army worked its way northward from the Lower Don to an area between the the Donets and the Dnieper bend on the western wing of Army Group Don. Manstein moved his headquarters from Stalino to Zaporozhye where he could more easily control developments on the north-west wing of Army Group Don.

In critical sectors the Red Army now enjoyed a numerical superiority of 8:1. The companies of First Panzer Army, reduced in some cases to twenty men, were holding sections up to half a mile wide, constantly threatened at night with encirclement by Soviet ski battalions. To plug the gaps as they opened up, staff up to divisional level formed strongpoints in the principal defence zones. A reinforced company was formed from First Panzer Army's headquarters personnel and sent straight into action.

On 8 February General Ivan Chernyakhovsky's Soviet Sixtieth Army took Kursk, 120 miles north of Kharkov. Six days later Rostov was abandoned. On the same day the Soviet encirclement of Kharkov was almost complete. Soviet tanks had pierced the northern and south-eastern defences and were nosing into the outskirts of the city. As the situation on the southern wing deteriorated, OKH reshuffled the command boundaries. On 12 February Manstein's command was redesignated Army Group South. Twenty-four hours later Army Group B, over which Manstein had vainly been attempting to exercise control, was broken up and its staff organization withdrawn to Germany. Its strongest component, Second Army, was transferred to Field Marshal Gunther von Kluge's Army Group Centre and the remainder of its battered formations absorbed into Army Detachment Lanz, defending Kharkov.

By now two of I SS Panzer Corps's three panzer grenadier divisions, Leibstandarte and Das Reich, and Panzer Grenadier Division Grossdeutschland, were in danger of being trapped in Kharkov. In command of I SS Panzer Corps was the sixty-three-year-old General Paul Hausser, a tough customer who had lost his right eye to a piece of Russian shrapnel. He had no intention of losing his divisions in a senseless battle against odds. On 14 February he asked General Lanz to authorize a break-out. The Corps diary for that day reads:

> Enemy facing Kharkov's eastern and north-eastern fronts greatly strengthened on 14:2. Attack along Chuguyev and Volchansk roads repulsed by last reserves. Enemy penetrated eight miles deep near southern airfield as far as Osnova. Mopping up now in progress but with inadequate force. No forces available for sealing off enemy penetration north-east of Kharkov at 'G-D' Division. All offensive troops tied down in the south for the moment. 320th Infantry Division not yet absorbed into the main defensive line. Its condition, according to general staff reports, precludes offensive employment for next few days.
>
> Inside Kharkov mobs firing at troops and vehicles. No forces available for mopping up since everything in front line. City,

including railway, stores and ammunition dumps, effectively dynamited at Army orders. City burning. Systematic withdrawal increasingly improbable each day. Assumptions underlying Kharkov's strategic importance no longer valid. Request renewed Führer decision whether Kharkov be defended to the last man.

It was highly improbable that Hitler would abandon his assumptions about the strategic importance of Kharkov. General Lanz may have sympathized with Hausser, but he merely reiterated Hitler's orders that Kharkov be defended to the last man and the last round. Hausser repeated his request to withdraw; Lanz stonewalled. By noon on 15 February there was only a small gap in the Soviet ring around Kharkov, to the south-east of the city. Its closure would seal the fate of Hausser's corps and Grossdeutschland.

Fully aware that to disobey the Führer could lead to his execution, Hausser took matters into his own hands. On the 15th he signalled Lanz: 'To avoid troops being encircled and to save material, orders will be given at 1300 to fight way through behind Udy sector on edge of city. Fighting through enemy lines in progress, also street fighting in south-west and west of city.'

Ignoring Lanz's frantic reply – 'Kharkov will be defended under all circumstances' – Hausser broke out of Kharkov. Twenty-four hours later the rear parties of Das Reich were the last to fight their way out of the blazing city. The Red Flag was raised in a ghost town. Two thirds of Kharkov's population had fled, another 250,000 had perished during the fifteen-month German occupation, deported as slave labour or killed by cold and starvation.

For Stalin and the Red Army's high command the German abandonment of Kharkov was proof positive that the enemy was in full retreat. Dazzled by the prospect of seizing the Dnieper crossings and amputating the entire southern wing of the Ostheer, Stalin announced that 'the mass expulsion of the enemy from the Soviet Union has begun'. His principal concern was the race the Red Army was now running against the onset of the *rasputitsa*, the twice-yearly wet season caused by the spring thaw and the autumn rains which turned Russia's dirt roads to quagmires and the surrounding steppe to swamp. Since 12 February, Vatutin had been broadening his South-Western Front's offensive. Now Major-General Kharitonov's Sixth Army was to cross the Dnieper on his right wing between Dnepropetrovsk and Zaporozhye. On Kharitonov's left General Popov's 'Front mobile group' had pushed through Slavyansk to close with First Panzer Army.

Manstein watched these developments with his customary calm. As he had anticipated, Stalin was once again over-reaching himself and exposing his spearheads to a counter-blow. As he pondered enemy movements on the map, correctly reading the Soviet intention to wheel south to drive Army Group South into the Black Sea, one of his staff officers heard him murmur, 'And the best of luck to you.'

The Red Army's luck was about to run out as exhaustion set in, supply lines stretched to breaking point, tactical air support fell away, and the sheer scale and speed of advance took its toll on the armoured formations. South-Western Front had lost half its armour through loss and battle damage. Popov's 'Front mobile group', comprising four corps (4th Guards, 18th, 3rd and 10th Tank Corps), had lost ninety tanks in two days of fighting and was now down to fifty-three battleworthy tanks. On Golikov's Voronezh Front, Third Tank Army's two tank brigades, 88th and 113th, could muster only six tanks between them. Nevertheless, this was considered adequate to pursue a beaten and retreating enemy.

Hitler had now had time to repent the accommodation he had made with Manstein on 6 February. Fighting the war from the map at Rastenburg, and lacking Manstein's strategic insight, he can perhaps be forgiven for thinking that the freedom of manoeuvre he had ceded to the commander of Army Group South was accelerating the collapse of the southern wing. On 16 February he decided to fly to Manstein's new headquarters at Zaporozhye, the site of a huge hydro-electric power station which had just been rebuilt by AEG.

That day Hitler's secretary, Martin Bormann, wrote in his diary: 'Our southern sector is by no means a "front" even now. Over vast areas we have just a void. To master this extremely tricky and dangerous situation the Führer . . . is going to fly out there with a small escort of intimates.'* In Zaporozhye Hitler returned to a familiar theme. There were to be no more withdrawals. Lanz was to be removed from his command (he was replaced by General Kempf) and Kharkov retaken immediately by I SS Panzer Corps. Manstein's plan to slice into the increasingly exposed flanks of Kharitonov's Sixth Army was to be set aside until Kharkov was back in German hands.

Manstein waited for the storm to blow itself out. On the 18th, at a second conference, he explained that the further the Red Army's offensive carried it to the west and south-west, the more effective would be his counter-blow. Vatutin's South-Western Front now had its head in a bulging salient whose northern shoulder was anchored by Army Detachment Kempf and on whose southern flank, concentrating for the counter-blow, were First and Fourth Panzer Armies, positioned in the neck of ground between the Donets and the Dnieper, across which Vatutin was driving to break into the German rear. Continuing, Manstein pointed out that the Russians were now 200 miles from their supply bases, their lines of communication stretching back over a wasteland left by the withdrawing Germans who had dynamited bridges, airfields and railway lines, and broken up long stretches of the few passable roads. Now was the time to strike at the Russians in the open, before the ground unfroze in the spring thaw. The counter-blow would be the essential preliminary to the retaking of Kharkov.

Hitler wavered. Manstein had taken the calculated risk of stripping the Mius line of its panzer divisions, leaving the two corps of Army Detachment Hollidt to hold five Soviet armies. On the 18th the line, built by Army Group Don the year before, was pierced by 3rd Guards Mechanized Corps, which trundled west for eighteen miles before a sudden thaw enabled the defenders to encircle and seal it off. Zaporozhye itself was threatened by the straining head of the Soviet salient. Between Vatutin's leading elements and Manstein's headquarters there were only scattered German anti-aircraft units and the headquarters defence company. On the 19th the Führer's mind was concentrated when advanced units of

---

* In the party were Generals Zeitzler and Jodl, General Schmundt, Hitler's adjutant, his diplomatic liaison officer, Hewel, and Dr Morell, his personal physician.

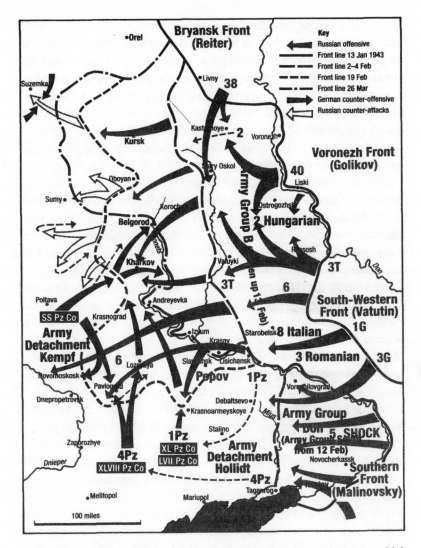

January–March 1943. The Soviet counter-offensive and Manstein's riposte, which left intact the huge Kursk salient

25th Tank Corps reached Sinelnikovo, only forty miles from Zaporozhye, cutting the rail link with Army Detachment Hollidt. As they probed towards Manstein's headquarters, Hitler was reminded by General Schmundt, his military adjutant, that he had an urgent appointment with General Heinz Guderian, recently appointed Inspector-General of Armoured Troops. The distant gunfire of Russian tanks could be heard as the Führer's FW200 Condor flew off into a grey winter sky. Manstein now had a free hand to deliver his counter-blow.

Still in the grip of victory fever, the Soviet high command was misreading a steady accumulation of danger signals. The westward movement of German armoured and motorized formations had not escaped the attention of Soviet intelligence but was interpreted as further evidence of retreat from the Donbas to the Dnieper. A stream of aerial reconnaissance reports of German armoured concentrations around Krasnograd (I SS Panzer Corps) and Krasnoarmeyskoye (First and Fourth Panzer Armies) merely reinforced the *idée fixe* that the enemy was in headlong retreat, covered by his armour. Thus, when on 20 February Manstein's armoured shears slashed simultaneously into Vatutin's right and left flanks, the Russians were taken completely by surprise.

I SS Panzer Corps lunged south-east to bite deeply into the exposed flank of Kharitonov's Sixth Army; XLVIII Panzer Corps, the cutting edge of Fourth Panzer Army, struck north-west towards Pavlograd; and First Panzer Army's XL Panzer Corps slammed into Popov's depleted 'Front mobile group' which was reassembling to join Sixth Army's drive.

On the night of the 21st Popov, who was now down to twenty-five battleworthy tanks, requested permission from Vatutin to pull back and establish a line twenty miles to the north. Permission was refused by Vatutin who reiterated the order to Popov to cut off the German escape routes to the west. Simultaneously, Kharitonov was ordered to establish a bridgehead over the Dnieper at Dnepropetrovsk, push mobile formations on to Zaporozhye and prepare to drive south to Melitopol. As the situation collapsed around Kharitonov's and Popov's ears, Vatutin remained stubbornly convinced that 'the enemy is doing everything he can to speed the withdrawal of his forces from the Donbas to the Dnieper'.

Precisely the opposite was happening, but Kharitonov doggedly attempted to follow orders. A division of 25th Tank Corps fought its way to within ten miles of Zaporozhye and then, with its fuel tanks dry, ground to a halt. Behind it the rest of 25th Tank Corps, separated from the main body of Sixth Army and also running short of fuel, was being worked over by XLVIII Panzer Corps, commanded by General von Knobelsdorff. His chief of staff, Major-General F.W. von Mellenthin, later wrote:

> The terrain was almost completely open, slightly undulating, and cut here and there by narrow brooks which were then completely frozen. It resembled the area west of Stalingrad, and indeed was very much like the North African desert. Russian columns streaming back to the north were visible at a distance of eight to twelve miles and were taken under effective artillery fire at that range.

The Russians fleeing XLVIII Panzer Corps were soon taken under fire at closer range as SS Divisions Das Reich and Totenkopf* overhauled them on a parallel course. Rumbling across the frozen steppe at 25mph, the SS tanks and motorized columns drew alongside the retreating Russians and poured machine-gun fire at point-blank range into trucks packed with infantry. Entire companies of T-34s, stranded with empty fuel tanks, were blown to pieces. Twenty miles to the south the remaining tanks and artillery of Totenkopf and Das Reich threaded their way back and forth through a seemingly endless obstacle course of burnt and blackened vehicles, shooting anything that moved, while panzer grenadiers, supported by Ju87 Stuka dive-bombers, fanned out across the steppe to kill or capture as many of the enemy as possible.

One by one, Kharitonov's corps were being encircled while Popov, fighting to hold off XL Panzer Corps, was falling back on Barvenkovo. On the Voronezh Front Golikov now sensed disaster.

---

* Rushed from France to join I SS Panzer Corps, Totenkopf had been caught by a sudden thaw near Poltava and spent three days in the clutches of the mud before going into action.

During the night of the 21st he ordered Sixty-Ninth Army and Third Tank Army to abandon their westerly drive to the Dnieper and turn south to deal with the panzer formations chewing away at Kharitonov's right flank south of Kharkov. The two armies wheeled ponderously south on parallel tracks, short of ammunition and armoured support and with their progress slowed by thousands of hastily drafted conscripts, most of them still in their work-clothes. On the 23rd they were stopped in their tracks when they lurched into Grossdeutschland Division.

At Vatutin's headquarters a three-way struggle was now in progress between a growing realization of impending disaster, understandable reluctance,to disobey Moscow's strict instructions and the lingering self-deception which had driven operations for the last week and which still saw the prize of the Dnieper in the distance. But the Dnieper was now no more than a mirage. Having halted the Russian drive to Zaporozhye with separate actions against Sixth Army and Popov's 'Front mobile group', Manstein now developed a coordinated offensive north-east to the Donets.

By 24 February, Popov, in spite of reinforcements, could field only fifty tanks against the 400 German tanks operating against his left wing. At 5.30pm on the 23rd Vatutin, under intense pressure from Stalin to 'get that left wing of yours moving', signalled the hapless Popov: 'I wish to remind you emphatically that you are to use all means available to halt and annihilate the enemy in the Barvenkovo area. I am holding you personally responsible.' However, within twenty-four hours he could no longer ignore the painful fact that Popov's group was smashed beyond repair and that the bulk of Sixth Army was facing encirclement. On 25 February Vatutin suspended all offensive operations and informed Moscow of his true position. The scale of his losses meant that he could no longer dissemble, but reinforcement was out of the question. His tank repair units were stranded with the encircled corps, leaving the armour in the rear unfit for battle, awaiting the delayed arrival of two mobile tank workshops.

On the afternoon of 28 February 7th Panzer Division broke through to the Donets south of Izyum, annihilating the remnants of Popov's group. Behind the group, stretching back to Krasnoarmeyskoye, the furthest point of its advance, lay a trail of mangled armour, artillery, trucks and at least 3000 dead. Sixth Army was also in its death throes. In an attempt to distract the German armour preying on the carcase of Kharitonov's command, General Rybalko's Third Tank Army was detached from Golikov's left wing and ordered to counter-attack. Assembling for the attack, Rybalko was caught by German armour and the dive-bombers and ground-attack aircraft of Luftflotte 4 (Fourth Air Fleet). Within four days Third Tank Army was encircled and fighting desperately to break out to the south-west of Kharkov while Sixth Army and the badly mauled First Guards Army reeled back to the Donets on a line between Andreyevka and Krasny Liman.

The winter weather saved them from complete destruction. The intense cold, which forced troops to spend the nights under cover and near a stove, the inability of the advancing Germans to seal so huge a pocket in such difficult conditions, and the frozen Donets, enabled the surviving units to cross the ice into relative safety, leaving their equipment behind. In all, six tank corps, five rifle divisions and six independent brigades had been destroyed or very severely handled.

The elimination of Sixth Army and Popov's 'Front mobile group' had opened a 120-mile gap in the Soviet front, enabling Manstein to launch the second phase of his counter-blow, the retaking of Kharkov. By 9 March I SS Panzer Corps – now joined by its third division, Totenkopf – was deployed to the north and west of Kharkov. In its northern drive it had encircled and destroyed two tank corps and three rifle divisions of Third Tank Army and it was now poised to avenge the loss of Kharkov the previous month. At 9.20am on the 9th, General Hausser was ordered by Colonel-General Hermann Hoth, commanding Fourth Panzer Army, to 'seal off Kharkov tightly from west to north. Conditions inside the city are to be reconnoitred. Opportunities to seize the city by a coup are to be utilized.'

Accordingly, Hausser deployed Totenkopf and Leibstandarte to the north of Kharkov, to cut the road to Belgorod and then probe south, while Das Reich attacked from the west and south. Initially, Das Reich encountered only light resistance and this encouraged Hausser to strike into Kharkov to achieve a quick victory. Das Reich was ordered to regroup in the western suburbs while

Totenkopf continued to skirt round the western edge of the city. On 11 March Hausser detached one battalion from Totenkopf to join Das Reich and Leibstandarte to take Kharkov by direct assault. Three days of vicious street fighting followed, resulting in heavy casualties and reducing Leibstandarte's already depleted tank strength to fourteen. Using dug-in T-34 tanks and a network of strongpoints in huge apartment blocks, the defenders of Kharkov fought to the last man. Outside the city, Totenkopf completed its northern envelopment and then pushed south-east to capture the vital bridge crossings over the Donets at Chuguyev, trapping and destroying the 25th Guards Rifle Division in a fierce battle.

The last pocket of resistance in Kharkov, in a tractor factory on the eastern outskirts of the city, was silenced on 15 March. Two days later Hoth ordered Hausser's Corps to regroup north of Chuguyev and advance on Belgorod which lay astride the Donets thirty miles to the north-east. Belgorod was quickly taken, bringing not only Kursk under threat but also the rear of the whole of the Soviet Central Front which formed a huge echeloned westward bulge in the line. If Manstein could now coordinate his northward drive with a southward thrust by Field Marshal Kluge's Army Group Centre, the Soviet armies west of Kursk would be trapped and destroyed.

The Red Army had little with which to block a continued drive by Fourth Panzer Army. Sixty-Ninth Army, which, on 18 March, had withdrawn from Belgorod across the Donets, had no tanks and fewer than 100 guns. Its divisions were skeleton formations, all of them reduced to fewer than 1000 men and, in the case of 340th Rifle Division, just 275. But Kluge refused to coordinate a new offensive with Manstein, claiming that his Second Army and Second Panzer Army were in no shape to attack after successfully concluding a hard fight to stabilize the situation on the southern wing of his army group.

Meanwhile the Soviet high command was shoring up the front around Kursk, inserting Twenty-First Army north of Belgorod, concentrating First Tank Army at Oboyan and bringing up Sixty-Fourth Army to the line of the Donets. With the *rasputitsa* taking a glutinous grip on the steppe, the German chance slipped away and Kursk was secured. By the end of March the front line had stabilized from the Mius to Belgorod, the latter now anchoring the southern face of the Kursk salient, a clenched fist of territory the size of Wales jutting westward into the German line.

Major-General von Mellenthin succinctly summed up Manstein's achievement in February–March 1943:

> In a few weeks he had been able to carry out a successful withdrawal, to launch a counter-attack on a large scale, to eliminate the threat of encirclement, to inflict very heavy losses on a victorious enemy and to re-establish the southern front from Taganrog to Belgorod as a straight defensive line. In numbers of divisions the ratio of strength was 8 to 1 in favour of the Russians, and these operations showed once again what German troops were able to do when led by experts in accordance with accepted tactical principles, instead of being hampered with 'holding at all costs' as the battlecry.

Once again the Ostheer had shown its remarkable powers of recovery, simultaneously demonstrating its tactical superiority in mobile operations, even when greatly outnumbered. Some 23,000 Russian dead had been left on the battlefield, but only 9000 prisoners had been taken; 615 tanks and 354 guns had been captured. Having recovered its composure after the shock of Stalingrad and the initial inroads made by the Soviet counter-offensive, OKH (Oberkommando des Heeres, the German Army High Command) could now contemplate renewing offensive operations in the summer of 1943.

CHAPTER 2

The Dictators

'Three months ago Red Army troops began an offensive at the approaches to Stalingrad. Since then the initiative has been in our hands . . . The balance of forces on the Soviet front has changed.' Josef Stalin, 23 February 1943

'I cannot understand it; what has happened?' Adolf Hitler, March 1943

On 10 March 1943, as Fourth Panzer Army opened the fourth battle fought over the city of Kharkov since the German invasion of the Soviet Union, Adolf Hitler travelled to Field Marshal von Manstein's headquarters at Zaporozhye. In decidedly more relaxed mood than on 6 and 17 February, he added an Oak Leaf Cluster to Manstein's Knight's Cross and met, and took reports from, all the army and air corps commanders on the southern front.

During the meeting Hitler jokingly addressed everyone as 'Herr Feldmarschall', no doubt causing some of the company to shift uneasily at the thought that one of the officers most recently promoted to that rank was the unfortunate Paulus. At the same time the Führer happily encouraged Manstein to make slighting remarks about his two neighbouring army group commanders, Kleist and Kluge, with both of whom the commander of Army Group South was conducting his own private war.

Hitler confided in Field Marshal Wolfram von Richthofen, commander of Luftflotte 4, that

> he never wants to hear of the Romanians or our other gallant allies again; if he relies on them he only gets worked up because they don't stand firm; and if he arms them but doesn't use them, he gets just as worked up to see them standing around doing nothing.

Three days later, on the 13th, Hitler repeated the performance in Smolensk for Field Marshal von Kluge, commander of Army Group Centre, which was on the point of completing a phased withdrawal from the Rzhev salient to release sufficient forces to block any Soviet advance west of Kursk. That day the Führer signed Operations Order No.5, instructing Manstein and Kluge to take the initiative again when the spring muddy season was over. He then flew back to Rastenburg.*

Hitler did not linger in the military compound, codenamed Wolfsschanze (Wolf's Lair), in the gloomy Gorlitz forest. On the evening of 23 March his Mercedes headed a long procession of cars which swept up to the Berghof, the Führer's mountain retreat near the town of Berchtesgaden in southern Bavaria. He was not to return to the Wolf's Lair until 9 May.

In Russia the front had been stabilized. The holes torn in the southern front had been stitched together and the German line restored to that from which the summer offensive of 1942 had been launched. To the west of Moscow, in Operation Buffalo, Ninth Army and parts of Fourth Army had been successfully withdrawn from the Rzhev salient to a heavily fortified line between Spass Demensk and Dukhovshchina. Behind them they left a wasteland

---

* A bomb had been placed on Hitler's aircraft. The device, made from slabs of British-manufactured nitrotetramethanium and packed into a parcel, had been prepared by Major-General Henning von Tresckow and Major Fabian von Schlabrendorff, two of Kluge's staff officers, and armed with a half-hour setting. Tresckow had persuaded one of Hitler's staff officers, Colonel Brandt, to carry the parcel, telling him that it was a present of a couple of bottles of cognac for a friend at Rastenburg. The bomb failed to explode and Tresckow was able to retrieve the parcel from the unsuspecting Brandt. He discovered that the detonator cap had failed. After the failure of the July 1944 bomb plot against Hitler, Tresckow deliberately walked into Russian fire. Schlabrendorff was arrested and tortured after the July 1944 plot but survived the war.

of scorched earth and dismantled plant. When the Red Army pushed cautiously into the vacuum, it suffered heavy casualties in expertly laid minefields and booby-trapped buildings.

Nevertheless, Hitler could draw little comfort from these tactical successes. A whole year had passed and with it a remorseless rise in casualties. By February 1943 Army and SS losses in Russia from the beginning of the war exceeded one million for dead and missing alone. Hitler's Propaganda Minister, Dr Josef Goebbels, confessed that merely to look at a map of the East gave him the creeps; so much ground had been lost and the prospect of an Anglo–American invasion 'hanging over all of them' left him with a feeling of unease. For his part, Hitler expressed bafflement that the millions of casualties the Russians had suffered since June 1941 had not led to the collapse of Soviet resistance. Surely, Stalin must be reaching the end of his reserves.

The extravagant ambition which had fuelled Hitler's plans for Barbarossa now dimmed. The sweep of grand strategy gave way to endless discussion of the new weapons which would give Germany the technical superiority to hang on to that which been won since September 1939. The walls were going up around Hitler's 'Fortress Europe': the Atlantic Wall along the west coast and, after August 1943, the East or Panther Wall in Russia, running from near Leningrad due southwards to the line of the Dnieper.

Within and without these walls the tide of war was turning against Germany. The Battle of the Atlantic had reached a crisis in March 1943 when three of Grand Admiral Dönitz's U-boat 'wolf packs' had scored one of their greatest successes, plundering two convoys, SC122 and HX229, sinking twenty-two ships out of a combined total of ninety merchantmen and one of their escorts. That month the U-boats accounted for 108 ships in the North Atlantic, totalling 476,000 tons, and, as the British Admiralty put it, 'never came so near [again] to disrupting communications between the New World and the Old'.

For a brief moment shipping was being sunk at twice the rate it was being built. But the moment passed. The mid-Atlantic 'air gap' was closed by very-long-range B-24 Liberator bombers flying from Northern Ireland, Iceland and Newfoundland and equipped with the Mk24 'mine', a lightweight anti-submarine homing torpedo.

New escort carriers were introduced, operating at the heart of 'support groups', harrying U-boats in head-on engagements while the escorts steamed on with their convoys. High-frequency radio direction-finding (HF-DF or Huff-Duff) enabled escorts to detect and track shadowing U-boats when they were transmitting. Those escorts fitted with the Type 271 centimetric radar could pick up objects as small as a U-boat's conning tower, making surface attacks at night increasingly dangerous. Decoded signals between the U-boats and Dönitz's headquarters in Berlin allowed convoys to be re-routed and anti-submarine forces to be concentrated where they were most needed. At the point of contact, Hedgehog, a multi-barrelled spigot mortar which launched up to twenty-four contact-fused bombs in a pattern ahead of the escort, ensured that Asdic contact could be maintained with a submarine up to the moment of a hit.

This was a battle for technological superiority which the Kriegsmarine was losing hands down. In May 1943, forty-three U-boats were lost against a monthly launching rate of fifteen. Dönitz withdrew his 'wolf packs' from the North Atlantic to lick their wounds and seek less dangerous hunting grounds. In his memoirs Dönitz concluded that, at this point, 'we had lost the Battle of the Atlantic'.

Defeat was also looming in North Africa where the supply situation of Field Marshal Erwin Rommel's Army Group Africa in Tunisia was now critical. On 4 March Hitler, still preoccupied with Stalingrad, reflected, 'This is the end. Army Group Africa might just as well be brought back.' Five days later Rommel himself, haggard, depressed and already labelled a 'defeatist', arrived at Hitler's headquarters at Vinnitsa in the Ukraine. In talks over the next three days Rommel attempted to persuade Hitler to authorize the abandonment of Army Group Africa's positions along the Mareth line* and a withdrawal into a short perimeter of 100 miles around Tunis. Hitler agreed to some shortening of the Axis front but insisted that the Mareth line be defended. He assured Rommel

---

* A system of field fortifications built by the French and running from the shores of the Gulf of Gabes (close to Mareth) inland to the foot of the Matmata Hills, a distance of about thirty miles. It was firmly based on the Wadi Zigzaou, a dried-up river bed and formidable obstacle.

that the Italian dictator Benito Mussolini would increase supplies to First Italian and Fifth Panzer Armies to at least 150,000 tons a month.* Hitler then awarded the Field Marshal the Diamonds to his Knight's Cross, the first such award to an Army officer. He was given leave of absence, a decision which was kept secret lest it affect morale.

Rommel's successor as commander of Army Group Africa, Colonel-General Hans von Arnim, could not hold the Mareth line and by mid-April was clinging to the north-eastern tip of Tunisia. His 100,000 fighting troops (about 60,000 of whom were German) and fewer than 100 tanks faced an Allied combat strength of 300,000 men and 1400 tanks. By 12 May Axis resistance was over. With the fall of Tunisia more than 230,000 Axis prisoners, nearly half of them German, tramped into Allied captivity. In spite of his gloomy forebodings on 4 March, Hitler was once again unable to bring himself to liquidate a front; as a result, he presided over another Stalingrad on the southern shores of the Mediterranean.

Within the Reich itself, Fortress Europe had no roof to shield its civilian population from the increasingly heavy blows delivered by the British and American combined bombing offensive. The year had opened with a small but dramatic demonstration of the limitations of the Luftwaffe's air-defence system. On the morning of 3 January 1943 a 'nuisance flight' of three RAF Mosquitos arrived over Berlin to disrupt a speech given by Josef Goebbels. During the afternoon a second flight arrived to wreck a rally attended by the Chief of the Luftwaffe, Reichsmarschall Hermann Göring.

These pinpricks were the preliminaries to the Battle of the Ruhr which was opened on 5 March 1943 when Air Chief Marshal Sir Arthur Harris, AOC-in-C RAF Bomber Command, despatched 442 aircraft, led by thirty-five Pathfinders, to attack the industrial city of Essen. The main force, carrying bombloads of one third high-explosive and two thirds incendiaries, attacked in three waves, concentrated within forty minutes. For the loss of only fourteen aircraft, severe damage was inflicted on the Krupp

---

* The minimum requirement to keep the combat troops of Army Group Africa in the field was 70,000 tons a month. In January and February the Italian merchant marine, suffering heavy losses, managed to deliver just 46,000 tons.

armament complex and 160 acres of Essen laid waste. Bomber
Command enjoyed its most effective night of the Battle of the Ruhr
on 29–30 May when a force of 719 aircraft attacked Wuppertal,
destroying 1000 acres of the built-up Barmen district and killing
some 3500 people.

Two weeks earlier, on the night of 16–17 May, Avro Lancasters of
No.617 Squadron had breached the Möhne and Eder dams which
supplied the Ruhr with much of its hydro-electricity. Although the
resulting damage to German war industry was slight, the raid was
a landmark in precision-bombing techniques and had a profound
psychological effect. The pattern of the future was already clear to
Goebbels in March when he confessed that he 'feared to think
what Germany would look like at the end of only another three
months' and that 'by next spring a greater part of the Reich will be
in ruins'.

The Luftwaffe's air defences had not lost the power to hit back.
During the Battle of the Ruhr, which ended in mid-July, Bomber
Command lost 872 aircraft over Germany. More significantly, however, by the end of July not only had all these losses been replaced
but another 300 heavy bombers had also been added to the
strength of Bomber Command. Similarly, when the USAAF's Eighth
Air Force began to make deeper penetrations into Germany in the
spring of 1943, its unescorted bomber formations suffered mounting losses which led, in October, to a temporary suspension of
operations. The situation underwent a dramatic change in the
winter of 1943 with the introduction of the powerful P-51 Mustang
long-range escort fighter, capable of accompanying the bombers
to and from their targets and wresting air superiority over the
Reich from the Luftwaffe.

Goebbels was no military man, but he grasped that Germany,
with its restricted capacity for the manufacture of aircraft, acute
fuel and growing manpower shortages and incompetent Luftwaffe
high command, could not hope to retain air superiority against
three enemies – the British, Americans and Russians – each of
whose aircraft production figures exceeded those of the Reich
(in the case of the Americans by many times). Perpetual air inferiority not only removed the essential condition of victory, it also
precluded the conduct of a successful *defensive* strategy. The

exposure of the German heartland, its population and industries to regular air attack, with its attendant effects on morale and war production, completed the vicious circle.

On 13 January 1943 Hitler issued a decree stating, 'The total war confronts us with tasks which must unequivocally be mastered.' But there was much that was equivocal about the war effort of the Third Reich. Up to the end of 1942 economic planning had been governed by the assumption that the war would soon be over. The output of domestic product was only 12 per cent less than in 1938. In 1942 the technocrat Armaments Minister, Albert Speer, had increased war production by 40 per cent in spite of the fact that the workforce in war industry between 1939 and 1942 had declined by almost 10 per cent. The German war economy was a mass of contradictions, with 6 million workers still producing consumer goods and 1.5 million women still employed as maids and cooks.

On 13 January Hitler named a three-man committee, consisting of Field Marshal Keitel, Martin Bormann and Hans Lammers, Chief of the Reich Chancellery, to mobilize all military, party and state agencies for the war effort. However, it was left to Goebbels publicly to grasp the nettle. On 18 February 1943, in an hour-long speech delivered at the Berlin Sportspalast, he ranged over the measures introduced in January to meet the demands of 'total war'. All men between the ages of sixteen and sixty-five and women between seventeen and forty-five were to be registered for compulsory war service. The Hitler Youth was to be drafted to work on farms and collect scrap. The prison population was to be given war-related work. The net result was the registering of about 3.5 million civilians of whom about 700,000 were put to work over the next twelve months. Additionally, all non war-related businesses were to be closed, including night clubs, luxury bars and restaurants, fashion and jewellery stores and establishments trading in postage stamps. The endemic corruption bred by the warring petty fiefdoms within the Nazi Party hierarchy ensured that there were many exemptions and much wastage in the implementation of these measures.

Also manoeuvring cautiously towards an exemption from their duties were Germany's allies. Hitler's Fortress Europe contained within its boundaries a combination of cowed occupied peoples and increasingly sullen allies. The latter were reluctant to make any more sacrifices on the Eastern Front where the Italian, Hungarian and Romanian armies had been swept away during the battle for Stalingrad and the subsequent Soviet counter-offensive. Their headquarters were now out of the front line, attempting to pull together the remnants of their forces. The Germans had openly regarded their allies as second-class troops; this did much to make them so. When Mussolini offered Hitler another 700,000 men, the latter observed that it would be pointless to equip them with German weapons which would be surrendered at the first opportunity, adding, 'They can't even be assigned "defensive" combat duties.' Even the Finns, whose fighting qualities no one could deny, had asked to withdraw their five remaining battalions from the German Twentieth Mountain Army serving in the Murmansk sector of the Eastern Front.

Finland, Hungary and Romania lay directly in the path of the Soviet advance to the west. If it gathered momentum, they would quickly find themselves in the front line. The Hungarian Prime Minister, Miklos von Kállay,* was already extending secret peace feelers to the British and the Americans, using intermediaries in Turkey, Switzerland and the Vatican. In Madrid and Ankara Romanian ministers were also opening clandestine negotiations with the enemy. Hitler was aware of these rustlings in the diplomatic undergrowth; his intelligence services had given him hard evidence of this queasy manoeuvring. On 12 April, at the Berghof, the Romanian premier, Marshal Antonescu, who had authorized the approaches, attempted to bluff it out with Hitler as did the Hungarian leader, Admiral Horthy, when he was confronted by the Führer a few days later. Hitler tartly reminded him, 'We are all in the same boat. If anybody goes overboard now, he drowns.'

The pressures of *sauve qui peut* bore down most heavily on Benito Mussolini. Never an equal partner with Germany, Italy was a broken reed. At Stalingrad the Italian Eighth Army, originally

---

* Kállay had been encouraged by Churchill's proposal to the Turkish government that a Balkan League be formed, comprising Turkey, Hungary and Romania, as a future counterweight to Soviet power.

200,000 strong, had been torn to shreds. In Tunisia another 200,000
Italian troops faced the prospect of becoming prisoners-of-war.
The clearing of North Africa by the Allies would provide them
with a base from which to carry the war to Sicily and the Italian
mainland. Now that the Duce's star was waning, many of
his senior commanders conveniently discovered that they were
royalists rather than fascists and were reconsidering their position. Hitler was aware of Mussolini's vulnerability. On 14 March he
told his generals: 'In Italy we can rely only on the Duce. There are
strong fears that he may be got rid of or neutralized in some way.'
This was inevitable for, as John Keegan has pointed out, 'There was
a final and ultimately disabling impediment to Italy's effective commitment to war on Germany's side: the Italians harboured little or
no hostility towards the enemies Hitler had chosen for them.'

In December 1942 Mussolini had sent his Foreign Minister,
Count Galeazzo Ciano, to the Wolf's Lair with a proposal that a
separate political settlement be made with the Soviet Union to free
the Axis for the fight against Britain and the United States. On
7 April the Duce met Hitler at Salzburg. A shadow of his former
strutting self, hollow-cheeked and constantly in need of a supporting arm, Mussolini sat listlessly through a series of carefully
staged briefings which said more about Hitler's lingering loyalty
to his old ally than the reality now pressing in on them both.
Before Mussolini's arrival Hitler had unsuccessfully attempted
to persuade the OKH Chief of Staff, Colonel-General Kurt Zeitzler,
to display wholly imaginary maps of the Eastern Front at the meetings as had been done on happier occasions in the past.

Once again Mussolini raised the question of seeking a separate
peace with the Soviet Union. At this stage in the war Hitler had no
illusions about the unlikelihood of dividing the grand alliance
against him. The Duce was sent on his way with a variation on the
'no surrender' theme, padded out with interminable lectures on
Frederick the Great and worthless promises of more oil for the
Italian navy.

Yet Hitler was increasingly concerned about the Mediterranean
theatre. Here, too, he was determined to hang on to every foot of
occupied soil. After the fall of Tunis, his eyes ranged back and
forth over the map as he pondered the most likely objectives for

an Allied landing. OKW considered Sicily the obvious target; Hitler thought it might be Sardinia. The approaches to the Balkans also occupied his attention, particularly the Pelopponese and the Dodecanese islands lying off the south-western coast of Turkey. The Allies encouraged this guesswork with an ingenious deception plan, Operation Mincemeat. On 30 April a corpse with the false identity of a Royal Marines officer was floated ashore on the coast of Spain. A briefcase chained to his wrist contained equally false papers which quickly reached German military intelligence. They indicated that the Allies would make a feint attack on Sicily as a cover for their real target of Sardinia, the springboard for the invasion of northern Italy and the Balkans.

Through all this Hitler remained temperamentally incapable of settling on priorities. To keep the Allies away from the borders of the Reich, Italy would have to be defended, not least because of Hitler's well-founded doubts about the willingness of the Italians to stay in the war. As he wryly observed, 'The Italians never lose a war; no matter what happens, they always end up on the winning side.' Italy would need to be covered by garrisons in Corsica, Sardinia and Sicily. To secure the Balkans against Allied attack, strong forces were needed in Crete and Rhodes and dozens of smaller islands in the eastern Mediterranean. Hitler reasoned that the island garrisons would serve a double purpose, denying the British access to the Dardanelles and thus preventing the establishment of a direct seaborne supply route to the Soviet Union; and also deterring Turkey from entering the war on the side of the Allies. In the Mediterranean, as on the Eastern Front, Hitler's first instinct was to defend everything along the perimeter. Although he liked to compare himself with Frederick the Great, he had forgotten one of the Prussian king's most famous dicta, that he who defends everything defends nothing.

If Hitler distrusted anyone more than his allies, it was his field commanders. After Stalingrad he had declared: 'There will be no more field marshals* in this war. We'll only promote them after the end of the war. I won't count my chickens before they are

---

* In fact Hitler created four more field marshals, von Richthofen, Model, Schoerner and von Greim.

hatched.' In his diary for 9 May 1943, Goebbels reflected on Hitler's disenchantment with his commanders:

> He is absolutely sick of the generals. He can't imagine anything better than having nothing to do with them. His opinion of all the generals is devastating. Indeed, at times it is so caustic as to seem prejudiced or unjust, although on the whole it no doubt fits the case . . . All generals lie, he says. All generals are disloyal. All generals are opposed to National Socialism. All generals are reactionaries . . . he just can't stand them. They have disappointed him so often.

The process of disillusionment had been gathering pace since February 1938 when Hitler had proclaimed himself the actual – as opposed to titular – Commander in Chief of the Armed Forces. In December 1941 he had dismissed the Army's C-in-C, the ailing Field Marshal von Brauchitsch, and had taken personal control of operations on the Eastern Front. The Führer had told Colonel-General Franz Halder, Army Chief of Staff and Zeitzler's predecessor, that 'Anyone can do the little job of directing operations in war . . . I have therefore decided to take over command of the army myself.'

The immediate effect of Hitler's self-promotion was that OKH, the designated high command for operations on the Eastern Front, ceased to be a high command in all but name. Henceforth operations in Russia, down to battalion level, were executed according to the Führer's direction.

Hitler's chosen method of controlling the Nazi state had always been that of divide and rule, encouraging a chaos of competing empires and thus ensuring his personal supremacy. When the same principle was applied to the armed forces, it fatally fractured the unity of the German high command. OKH, its operations confined to the Eastern Front, was broken up and the Army General Staff retained as the instrument of Hitler's will. It was now reduced to the status of OKW which exercised responsibility for all other theatres. OKW had never fulfilled its envisaged role as a supreme joint services command and, in the hands of its Chief of Staff, Colonel-General Alfried Jodl, merely duplicated the general staff of OKH.*

---

* Nor did OKW have any control over the Navy and Luftwaffe high commands, OKM and OKL, whose chiefs reported directly to Hitler.

Jodl's attempts to wrest operational control of the Army from OKH served only to increase tension within the German high command. As he was only Hitler's executive, however, and had no active experience of command, his occasional spoiling forays were confined to matters of routine. Jodl's importance rested in the fact that, throughout the war, he was the officer closest to Hitler, personally briefing him every day and discussing the plans and operational orders which he drafted in the Führer's name. Jodl's loyalty to Hitler, whom he regarded as a military genius, overrode the private misgivings he had about the conduct of the war from 1942. Content with such submissiveness, Hitler told Göring that he considered Jodl 'a very good and solid worker with an excellent general staff training'.

While Jodl remained an irritant to OKH, unqualified contempt was reserved for his superior, Field Marshal Wilhelm Keitel, Chief of OKW. Keitel exercised no influence over operations, acting merely as a functionary, faithfully carrying out the Führer's orders in a style which prompted Hitler to refer to him as 'treu wie ein Hund'. In less charitable mood Hitler observed that Keitel had the brains of a cinema commissionaire. Mussolini's assessment was that Keitel was a man who was very pleased to be Keitel. Young staff officers referred to him as Lakaitel (a pun on the German for servant) or 'nodding donkey', a reference to Keitel's constant readiness to agree with the Führer. General Walter Warlimont, Deputy Chief of Operations at OKW, recalled Keitel's conduct at the daily Führer briefings: 'He could hardly wait for some catch-word or pause in Hitler's flow of speech to indicate by some word or gesture that, without further ado, he was in agreement.'

From the winter of 1941 Hitler had taken on the mantle of Feldherr, the warlord in control of Germany's destiny and in personal command of all air, naval and ground forces. He controlled the field formations in every theatre through two separate and squabbling staffs. And he exercised a direct hold over every officer, from lieutenant to field marshal, through the Army Personnel office which, in the autumn of 1942, was removed from OKW and placed under the Führer's military adjutant and devoted admirer, General Rudolf Schmundt.

Hitler had successfully concluded his crusade against the

Prussian military caste he so heartily loathed. In a radio broadcast of 30 September 1942 he told the German people that victory had been secured, not over the enemy but over the 'old world' of hidebound military tradition represented by the red trouser stripes and silver collar tabs of the General Staff. In Hitler's 'classless' society the future belonged to the brave and loyal Party man. Half-hearted attempts to persuade Hitler to merge OKW and OKH were brushed aside, as were suggestions from Manstein that a C-in-C Eastern Front (doubtless Manstein himself) be appointed. But, as Warlimont gloomily observed of the doomed efforts to effect a merger of OKW and OKH:

> A combination of these two offices in the hands of one man would have been entirely opposed to Hitler's innermost conviction, for he always followed the principle of division of authority . . . Hitler did not want unity, he preferred diversity, such unity as there was being concentrated in his person alone.

While Hitler saw himself as the reincarnation of a military genius like Frederick the Great, Josef Stalin, the Soviet Union's Supreme Commander,* Commissar for Defence and Chairman of the Council of People's Commissars, took on the Russian role of Vozhd, the all-seeing leader, in whom all knowledge, insight and ability reside.

In the person of Stalin also resided all authority. He dominated the Russian war effort, establishing his supremacy over the Soviet military from the outset, possibly because of his personal experience of operations as commissar of the First Cavalry Army during the Civil War. Nevertheless, in the first days of the German invasion of the Soviet Union it seems that he came close to a nervous breakdown. When he recovered his poise his characteristic reaction was to consolidate control of the war in his hands. To have done otherwise would have been to cut himself adrift from the state and military systems he had built up around himself in the 1930s. In June 1941 he created the State Defence Committee, or GKO, which oversaw all political, military and economic aspects

---

* Although Stalin had secretly become Supreme Commander on 8 August 1941, he was always officially referred to as Commissar for Defence.

of the war. Its original members were Stalin, Foreign Minister Molotov, Malenkov (Stalin's right-hand man in the Communist Party organization), Marshal Voroshilov, who had served as Commissar for Defence from 1925 to 1940, and Beria, head of the secret police, the NKVD.

GKO administered military matters through the Stavka of the high command; this became the highest organ of field direction of the armed forces of the Soviet Union. The Stavka drew up battle plans and through its adjunct, the General Staff, directly organized the preparation and execution of strategic operations. Representatives of Stavka made frequent trips to the fronts and, in accordance with the strategic plan, organized important on-the-spot operations, exercising control over the execution of Stavka orders and coordinating the actions of different fronts.

In all probability Stalin saw Stavka as a kind of 'military Politburo' of top commanders, later augmented by technicians, who could present options and the supporting facts for discussion. At the end of the process Stalin would make the final decision. Thus behind the facade of collegial command Stalin continued to wield untrammelled power as Commander in Chief, relying throughout the early crises of the war on the fear he had always instilled in his subordinates. Visiting Moscow in October 1941, General Sir Hastings Ismay, Churchill's military aide, noted that when Stalin entered a room 'every Russian froze into silence and the hunted look in the eyes of the generals showed all too plainly the constant fear in which they lived. It was nauseating to see brave men reduced to such servility.'

Fear may have eaten away at the soul of many of Stalin's commanders – the penalty for failure was often the penal battalion, sometimes death – but there were some important exceptions, most notably Marshal Georgi K. Zhukov, who, in August 1942, was appointed Deputy Supreme Commander of the Red Army.

Zhukov had been conscripted into the Tsarist Army at the beginning of the First World War. He supported the Bolshevik revolution of 1917, joining the Red Army on its foundation, and served as a cavalry commander during the Civil War and the invasion of Poland. Zhukov subsequently became a specialist in armoured warfare, teaching the subject at the Frunze military academy. In the early 1930s, during the period of military cooper-ation between Hitler and Stalin, he studied military science in Germany. Most important of all, he contrived to avoid the purges which cut a swathe through the upper echelons of the Red Army during the late 1930s. In 1939 Zhukov was given command of Soviet forces in the Far East where there had been border clashes with the Japanese along the Manchurian frontier. In May 1939 the brutal jockeying for position in the region between Japan and the Soviet Union came to a head when Japan launched an attack on Mongolia, effectively a satellite of the Soviet Union. Invoking a mutual defence treaty, Stalin went to the aid of the Mongolians. In the subsequent battles of Khalkin Gol the Japanese Sixth Army was encircled and heavily defeated. On 16 September the Japanese signed an armistice.

Although over 250,000 men were involved in the fighting, the Khalkin Gol battles were virtually ignored in the West, pre-occupied as it was with Hitler's invasion of Poland. Nevertheless, the outcome had a profound strategic effect on the Japanese who never repeated their move against the Soviet Union, even in the autumn of 1941 when Barbarossa seemed likely to achieve its objectives. Zhukov had handled the operation with massive competence, rather than flair, disposing of over 500 tanks and demonstrating his 'stern character', a Soviet euphemism for ruthlessness and the summary disciplining or dismissal of subordinates who were squeamish about casualties.

General Ivan Bagramyan, who had served with Zhukov at the Higher Cavalry School in Leningrad in 1925 and was to end the war in command of the Red Army's First Baltic Front, has left a vivid picture of Zhukov in 1940 when he was commanding the Kiev Special Military District:

> Georgi Konstantinovich had not changed too much. Actually he was still thickset, his hair was slightly thinner and the lines of his face more deeply etched; which gave him a more serious expression. Yet, in those fifteen years he had been more successful than his classmates. But his success did not surprise me. Of all the outstanding military commanders who rose with lightning speed in the prewar years, he was

without doubt the most brilliant and gifted personality. In the period of our training together in Leningrad, among all of us he was distinguished not only by a truly iron-hard persistence* in attaining an established goal, but also by a particular originality of thought. In our exercises he frequently amazed us with something unexpected. His decisions always evoked the greatest controversies and he usually was able with rare logic to defend them . . . his strictness with his subordinates – thanks to his outstanding mind and highly developed intellect – seldom turned into the outspoken rudeness which characterized a number of military chieftains at the time. He was a terror only for the good-for-nothing.

Success in the field secured Zhukov's appointment as Chief of General Staff in January 1941. In July he was removed from the post by Stalin for advocating a withdrawal at Kiev, but in September he was given control of forces in the field, directing the holding operation which denied the city of Leningrad to the enemy and led to a 900-day siege. A month later he was given command of the buckling Western Front, the central sector of which was threatened by a renewed German drive on Moscow.

Feeding reinforcements and material into the line, Zhukov halted the German advance and then, as the Russian winter took a ferocious hold on the front, launched a counter-offensive which drove the enemy back 200 miles before the front congealed in the spring thaw. Zhukov's handling of the defence of Moscow had demonstrated the essence of his method: an acute reading of the enemy's intentions; an ability to juggle scant resources under great pressure in the front line while calmly amassing a powerful reserve in the rear; and the nerve to withhold the reserve – the thirty fresh divisions transferred from Siberia – until the moment when he judged that the enemy had reached the end of his tether.

Zhukov clashed a second time with Stalin, on this occasion over the scale of the counter-offensive launched after the defeat of the Germans in front of Moscow. In August 1942, however, he was appointed Deputy Supreme Commander of the Red Army, a post he held until the end of the war. The official Soviet history comments that, by appointing a deputy supreme commander, Stalin

---

* Another Soviet military euphemism for extreme ruthlessness.

had introduced 'a new element in the leadership at the strategic level', and that Zhukov and his new Chief of Staff, General Aleksandr M. Vasilevsky (appointed in June 1942), were 'provided with plenipotentiary powers and possessed great authority over the fighting forces'. Crucially, with the appointment of Zhukov as his deputy, Stalin inserted into the chain of command (above the operational) a battle-hardened military professional who had proved his worth as his 'fireman' in 1941 when the survival of the Soviet Union hung in the balance.

Zhukov and Vasilevsky provided the points around which a recognizable high command could coalesce. The planning and execution of the counter-offensive at Stalingrad had not only been overseen personally by Zhukov but had also brought the commanding general of the air force, Aleksandr Novikov, and the chiefs of artillery and armour – who had previously held largely administrative posts in the Defence Commissariat – into the line of command under Zhukov and Vasilevsky. In December 1942 the Red Army's artillery, armoured and mechanized forces joined the air force in being accorded branch status; their chiefs became commanding generals and deputy defence commissars. The system, still essentially ad hoc, assumed permanent form in May 1943, when Zhukov's and Vasilevsky's appointments as First and Second Deputy Defence Commissars placed them at the head of both the line and staff military chains of command.

Zhukov's position came as close as Stalin would allow to that of commander in chief. Certainly, Zhukov never quailed before Stalin in the manner recorded by General Ismay. In his memoirs General P.A. Belov, who commanded Sixty-First Army at Kursk, recalled Zhukov's impressive presence at a meeting with Stalin in 1941. Although allowances must be made for the spin given to the passage by 'de-Stalinization', it nevertheless underlines Zhukov's importance to Stalin and his status as the man of the hour:

> Zhukov presented me to Stalin, who stood in the centre of the office. Now, calling to mind the past, I automatically remember the small, insignificant details, the first impressions which surprised and puzzled me. In those years much was written about Stalin in the papers, calling him strong, wise and a genius – in a word, they did not spare epithets. I had not seen him since

1933. Since that time he had changed greatly; before me stood a man of short height with a tired, sunken face. In eight years he had aged, it seemed, twenty years. In his eyes there was not the former strength (and) in his voice confidence was not felt. But the behaviour of Zhukov surprised me even more. He spoke sharply, in an imperious tone. The impression was such that the senior chief might have been Zhukov. And Stalin perceived it properly. At times he even had a somewhat perplexed look on his face.

In 1942 both Stalin and Hitler had tested their powers as supreme commanders almost to destruction. On 28 July 1942, echoing Hitler in December 1941, Stalin had issued his 'not a step back' order; this was read to every Soviet soldier and applied, most sternly of all, to the troops in the Stalingrad sector. Nevertheless, Stalin was prepared to countenance some flexibility *in extremis*. Earlier in July, as the Red Army faced a series of encirclements which threatened to repeat those of 1941, Vasilevsky had persuaded Stalin that 'stand fast' orders issued merely for their own sake were only one step away from strategic bankruptcy. He thus ensured the withdrawal and survival of a significant part of Marshal Timoshenko's forces in the Don-Donets corridor.

On 13 September, at a meeting in the Kremlin with Vasilevsky and Zhukov, now in overall command of the Stalingrad sector, Stalin dropped his initial objections to their plan for a wide encirclement of the German forces on the Lower Volga and the destruction of Paulus's Sixth Army at Stalingrad. Stalin's argument for a narrow encirclement was dismissed, as were his doubts that there were sufficient forces available for the operation. Zhukov and Vasilevsky assured him that these could be assembled and equipped within forty-five days. Stalin withdrew his objections, adding the rider that the 'main business' was to ensure that Stalingrad did not fall.

By the autumn of 1942 Stalin was beginning to learn to temper his over-confidence and impetuosity with a caution acquired at the cost of millions of men and thousands of tanks. Only the Soviet Union could have suffered such a prodigal waste of manpower and material and yet remain in the field. Vasilevsky later wrote:

> The Stalingrad battle was an important turning point [in
> Stalin's development as a military leader]. J.V. Stalin began not
> only to understand military strategy well . . . but also found his
> way about well in the operational art. As a result he exercised
> a strong influence on the working of operations.

At the same time Hitler and Stalin had arrived at a system of
command which suited their particular temperaments. However,
while Hitler's solution left him in a permanent state of decidedly
uncreative tension with his generals, Stalin was able to make the
best possible use of the outstanding military professionals who
had emerged since June 1941 without undermining his final
authority over the armed forces. Unlike Hitler, who was a fatal
combination of the dilettante and the doctrinaire, imposing his
own blueprint on every operation, Stalin tended to collect the
opinions of those who mattered most, weigh the pros and cons
while applying his detailed knowledge of the overall situation and
then reach a decision. Usually he sanctioned a course of action on
which Stavka had already been deliberating, as that concerning
Stalingrad. Thus the view of the majority became Stalin's, encouraging the collective initiative of his commanders and allowing indi-
viduals to put forward radical ideas for discussion.

In the final analysis the majority – those commanders who had
proved themselves by performance in battle – was of Stalin's own
making and there for the breaking, too, if the occasion demanded
it. Descending on the fronts, Zhukov, Vasilevsky and other Stavka
representatives could wield great powers, but they held these
only at Stalin's pleasure. When it suited him, the distance between
the Supreme Commander and his deputies could yawn as wide as
the gulf between a marshal and a private.

Hugh Trevor Roper has suggested that Hitler and Stalin were
not so much ideological antipodes as serious rivals in the deadly
game of dictatorship. They admired each other's ruthlessness and
studied each other's methods. They reserved for each other the
respect due between those at the top of their profession.

In the war their patterns of working were curiously similar, con-
forming to a secretive, nocturnal routine which reversed night and
day. From the beginning of the Russian campaign Hitler had fought
the greater part of the war from the Wolf's Lair deep in the drip-

ping Gorlitz forests of East Prussia. Behind the barbed wire and minefields which surrounded Security Zone One he retreated into a self-imposed isolation, moving in an airless world of map tables and military conferences.

Freezing in winter and stiflingly hot in summer, the Wolf's Lair fed off the Führer's enervation and gloom. Count Ciano, Mussolini's Foreign Minister, found the atmosphere there intensely depressing: 'One does not see a single colourful spot, not a single lively touch. The ante-rooms are full of people smoking, eating and chatting. Smell of kitchens, uniforms, heavy boots.'

Those who came and went, waited and smoked, or stood awkwardly silent as the Führer shuffled through the compound with his Alsatian bitch Blondi at his side, were mere extras in a drama whose last act was being written by a man retreating step by step from reality. After Stalingrad, Hitler strove to conceal his growing depression and deteriorating health behind a mask of rigid self-control. But the mask kept slipping and his physical appearance shocked those who had not seen him for some time. Visiting Hitler at his headquarters in the Ukraine on 20 February 1943 to confirm his own appointment as Inspector-General of Armoured Troops, Colonel-General Guderian found him greatly changed since their last meeting in December 1941: 'His left hand trembled, his back was bent, his gaze was fixed, his eyes protruded but lacked their former lustre, his cheeks were flecked with red. He was more excitable, easily lost his composure and was prone to angry outbursts and ill-considered decisions.'

Nevertheless, Hitler maintained his routine in all its stupefying monotony. He rose late in the morning and, at midday, accompanied by his *maison militaire*, he attended a briefing conference lasting two to three hours. In the stuffy, crowded conference room Hitler was the only one who was seated, although an upholstered stool was usually provided for the corpulent Göring. Around the map table, illuminated by desk lamps with long swinging arms, stood Hitler's adjutants, OKW staff officers and the Army General Staff, and the Führer's liaison officers with the Luftwaffe, Kriegsmarine, Waffen-SS and Himmler's Ministry of the Interior. Albert Speer recalled that, 'on the whole, they were rather young men with likeable faces, most of them holding the rank of colonel or major'. Keitel, Jodl and the Army Chief of Staff, Colonel-General Kurt Zeitzler, stood casually among them. Throughout the conference there was a low background hum of whispered conversation.

The Eastern Front was the first item on the agenda. On the situation table Hitler would work his way from north to south on four large strategic maps, pasted together and each measuring about eight by five feet; these carried information on the previous day's events down to the activities of patrols. The layman Speer was 'astonished at the way Hitler, in the course of hearing the reports, made deployments, pushed divisions back and forth, or dealt with petty details'.

As the war progressed, Hitler's tendency to indulge in unrestrained monologue frequently prevented the rational consideration of the day's business. Warlimont recalled that

> urgent concrete questions and proposals under discussion would be drowned in this ceaseless, repetitive torrent of words in which matters old and new, important and unimportant, were jumbled up together. There would also frequently be long-winded telephone conversations with senior commanders at the front; sometimes the latter used the knowledge of the time at which the briefing conferences took place to try to get urgent decisions out of Hitler; alternatively he would call them up in the vague hope that they would be able to provide him with more pleasant information than that presented by Halder.*

Technical experts, often from the traffic-control authorities, ministers and secretaries of state were regularly summoned to these conferences to be 'questioned, lectured or threatened'. Hitler no doubt felt that their presence injected a sense of purpose and unity into the proceedings, but this was frequently dispelled by the delight he took in browbeating senior officers with barrages of statistics carried in his head. Manstein observed of this *rage*

---

* Zeitzler's predecessor, Colonel-General Franz Halder, who was appointed Chief of Staff in 1938 and dismissed on 24 September 1942 after an argument with Hitler over the latter's policy of simultaneous advance on two fronts; this led to the disaster at Stalingrad.

de nombre: 'He was amazingly familiar with the effects of the very latest enemy weapons and could reel off whole columns of figures on both our own and the enemy's war production. Indeed, this was his favourite way of sidetracking any topic that was not to his liking.' Both Warlimont and Speer concluded that the hours taken up by the briefings, and the preparations for them, were a great waste of time.

Lunch was taken at a long, oblong table with the attentive Jodl at the Führer's left and a visitor such as Göring or Speer on his right. Liaison officers and young adjutants, ranged down the table, were all ears as Hitler's table talk unreeled on a nightmarish loop. After Stalingrad, however, the Führer increasingly took to eating his meagre vegetarian meals alone. After lunch there were more meetings and conferences before Hitler took a break to guzzle cream cakes with his female secretaries in a forlorn attempt to provide them with a 'congenial atmosphere'. Late at night, after the last meeting, Hitler would reassemble this captive audience and continue talking until dawn, regaling them with crude invective about Churchill ('an alcoholic bullshit'), Roosevelt ('a cracked fool') and generals like Manstein ('a pisspot strategist') and lurching seemingly at random between subjects both ludicrous and sinister: Ice Age catastrophes, the 'stunted smears' of modern art, cannibalism among the defenders of Leningrad, the best way of dealing with a mutiny in Germany ('shoot a batch of a few thousand people') and the good sense of the Soviet system which did not bother with 'all that humanitarian blather'.

A secretary who regularly attended these marathon sessions wrote in July 1941: 'I really must start writing down what the Chief says. It's just that these sessions go on for ages and afterwards you are just too limp and lifeless to write anything.' After a while, sitting up with the insomniac Führer must have become almost unendurable. Release came at dawn when, as Guderian recalled, 'Hitler would lie down for a brief sleep, from which the pushing brooms of the scrubwomen at his bedroom door would awaken him by nine o' clock at the latest.'

Stalin's working day imposed similar strains on those around him. Like Hitler's it began at midday when he rang the operations directorate of the General Staff for a briefing on the events of the previous night. The answering officer would describe the situation to Stalin as he walked from one map to another, a ten-yard-long telephone lead trailing behind him. Stalin followed the reports on a corresponding set of maps in his office which were updated every five days. He dealt with the most important fronts first, referring to the larger formations by their commanders, the lesser by their numbers and designation. Sometimes he would interrupt the briefing to dictate an order to be sent to a particular front.

A second briefing followed at 4pm, occasionally by telephone but usually presented in person by General A.I. Antonov, who had been appointed Chief of Operations in December 1942. (As Vasilevsky was so frequently in the field directing operations, Antonov was the de facto Chief of Staff.) A gifted and extremely efficient staff officer, Antonov had previously served as Chief of Staff to the Trans-Caucasus Front. His predecessors as Chief of Operations had come and gone as if through a revolving door, but Antonov made the job his own. He delayed his first appearance at a Stavka meeting for a week while he immersed himself in the general situation. When the summons came, he was well prepared. Thereafter he streamlined the decision-making process, presenting material to Stalin in three sets of files: red for urgent matters (draft directions and orders); blue for less pressing business; and green for promotions and appointments. The presentation of the last required all of Antonov's considerable powers of timing.

Shortly after midnight the final briefing took place, either at Stalin's dacha outside Moscow or in his quarters at the Kremlin. The way to Stalin's apartments lay through the office of his secretary, Poskrebyshev, and past a cubby hole occupied by the chief of the dictator's NKVD bodyguard. Inside, under a vaulted ceiling and surrounded by light oak panelling from which hung portraits of Suvorov, Kutuzov, Marx and Engels, Stalin, Stavka and members of GKO and the Politburo awaited the briefing presented by Antonov and his head of operations, General Sergei M. Shtemenko.* In his memoirs, Shtemenko recalled:

---

* The work of the General Staff was organized on a twenty-four-hour basis. Antonov was relieved from duty from 6am to noon and Shtemenko from to 2pm to 6pm.

In the left part of (Stalin's) *Kabinet*, a small way from the wall, stood a long, rectangular table. We spread out the maps* on it and delivered a report on each front separately, beginning with those where the main events were taking place. We made no preliminary notes, since we both knew the situation from memory and it was outlined on the map. Behind the table, in the corner, a large globe of the world stood on the floor.

Usually attending these midnight briefings were the heads of the main arms and services: Fedorenko (chief of armoured forces), Voronov (artillery), Yakovlev (artillery administration), Novikov (air force), Khrulev (rear services), Peresypkin (signals), Vorob'ev (engineers).

During the briefing, which normally lasted about three hours, Stalin paced back and forth in front of a death mask of Lenin, his hands behind his back and puffing steadily at his pipe. Finally, came the drafting of Stavka directives and orders which were often dictated by Stalin on the spot, noted and corrected by Shtemenko and then immediately transmitted to the fronts from Poskrebyshev's signals centre just a few yards away.

Stalin maintained his control over the fronts not only with the Stavka supervisors but also with civilian representatives who joined the military soviets as the political member, serving alongside the commander and Chief of Staff. On the Southern Front the political member was Lieutenant-General Nikita Khrushchev. He was there to ensure that the Kremlin's orders were carried out, to report on the loyalty of the front's senior officers and Party members and to cooperate with the NKVD troops who stood between the front line and retreat. In his memoirs Khrushchev recalled being ordered by Stalin to keep a close eye on the front's then commander Malinovsky:** 'When you return to the Front,

---

* The maps were on a scale of 1:200,000 for each front with positions down to division and, in some cases, regiment.

** Stalin's suspicions about Malinovsky, whom he had never met, were fuelled by the suicide of a member of the military council of Second Guards Army, Larin, who had left a note which concluded, 'Long live Lenin.' Malinovsky himself was considered politically unreliable because he had been part of the Tsarist expeditionary force to France in the First World War and had been on White-occupied territory when he had joined the Red Army. Malinovsky ended the war as a Marshal of the Soviet Union, commanding the Trans-Baikal Front.

you'd better keep a close watch on him. I want you to keep a close eye on Second Guards Army HQ, too. Check up on all his orders and decisions. Follow his every move.' Khrushchev followed orders: 'I had to spy on Malinovsky every hour of the day. I had to watch him even when he went to bed to see if he closed his eyes and really went to sleep. I didn't like having to do this one bit.' But do it Khrushchev did. Although in his memoirs he claimed that, on several occasions, he intervened personally in attempts to mitigate the disastrous consequences of Stalin's orders, Khrushchev knew that he could venture only so far into such dangerous waters:

> It was as though the Devil himself held a string attached to Stalin's main nerve, and no one knew when the Devil would give the string a jerk, sending Stalin into one of his fits of rage. Both Stalin's temper and his self-control were developed to an advanced degree. He was, in short, an overpowering personality.

CHAPTER 3

The Vanishing Army

'The number of the dead is increasing, the number of the wounded is frightful. In my black book there is already one black cross after another, my whole community is either dead or wounded.' The chaplain of 18th Panzer Division, 9 July 1942

THE INVASION OF the Soviet Union in June 1941 was planned as the last of Hitler's Blitzkrieg campaigns. In the summer of 1943, however, the fighting in the East was absorbing the greater part of the German war effort. On the Eastern Front there were 168 divisions (3.1 million men), with six SS and twelve Luftwaffe field divisions, and 3000 tanks. In other theatres there were seventy-five divisions (1.4 million) men, with five SS and ten Luftwaffe field divisions, and 1300 tanks. In France, where an Allied invasion loomed, there were forty-four field divisions, mostly of poor quality, and 860 tanks, of which half were captured French vehicles. In Italy, which was now more immediately threatened, there were seven divisions and 570 tanks.

The successful conclusion of Manstein's counter-offensive could not mask the declining strength of the Ostheer. General Thomas, head of the economics section at OKW, estimated that, while losses in the East up to Stalingrad represented the equivalent of about fifty fully equipped divisions, in the battle for Stalingrad alone the equivalent of forty-five divisions were lost. At the end of March 1943, as the front stabilized in the East, the Ostheer was 470,000 men below establishment.

Front-line formations had been shredded by the fighting. The 18th Panzer Division, established in the autumn of 1940, began the war against the Soviet Union as a formation of 17,174 (including 400 officers and administrative personnel) in Guderian's Panzer Group 2. In the first three weeks of the invasion the division lost 60 per cent of its tanks, and on 11 July the divisional commander expressed fears that the loss of men and equipment would prove insupportable 'if we do not intend to win ourselves to death'. In August 1941 18th Panzer was re-equipped, but by November it had lost all its tanks. When the Soviet counter-offensive burst upon the Ostheer on 6 December 1941, the division had only 50 per cent of its original combat strength and 25 per cent of its vehicles. The divisional chaplain wrote in his diary: 'This is no longer the old division. All around are new faces. When one asks after somebody, the same reply is always given: dead or wounded. Most of the rifle company commanders are new, most of the old ones are gone.' The division spent 1942 in the Zhisdra area where, in July, it sustained 1406 casualties in the first four days of the German summer offensive. The chaplain noted that the colonel of one of the worst hit regiments 'stands silently in front of the long row of graves: "There lies my old guard. In reality we should also be there. Then it would all be over."'

In September 1941, 18th Panzer had a combat strength of 9616 men (293 officers and 9323 other ranks). By April 1943 this had shrunk to 3906 men (124 officers and 3782 other ranks). Attrition left the division with a high proportion of inexperienced officers and freshly promoted NCOs, while the NCOs' positions were occupied by privates. An attempt was made to tackle the manpower shortage by the employment of armed Russian 'volunteers', the Hilsfreiwillige (or Hiwis), on lines-of-communications duties. By December 1942, there were nearly 400 Hiwis serving with 18th Panzer, a figure which was quickly quadrupled by a policy of forcible recruitment. By mid-summer 1943 there were 1659 Hiwis in the division's Voluntary Russian Rear Security Companies and another 1006 workers building field works and undertaking local guard duties. Few were willing wearers of German uniform.

By the spring of 1943 the high rate of casualties and the lack of reserves made it impossible to bring depleted divisions up to full strength. Logic dictated that divisions should be merged to maintain a sustainable ratio between combat troops and those in the auxiliary tail. This would have encouraged the economic use of experienced officers, NCOs and specialists and more effective employment of motor vehicles, equipment and horses.* Hitler's obsession with numbers frustrated any such rationalization. For the Führer, what mattered was the number of divisions in the order of battle, not their quality. Thus, every one of the divisions lost at Stalingrad was reconstituted, along with four of the six lost in Tunisia. In the twelve months from July 1942 the number of field divisions in the Army, SS and Luftwaffe rose by fifty-five. The creation of twenty-two Luftwaffe divisions was particularly shortsighted, although typical of the free-for-all at the top of the Nazi hierarchy, encouraged by Hitler. The men would have been more efficiently absorbed into existing divisions in the Army, but Hitler accepted Göring's objections to 'good young National Socialists being dressed in the grey (i.e., reactionary) uniform of the Army'.

The additional Luftwaffe divisions gave Hitler another stick with which to beat the generals, but they were a signal waste of manpower as the divisions were never efficient fighting formations. OKW finally secured their incorporation into the Army in October 1943, but they were to remain a constant liability in battle.

In March 1943 the greatest cause for alarm was the parlous state of the panzer arm. At the end of January 1943 there were only 495 battleworthy tanks on the Eastern Front, the great majority of them being PzKw IIIs and IVs which, in spite of being upgunned and more heavily armoured, were matched by the Red Army's T-34/76. Nearly 8000 German tanks had been lost in the fighting since June 1941. In the first three months of 1943 losses totalled 2529, representing 59 per cent of the total production for

---

* For all its vaunted armoured spearheads, the German Army depended on horses for over 80 per cent of its motive power. Some 2.5 million horses served on the Eastern Front and, on average, 1000 of them died every day. To obtain replacements, a vast remount organization was set up throughout occupied Europe.

1942. The morale of the panzer troops, now contemplating their numerical and technical inferiority to the enemy, was low. Battle fatigue eroded morale. Early in 1943 the operations officer of the elite Grossdeutschland Division reported that 'fatigue within the division has become so severe that the feeling of indifference is spreading and cannot be opposed by any means'.

The decline in the panzer arm owed much to the procurement and manufacturing muddles caused by Hitler's persistent meddling in the technical matters which so absorbed him. The arrival in numbers on the Eastern Front of the Russian T-34 in the autumn of 1941 had given the Ostheer an unpleasant shock. Guderian later wrote: 'Up to that time we had enjoyed tank superiority, but from now on the situation was reversed.' In the winter of 1941 a German tank sergeant wrote of the impact made by the T-34:

> There is nothing more frightening than a tank battle against superior force. Numbers – they don't mean much, we were used to it. But better machines, that's terrible. You race the engine but she responds too slowly. The Rusian tanks are so agile, at close range they will climb a slope or cross a piece of swamp faster than you can traverse the turret. And through the noise and the vibration you keep hearing the clang of shot against armour. When they hit one of our panzers, there is so often a deep, long explosion, a roar as the fuel burns, a roar too loud, thank God, to let us hear the cries of the crew.

The T-34's sloped armour, speed and manoeuvrability brought about a profound change in tank design. At first, serious consideration was given to producing a straightforward German copy of the T-34, incorporating important modifications like universal radio installation and powered turret traverse. The designers demurred, however, not solely from offended pride but also because of the technical difficulties involved in manufacturing the aluminium components in the diesel engine. Having ruled out military plagiarism, the decision was made to continue with the production of the 60-ton PzKw VI Tiger I heavy battle tank, which had started production in August 1942, and to design a lighter tank, the PzKw V Panther, weighing 45 tons, which would incorporate the outstanding features of the T-34.

The Tiger, whose origins lay in a 1937 specification for a heavy 'breakthrough' tank, had endured a troubled development history. In 1941, after the first encounters with the T-34, the 1937 concept was revived, resulting in a specification for a heavy tank capable of mounting the formidable 88mm high-velocity gun in a turret with a full traverse and carrying sufficient armour to defeat all present and future anti-tank weapons. Two firms, Porsche and Henschel, submitted prototypes for this second-generation panzer.

Dr Ferdinand Porsche, one of Hitler's intimates, was a brilliant designer of motor-cars, notably the Volkswagen and the brutally powerful Auto Union Grand Prix racer, but, like the Führer, he was more of a visionary than a nuts-and-bolts man. Porsche's plans for the Tiger were unconventional, including provision for electric transmission, and were rejected by the Army Ordnance Office. Undaunted, Porsche pressed on, securing from Hitler backing for the development of a mammoth tank weighing 180 tons, the Maus (Mouse), which reflected the Führer's growing obsession with bizarre weapons systems.

At the same time Porsche profited from the artillery arm's urgent demands for powerful self-propelled tank destroyers (Jagdpanzer) and infantry support guns (Sturmgeschutze) to supersede the obsolescent 37mm and 50mm towed anti-tank guns which were wholly ineffective against the T-34. Improvised first-generation tank destroyers – Marders – had appeared in 1942, consisting of a 75mm anti-tank gun mounted on the chassis of an obsolescent German or foreign tank (PzKw IIs and Czech 38-Ts). The fighting compartment was protected by a fixed open-topped superstructure of armour plate. Hitler immediately grasped that the production of Jagdpanzer was not only quicker and cheaper than that of tanks but that it also provided a fast road to boosting the strength of the panzer arm. In this he received partisan encouragement from the artillery arm which had been careful to retain the assault guns and tank destroyers within its command structure.

Dr Porsche was now able to regain some of the ground lost by the rejection of his Tiger prototype; he peddled to Hitler a Jagdpanzer variant based on the Tiger chassis and known variously as the Ferdinand and the Elefant. The Elefant heavy tank destroyer carried an 88mm gun on a fixed superstructure at the rear of the hull and was protected at the front by 200mm of belly armour. At first sight the Elefant was a formidable beast, but it was expensive to produce in comparison with the Marder; it also shared the latter's limitations of narrow field of fire and restricted accommodation. The Elefant also lacked secondary armament, a flaw which was to prove fatal in the Kursk salient at the beginning of July 1943.

Porsche's political footwork had diverted resources from the development of the successful Tiger prototype submitted by Henschel which was prematurely committed to battle in August–September 1942. Like a schoolboy with a birthday train set, Hitler always wanted to use his new weapons immediately they became available, forfeiting the advantages of surprise and employment en masse in the most favourable conditions. Instead, the first batch of Tigers was thrown into action piecemeal in a secondary operation in the swampy forests near Leningrad where the terrain was quite unsuitable. Lumbering in single file along the forest tracks, the Tigers were picked off by Russian anti-tank guns.

Nevertheless, the Tiger emerged from this discouraging combat debut as the most powerful tank in the world. Its 88mm gun, which had ninety-two rounds of ammunition, packed a heavy punch and outranged the T-34. Its armour was not well sloped, as was that of the Panther, but it was 100mm thick at the front and 80mm thick around the sides. Its weight made it slow, however with a cross-country speed of only 12mph; this limited its operational range to about sixty miles and imposed a severe strain on its gear-box which required frequent maintenance and repair. By November 1942, production of the Tiger had reached twenty-five a month.

As if in anticipation of the minefields they would encounter in service, the new armoured vehicles had to nose their way across a development obstacle course of Hitler's devising. While events demanded a ruthless standardization of German armour, that great military dilettante indulged in ever wilder flights of fancy: an Elefant equipped with a 210mm mortar; the development of Ram Tigers for street fighting; the transformation of the Gustav 800mm railway gun into an anti-tank weapon; and, most extraordinary of all, a specification drawn up for a 1000-ton 'land monitor', final proof of the galloping gigantism which had overtaken Hitler's military thinking. The result of this eclecticism, when applied to models already in production, was, as Guderian noted, 'the . . . creation of countless variations to the original type, each of which would need innumerable spare parts. The repair of tanks in the field became impossible.' All this occurred at a time when the Soviet Union was concentrating on the mass production of the T-34.

The crucial factor remained the number of tanks in the field. Here the picture was grim. The panzer divisions had originally been designed to contain four tank battalions with a total strength of approximately 400 tanks per division. By the beginning of 1943 there were only three battalions in a division, one of which was equipped with Jagdpanzer. Matters were complicated by the withdrawal of the obsolete PzKw II, which was little more than a death trap, and the difficulty that commanders of old formations faced when attempting to secure allocations of new tanks which were reserved for the building-up of fresh divisions. The reluctance of these commanders to send vehicles in need of major overhaul back to Germany also meant that many tanks remained stranded in divisional garages not best equipped to repair them. As a result, panzer divisions seldom mustered more than 100 tanks, and the average hovered between seventy and eighty. Firepower was further reduced by the division of authority between the panzer arm and the artillery, which enabled the latter to draw off the Jagdpanzer for the motorized infantry and the Waffen-SS.

As Hitler's disillusion with the Army grew, his faith in the Waffen-SS increased. He saw the SS which, by 1944, numbered thirty-eight divisions (600,000 men) as the historic successor to the Order of Teutonic Knights and the true repository of National Socialist virtue. The expansion of the Waffen-SS which, in June 1941, had contained 150,000 men disposed among five divisions, had been accomplished at the expense of the Army, although the latter retained control of the Waffen-SS in the field. Nevertheless, SS armoured divisions were more lavishly equipped than their Army counterparts. The armoured units of an elite Waffen-SS panzer grenadier* division, like Leibstandarte Adolf Hitler, deployed the same firepower as an Army panzer division.

That even Hitler realized that some order had to imposed on the armoured forces was confirmed by his appointment in February 1943 of Colonel-General Heinz Guderian as Inspector-General of Armoured Troops. His brief was to oversee 'the future development of armoured troops along lines that will make that arm of the service into a decisive weapon for winning the war'.

Guderian, the Army's leading theorist and practitioner of armoured operations, had been removed from the command of Panzer Group 2 on Christmas Day 1941 after conducting a tactical withdrawal from an exposed position as the Red Army launched its counter-offensive before Moscow. Plagued by heart problems, Guderian had kicked his heels in the OKH officers' reserve pool until summoned to Vinnitsa to assume control of the organization, training, manning and equipping of all panzer and panzer grenadier units.

Guderian met Hitler on 20 February, later recording his surprise at how ill the Führer looked and his pleasure at seeing copies of his books on armoured tactics prominently displayed in the Commander in Chief's quarters. The Führer gave him the same emollient welcome he had accorded Manstein two weeks earlier, telling him, 'Since 1941 our ways have parted; there were numerous misunderstandings at that time which I much regret. I need you.'

The assignment of duties which Guderian subsequently drew up with Keitel and General Friedrich Fromm, the commander of the Replacement Army, was signed by Hitler on 28 February. Guderian had made his return to active duty conditional on the granting of sweeping powers to the Inspectorate-General, which was to report directly to Hitler, bypassing OKW, the Replacement Army and the Chief of the General Staff whom

---

* The panzer grenadier division had evolved within the German Army as a motorized infantry formation to augment the true panzer division but, as the war progressed, the distinction between the two became increasingly blurred, particularly within the SS as their allotment of armoured fighting vehicles (AFVs) grew larger. Leibstandarte, which had achieved divisional status in 1942, fielded two tank battalions, one of Tigers and one of Mk IVs, two panzer grenadier regiments and mobile anti-tank and assault-gun detachments.

Guderian was obliged only to 'consult'. Luftwaffe and SS armoured units were to come under his control. Guderian had effectively secured independent command of panzer troops within the Reich, with complete responsibility for all panzer troops in the armed forces. OKW and OKH, already at each other's throats, were now presented with a new rival over which only Hitler exercised control.

Guderian himself was aware of the chaos created by the clashing personalities and overlapping staffs within the high command, although his memoirs contain no hint that the manner of his own elevation to the Inspectorate-General was a symptom of the problem rather than part of its solution. On 3 March, while visiting Goebbels, Guderian raised with the Propaganda Minister the question of the 'confusion of leadership' and Hitler's growing tendency to interfere in matters of subordinate importance. He suggested that the Führer would be 'well advised to appoint some Chief of the Armed Forces General Staff as his assistant; and that the man chosen should be one who understood how to function as an operational commander and who was more qualified to fill this difficult office than was Field Marshal Keitel'.

Guderian then pointed out that, as an intimate of the Führer and a civilian, Goebbels (rather than one of the hated generals) might more readily persuade Hitler to reconsider the situation. Goebbels, doubtless wishing that Guderian had not bowled him this unwelcome ball, replied that, indeed, this was a 'thorny problem'; he promised to do his best, when a suitable occasion arose, to lead the conversation along the lines Guderian had proposed and to urge Hitler to 'reorganize his supreme command in a more practical form'. Not surprisingly, Goebbels never found the *moment juste* to tackle the 'thorny problem'.

Meanwhile, Guderian had problems of his own as the Army, which had long been hostile to an independent panzer arm, regrouped to undermine his position. In the draft of his assignment of duties Guderian had included a footnote defining the term 'armoured troops' and including within it assault guns. Once the draft was out of Guderian's hands, the artillery changed the footnote, limiting his control to *heavy* assault guns which were only just entering production. The artillery's continued grip on assault guns had serious consequences as they were urgently needed to arrest the wasting disease in the armoured divisions, particularly as assault guns now made up one third of the total output of all armoured fighting vehicles.

Guderian then made a second tactical error, providing Hitler's adjutants' office with a summary of the paper – on the panzer arm – that he planned to deliver at a Führer conference at Rastenburg on 9 March. When he arrived, he found a large and hostile OKW and General Staff audience waiting for him. Later he wrote:

> All these gentlemen had some criticism to make of my plans, in particular of my expressed wish that the assault guns be placed under my General-Inspectorate and that the anti-tank battalions of the infantry divisions be re-equipped with assault guns in place of their present ineffective weapons drawn by half-tracks.

Guderian's arguments fell on deaf ears. Hitler's chief adjutant observed that the assault artillery was the only weapon which enabled gunners to win the Knight's Cross. The coup de grâce was delivered by Hitler who, gazing pityingly at Guderian, told him, 'You see, they are all against you. So I can't approve either.' Guderian left the conference after a four-hour battering and fell to the ground in a brief blackout which mercifully went unheeded.*

---

* Guderian's problems in the spring of 1943 were exacerbated by his simmering feud with Field Marshal von Kluge, commander of Army Group Centre, with whom he had clashed bitterly in Russia in the winter of 1941. In May 1943 von Kluge wrote to Hitler, asking the Fuhrer to act as his second in a duel with Guderian. The affair was smoothed over, but it did little to improve the atmosphere within the German high command during the build-up to the offensive at Kursk.

CHAPTER 4

Red Army Rising

'Our generals are making their old mistakes again. They always overestimate the strength of the Russians. According to all the front-line reports, the enemy's human material is no longer sufficient. They are weakened; they have lost far too much blood. But of course nobody wants to accept such reports. Look how badly Russian officers are trained. No offensives can be organized with such officers. We know what it takes. In the short or long run the Russians will simply come to a halt. They'll run down. Meanwhile we shall throw in a few fresh divisions; that will put things right.' Adolf Hitler, 19 November 1942

'The real struggle is only beginning.' Josef Stalin, 23 February 1943

NAZI IDEOLOGY ENSURED that the war in the East was fought with unparalleled savagery. Hitler's invasion of the Soviet Union was the culmination of the obsessions which had driven him throughout his career. German hegemony in Europe could be secured only by the seizing of *Lebensraum* ('living space') in the East and, with it, the industry and agricultural land which would ensure Germany's survival as a world power. Just as in the Middle Ages people of Germanic stock colonized the Baltic lands and pushed on into Russia, so their twentieth-century counterparts would repeat the process on a vastly greater scale. Deutschstum's consolidated eastern front in central Europe would be expanded by conquest to a line stretching from Archangel to Astrakhan.

In the process the 'Jewish-Bolshevist' government of the Soviet Union would be destroyed and its 'human material', both Slav and Asiatic, enslaved or expelled into a wasteland beyond the battlements of German *imperium*. This was to be a colonial war, akin to those of the nineteenth century but directed against one of the great powers of Europe with the intention of utterly destroying it.

The language which described this struggle is saturated with the contempt and disgust which Hitler harboured for those he considered sub-human, the *Untermenschen*. This was reinforced by the German *Volk*'s lingering race memory of the Mongol hordes who might once again threaten to submerge Europe under an 'Asiatic tide'. Thus drained of their humanity, the enemy were seen, in John Keegan's words, as a 'nation of 200 million Calibans quailing under the eye of a Prospero corrupted by absolute power', a telling mirror image of the *Volk* itself. Victory against such an enemy could only be won by 'annihilation'. On 30 March 1941, in the Reich Chancellery, Hitler had delivered a two-and-a-half-hour address to some 250 officers from all branches of the service on the nature of the coming war in the East. Afterwards, Halder, Hitler's Chief of Staff, noted in his diary:

> Our tasks in Russia: smash the armed forces, break up the State . . . Struggle of two ideologies. Annihilating verdict on Bolshevism, is equivalent to asocial criminality. Communism tremendous danger for the future. We must abandon the viewpoint of soldierly comradeship. The Communist is no comrade before and no comrade afterwards. What is involved is a struggle of annihilation . . . The struggle must be waged against the poison of sedition. That is no question of courts-martial. The commanders of the troops must know what is at stake. They must lead the way into the struggle . . . Commissars and GPU men are criminals and must be treated as such . . . The fight will be very different from the fight in the West. In the East harshness is kindness towards the future. The leaders must demand of themselves the sacrifice of their scruples.

Hitler's pitiless view of the war was transmitted directly to the front line. At the beginning of Barbarossa, Field Marshal Walther von Reichenau issued an order to Sixth Army, copies of which were later distributed to all troops of the *Ostheer.*

The essential goal of the campaign against the Jewish-Bolshevik system is the complete destruction of the sources of power and the eradication of the Asian influence on the European cultural sphere ... The soldier in the East is not only a fighter by the rules of war but also the carrier of an inexorable racial concept and the avenger of all bestialities inflicted on the Germans ... For this reason the soldier must have complete understanding for the necessity of harsh but just measures against Jewish sub-humanity ... Only in this manner will we do justice to our historical task, to liberate the German people for once and for all from the Jewish-Asiatic danger.

Thus the racial and cultural inferiority of the enemy, characterized as a demon in human form and an historic threat to German racial purity, freed the Wehrmacht from the obligation to observe the accepted rules of military conduct.

The descent into barbarism was also sanctioned by the so-called Commissar Order of 6 June 1941 which specified that the political commissars of the Red Army, being 'the authors of ... Asiatic methods of fighting ... when captured in battle or in resistance are, on principle, to be disposed of by gunshot immediately'. The message was rammed home in the *Mitteilungen fur die Truppe* (*Information for Troops*):*

Anyone who has ever looked at the face of a Red commissar knows what the Bolsheviks are like. Here there is no need for theoretical expressions. We would be insulting the animals if we were to describe these men, who are mostly Jewish, as beasts. They are the embodiment of the Satanic and insane hatred against the whole of noble humanity. The shape of these commissars reveals to us the rebellion of the *Untermenschen* against noble blood.

Inevitably, the sanctioning of one form of barbarity, against commissars, encouraged another, the random shooting of Russian prisoners-of-war. The ambivalent attitude to these casual shootings among senior Army officers is illustrated in an order issued to XLVII Panzer Corps by General Lemelsen on 25 June 1941, only

* *Mitteilungen fur die Truppe* was a bi-weekly newssheet issued by the Propaganda Section of OKW. Every division received 180 copies. There was a similar publication for officers.

three days after the invasion of the Soviet Union:

> I have observed that senseless shootings of both POWs and civilians have taken place. A Russian soldier who has been taken prisoner while wearing a uniform and after he put up a brave fight, has the right to decent treatment. We want to free the civilian population from the yoke of Bolshevism and we need their labour force . . . This instruction does not change anything regarding the Führer's orders on the ruthless action to be taken against partisans and Bolshevik commissars.

It was impossible, however, to isolate either the hatred directed against the 'Jewish-Asiatic' commissars, or the propaganda war against the *Untermenschen*, from the ordinary Russian soldier. The shootings continued and, five days later, we find General Lemelsen warning sternly:

> This is murder. The German Wehrmacht is waging this war against Bolshevism, not against the united Russian peoples. We want to bring back peace, calm and order to this land which has suffered terribly for many years from the oppression of a Jewish and criminal group. The instruction of the Führer calls for ruthless action against Bolshevism and any kind of partisan. People who have been clearly identified as such should be taken aside and shot only by order of an officer . . . (descriptions) of the scenes of countless bodies of soldiers lying on the roads, having clearly been killed by a shot through the head at point-blank range, without their weapons and with their hands raised, will quickly spread in the enemy's army.

Departures from OKH's 'instructions' on the treatment of prisoners-of-war meant little as these instructions fell far short of a minimum humanity. Denied any organized means of transport in their journey to the rear, tens of thousands of Russian prisoners died while marching vast distances or packed like cattle in open railway wagons in the depths of the Soviet winter. On 31 July 1941, Sixteenth Army issued instructions to its formations not to transport prisoners-of-war in empty trains returning from the front lest they be 'contaminated' by their human cargo. The huge number of prisoners taken during the opening weeks of Barbarossa caused immense logistical problems, but policy at the highest level was summed up by Göring's cynical observation that it would be a positive advantage if 'many scores of millions' of Russians died.

Lack of organization combined with deliberate neglect to swell the numbers of prisoners who died from disease or starvation. Winter took a terrible toll on those who had been stripped of their warm clothing by freezing German troops. When orders were issued to improve the conditions for prisoners, the necessary measures were invariably taken at the expense of the civilian population.

'Peace, calm and order' were unknown conditions anywhere near the war zones where civilians, and particularly refugees, ran the constant risk of being shot out of hand as 'partisans' or 'agents of subversion'. The institution of the body count, later a feature of the war in Vietnam, was familiar on the Eastern Front as bogus proof of a unit's success against partisans.

Peasants who stayed put were helpless against German 'scorched earth' tactics and anti-partisan sweeps. During the Russian winter offensive of 1941–2, 18th Panzer Division created a series of 'desert zones' as it withdrew. The adult male population of these zones was taken to the rear while the women and children were ordered at gunpoint to 'wander off' in the direction of the advancing Red Army with nothing more than the clothes they stood up in. All the houses in the zone were burned down, the wells poisoned with dead cattle and machinery and all other economic assets destroyed. Anti-partisan operations left a similar trail of devastation.

In mid-May 1943, 18th Panzer was pulled out of the line, given the codename 318th Infantry Division and, together with a number of 'volunteer' units, was given the task of clearing the forest area south of Bryansk, thought to harbour some 3500 partisans. During the operation, codenamed *Zigeunerbaron* (Gypsy King), all civilians in the area deemed unfit for military service were evacuated with rations for two weeks. Males between the ages of fifteen and sixty-five were treated as prisoners-of-war. All villages in the area were burned down. Red Army officers and commissars were handed over to the intelligence section, while soldiers, Party functionaries and Jews were used as guides or to clear minefields. During the two-week operation nearly 16,000 civilians were driven out of the area, many of them dying of exposure and starvation or falling victim to the *Einsatzgruppen*, SS units which roamed the rear areas executing Jews and other non-Aryan elements in the occupied territories.*

The net result of *Zigeunerbaron*, a routine operation, was 700 people killed or captured and the destruction of 207 'camps' and 2390 'battle positions', many of them people's homes. With crazy logic, 18th Panzer's report stated that 'it is quite clear that the operation will influence the civilian population of the adjacent area in a favourable propagandistic direction'. Anything calculated to produce precisely the opposite effect it is hard to imagine.

The brutality with which the war in the East was fought, not only by the Waffen-SS but also by the Army, was repaid in kind by the Red Army. The survivors of Stalingrad marched into a captivity every bit as grim as that endured by the long columns of Russians trudging westward after the great encirclements of 1941. An anonymous German soldier who surrendered during the Stalingrad campaign and survived the war recalled the aftermath of capture and the subsequent nightmarish march into captivity:

> After our last bits and pieces had been plundered, haversacks and blankets** stolen, medals and badges ripped from our coats with curses and imprecations, the thousands of those who had been assembled were driven out on the march by an enemy who knew no mercy ... Towards evening we reached the ruins of a place called Yersevko and stayed overnight there in the snow. In the morning we headed for Dubovka. We left behind in Yersevko thousands of our comrades; German soldiers who had died on the steppe where there was neither food nor shelter.

On the long march to the rear, thousands died of dysentery, cholera, typhus and starvation. At one collecting point 17,000 dead were left behind as their comrades trudged off to their final destination of Beketovka. Those too weak to join the column were

---

* At Nuremberg Otto Ohlendorff, commander of *Einsatzgruppe* D operating in the Ukraine, confessed that, in the first year of the war in the East, his unit murdered 90,000 men, women and children.

** The Red Army soldier was not issued with a blanket; as a consequence, he wore his greatcoat even in the heat of summer.

shot by their guards, supervised by Red Army officers. At
Beketovka the Germans found

> a large living area (which) had been cleared of civilians and sur-
> rounded by barbed wire. This was to be our prison camp. Those
> just arriving had a shock. The two-storey houses and the open
> places – in short the whole area surrounded by the barbed wire
> – was packed with the dead bodies of those who had been tak-
> en captive in the Stalingrad South pocket and who had died here
> of disease. The number of dead was thought to be 42,000 . . .

The Russian way of waging war inflicted a similar harshness on
its own people. A German soldier's letter home recorded the way
by which herds of humans were used to clear a path through
uncharted minefields for armoured formations:

> I saw other attacks which were preceded by solid blocks of
> people marching shoulder to shoulder across the minefields
> which we had laid. Civilians and Army punishment battalions
> alike advanced like automata, their ranks broken only when
> a mine exploded, killing and wounding those around it. The
> people seemed never to flinch nor to quail and we noticed that
> some who fell were shot by a smaller wave of commissars or
> officers who followed very closely behind the blocks of punish-
> ment victims.

This was a not unfeeling picture of the Russian, both soldier and
civilian, as a robot, part of the remorseless 'steamroller' which
crushed everything in its path. An infantryman with the German
Sixth Army recalled an attack during the autumn of 1941 when
the Soviet Thirty-Seventh Army was attempting to break out of the
Kiev encirclement:

> The Soviet assaults . . . were carried out by masses of men who
> made no real attempt at concealment but trusted in sheer
> weight of numbers to overwhelm us . . . The lines of men
> stretched to the right and left of our regimental front, overlap-
> ping it completely, and the whole mass of Russian troops came
> tramping solidly and relentlessly forward . . . At 600 metres we
> opened fire and whole sections of the first wave just vanished,
> leaving here and there an odd survivor still walking stolidly for-
> ward. It was uncanny, unbelievable, inhuman.

The final sentence underlines the dehumanization of the enemy, expressed by Hitler with horrible glee when he remarked to the Spanish ambassador Espinosa that the battles in the East were 'sheer massacres of human beings' in which wave after wave of Russian infantry were reduced to 'chopped meat'. On a more soldierly level the Sixth Army infantryman concluded:

> The whole assault was so ineptly handled that I found it difficult to believe that it was being carried out by a professional army, and this incompetence reinforced the belief held at that time by many German officers that the Red Army was being handled no differently than the Tsarist Army. It was the same old steamroller.

At the beginning of the war, what the Russian soldier lacked in leadership he made up for in courage. Waffen-SS General Max Simon, a former commander of Totenkopf Division, observed: 'The Russian infantryman . . . always defended himself to the last gasp . . . even crews in burning tanks kept up fire for as long as there was any breath in their bodies. Wounded or unconscious men reached for their weapons as soon as they regained consciousness.'

The Red Army soldier was extremely dogged in defence, digging in with an instinctive feel for terrain which made his positions all but impossible to detect. General Simon described this simple and effective approach to defensive systems:

> Trenches were discarded to a very great extent and, instead, deep, narrow holes were dug which held two or three riflemen. Machine guns were skilfully sited so that dead angles were avoided and snipers, of whom there were often as many as forty or fifty in a company, were given the best positions. Trench mortars were available in all calibres and flame throwers, often fitted with remote control, were used in conjunction with mortars so that the attacking troops ran into a sea of flames. Well-concealed tanks stood by to take part in counter-attacks or were dug in at intervals. This was defence in depth protected by barbed-wire entanglements and numerous minefields, and was a defensive system applied to all kinds of terrain.

Simon was also impressed by Russian battlefield discipline which allowed German units to drive unmolested through apparently deserted villages only for the follow-up troops to find themselves in the middle of a fortified position, defended by an

infantry regiment, reinforced by all arms, which had been concealed by the most cunning camouflage. He noted, however, that
this rigid discipline tended to break down if an attack was
launched from an unexpected angle. Von Mellenthin also noted
the volatility which formed part of the Russian character:

> There is no way of telling what the Russian will do next; he will
> tumble from one extreme to another . . . His qualities are as
> unusual and many-sided as those of his vast and rambling coun-
> try. He is patient and enduring beyond imagination, incredibly
> brave and courageous – yet, at times, he can be a contemptible
> coward. There were occasions when Russian units, which had
> driven back German attacks with ferocious courage, suddenly
> fled in panic before a small assault group. Battalions lost their
> nerve when the first shot was fired and yet the same battalions
> fought with fanatical stubbornness on the following day.

Independent of season and environment, expert at infiltrating
enemy lines, capable of sustaining himself on a fraction of the
supplies considered necessary by Western armies and, as the war
progressed, increasingly well equipped, the Red Army soldier was
a formidable enemy whom the Germans underestimated at their
peril. This was Ivan, as the Germans called him, a skilful and
enduring soldier, armed with the standard Mosin Nagant 7.62mm
rifle, two or three hand grenades and the PPSH sub-machine-gun.
He was the basic component in the Soviet war machine and, within the Russian scheme of things, treated as utterly dispensable
by Stavka. Up to the summer of 1943 infantry formations were
expected to manage on their initial ammunition issue (*boekom-
pletky*) which lasted about ten days. Little or no thought was
given to further supply as it was Red Army practice to let these
formations fight themselves into the ground before rebuilding
them again from scratch. Thus in a high-intensity battle it was calculated that infantry formations would not last beyond their initial
allocation of ammunition.

Since the disastrous summer of 1941 the Red Army had under-
gone a wholesale reorganization; nowhere was this more evident
than in the tank arm. In the 1930s the Soviet Union had been
a leader in the development of large armoured formations and
several mechanized corps had been formed. These owed much to

the strategic radicalism of Marshal Mikhail N. Tukhachevsky, Stalin's Chief of Staff, a former Tsarist officer and superb professional who was shot, along with seven other generals, on 11 June 1937 at the start of Stalin's purge of the military leadership. By the autumn of 1938 the firing squads had accounted for three of the Red Army's five marshals, thirteen of its fifteen army commanders, 110 out of 195 divisional commanders and 186 out of 406 brigadiers. The immediate result was to consolidate the power of military reactionaries like Marshal Klimenti E. Voroshilov,* an old crony of Stalin's and Commissar for Defence, who slammed Tukhachevsky's reforms into reverse. After misreading the lessons of both the Spanish Civil War and the dismal performance of the Red Army in the Finnish campaign of 1939–40, the mechanized corps were broken up.

Zhukov had drawn different conclusions about the employment of armour from his own experience in the Khalkin Gol battles and the success of the panzers in France. Zhukov's views prevailed and the decision was taken to recreate the tank divisions as a matter of the greatest urgency, but the launching of Barbarossa caught the Red Army in the middle of this hasty reorganization. By the end of 1941 all large Soviet armoured units had been destroyed or disbanded because of heavy losses and replaced by brigades, regiments and battalions used in an infantry-support role. Thus in the battles around Moscow which followed the Soviet counteroffensive of December 1941, the Red Army was unable to encircle large German groupings because it lacked the necessary tank formations in the front and in army organizations. Stavka concluded that there was little chance of developing tactical advantage into operational success without the addition of larger tank and mechanized corps and tank armies, rather than the small units forced on the Red Army by the reverses of the first six months of the war.

---

* By the summer of 1940 Voroshilov's influence was beginning to fade, and in May of that year he was replaced by Timoshenko and given the less demanding post of Deputy Chairman of the Defence Committee. He served on the GKO from the beginning of the war but his feeble performance while in command of the North-West Front, when he was unable to halt the German advance to Leningrad, led to his replacement by Zhukov. As an old Civil War comrade of Stalin, and unquestionably loyal, Voroshilov avoided disgrace or worse but, for the remainder of the war, held only staff or high-level liaison appointments.

These formations had duly appeared in the summer of 1942, only to be chewed up in the fierce battles in the south. Control by infantry officers unused to armour, tactical rigidity and superior German battlefield reflexes once again threw a question mark over the future of the Red Army's tank arm, but now there was a sufficient number of able and experienced corps commanders to convince Marshal Fedorenko, chief of the Main Administration for Armoured Forces and a hesitant convert in these matters, that there could be no turning back.

Among the rising stars of the Russian tank arm were General M.E. Katukov and General Pavel Rotmistrov. As commander of the 4th Tank Brigade in October 1941, Katukov had conducted a skilful defensive action in the Mtsensk area which, for a week, had slowed Panzer Group Guderian's advance to a crawl. Rotmistrov was a passionate advocate of tank armies; his slight frame, mournfully drooping moustache and hornrimmed spectacles gave him the air of an academic who had strayed on to the battlefield (before the war he had been a lecturer at the Stalin Academy of Mechanization and Motorization). But his appearance belied an incisive and aggressive military mind which made him an outstanding tactical and operational commander. In the spring of 1942 Stavka had activated twelve tank corps and two tank armies. In April Rotmistrov formed 7th Tank Corps which, in July, became part of Fifth Tank Army. In the battles around Voronezh, Stalingrad and Rostov, Rotmistrov began to formulate his method of operations based on a high degree of agility and powerful, direct, active manoeuvre. At the time, however, Fifth Tank Army remained no more than an infantry army with a strong armoured element, comprising two tank corps, six rifle divisions, a cavalry corps, an independent tank brigade,* motorcycle regiment and artillery. Rotmistrov was convinced that the mixture of tanks and infantry

---

* In theory an independent tank brigade had a tank regiment with three mixed-tank battalions, a lorried machine-gun battalion and a company each of anti-tank guns and mortars. In practice the independent brigade usually fielded just under fifty tanks in two tank battalions of about twenty-three tanks each. In the early stages of the war these units were better suited tactically to commanders who were learning the basics of armoured warfare in the middle of a campaign and needed small units to move quickly into gaps in the defence as they appeared.

was a mistaken policy and that the future lay with all-tank armies, combining one or two tank corps with a mechanized corps. His outspoken advocacy of armoured reform went beyond the boundaries of initiative normally allowed senior commanders, but Rotmistrov's brilliance, and the Red Army's continuing struggle to gain the edge over the Ostheer, licensed what, in other circumstances, might have been considered a dangerous individualism. Early in 1943 Stalin was persuaded by Fedorenko to authorize the creation of five tank armies proper, of which the First and Fifth Guards were to be commanded, respectively, by Katukov and Rotmistrov.

The mainstay of the tank armies was the T-34/76, a weapon of such basic excellence that it fought throughout the war without major modification. Dubbed *Prinadlezhit-Chetverki*, or Thirty-Four by the troops, the T-34 made no concessions to crew comfort; initially, it lacked a radio and a turret with an all-round sight for its commander but, nevertheless, remained a superb fighting machine. It had a crew of four: the driver and hull-gunner, who sat on armchair-style seats in the forward part of the tank, the latter operating the T-34's gas-operated Degtyarev 7.62mm machine-gun; and the turret crew of loader and commander (who also doubled as the gunner), laying and firing the gun in a cramped turret. The commander and the loader sat on padded seats mounted on a tubular support, each provided with a wide cushioned backrest fitted to the turret ring. Since the turret crew's seats were themselves attached to the turret ring, they did not revolve with the gun as the turret traversed, obliging both loader and commander to squirm in their seats as the gun swung round.

In battle the tank commander had his work cut out, shouting directions by microphone to the driver, who had only a restricted frontal view, bellowing orders to the loader as to the type of ammunition he wanted, ducking down to the periscope or cranked telescope sight to lay the gun, working out the range, opening fire and then keeping himself well clear of the 76.2mm gun as it lunged back for a full 14 inches on recoil. This left him little time to see what the other tanks in his formation were doing. By using a hand-trigger attached to the main armament to fire the gun, rather than the spring-mounted foot-pedal bolted to the gun mounting, the overworked commander could remain in the turret for longer periods. Life was further complicated by an electric-powered traverse which frequently broke down, requiring the commander-gunner to haul the T-34's heavy turret round with a manually operated traverse so awkwardly placed that it contorted him into a crouching position, his right hand stretched across his body, cranking away, while he strove to keep his head firmly pressed against the sight's rubber eyeguard which let in distracting amounts of light.

The loader, too, had his problems. Of the seventy-seven rounds carried by the T-34/76 (on average, nineteen rounds armour-piercing, fifty-three high-explosive and five shrapnel) only nine were immediately accessible – six in racks on the left-hand wall of the fighting compartment and three on the right. The remaining sixty-eight rounds were distributed in eight metal bins at the bottom of the turret, covered by rubber matting which formed the turret floor. Thus in any action in which more than a handful of rounds were fired without an appreciable pause, the loader had to start uncovering and dismantling the turret floor in order to replenish the gun. Struggling amid a tangle of bins and matting, he faced an extra hazard every time the gun was fired, discharging a very hot shell case into the debris.

These drawbacks were outweighed by the T-34's modified American Christie suspension which permitted high speeds, even over rough terrain, and its broad tracks which reduced ground pressure to a minimum. A rugged all-weather diesel engine gave an excellent power-to-weight ratio and a range of 186 miles, three times that of the Tiger and the Panther and of crucial importance in the great spaces of the Soviet Union. Sloping armour considerably increased resistance to shell penetration and an innovatory long-barrelled high-velocity 76.2mm gun completed a well-balanced design which combined the basic requirements of firepower, mobility and protection and facilitated rapid mass production and easy repair and maintenance in the field. In the T-34/76 and its successor, the T-34/85, which entered mass production in the winter of 1943, the Red Army had a war winner.

The T-34 accounted for 68 per cent of all Soviet tank production. In the field it was supported by the KV-1 heavy tank, named after

Stalin's old Civil War comrade, Klimenti Voroshilov, and also armed with the 76.2mm gun. During the summer of 1942 a lighter, faster version, the KV-1S, was introduced, to be followed in the summer of 1943 by the more heavily armoured and armed KV-85 which carried an 85mm gun. Mounted on a KV-1 chassis was the SU-152 assault gun, said to have been developed to prototype by the Kotlin Bureau in only twenty-five days after the capture of a Tiger on the Leningrad front in February 1943. Armed with a powerful 152mm howitzer mounted forward in a heavily armoured superstructure, the SU-152 went into production in March 1943. It was soon to prove capable of defeating both the Tiger and the Elefant, in the process earning the nickname of Animal Killer.

In stark contrast to the multiplicity of vehicles fielded by a German armoured division – often as many as twelve different types of armoured vehicle and twenty types of other vehicle – the Soviet mechanized formations relied on just two, the T-34 and the American Dodge truck, nearly 140,000 of which had been supplied by the United States by the summer of 1943. American Lend-Lease aid enabled Stalin's war factories to concentrate almost exclusively on the production of battle equipment. Stalin himself told Churchill that he wanted trucks more than tanks. The German General Fridolin Senger und Etterlir, who had commanded 17th Panzer Division in the abortive attempt to relieve Stalingrad, commented that the Russians

> had these principles to pick up the best type of machine wherever they could get it; to have only a very few types; to construct the type as simply as possible; and then to produce these types in large quantities . . . The Russian tank maintenance was also good. The bigger repairs were not carried out as fast as in the German Army, but their normal maintenance service was very efficient, and they had plenty of well-trained mechanics. Indeed, we came increasingly to employ Russian mechanics in our own tank-maintenance companies.

General Hasso von Manteuffel, a brilliant tactician who took command of 7th Panzer Division in August 1943, praised the Russian salvage and repair services, 'which in the armoured arm were never separated from the "troops" . . . They performed extraordinary feats by following the tank troops on foot to tow away

and repair the machines. I therefore issued orders that, on principle, tanks were to be set on fire.' Manteuffel was less complimen-
tary about Red Army tank tactics which he considered lacked the
'tactical mobility which, coupled with adequate personnel, is the
basis for operative mobility and adaptability'. General Senger confirmed this with the observation that 'Russian tank tactics were of
a simple nature, and carried out on a drill pattern that was carefully planned in advance, so as to avoid demanding too much in
the way of individual initiative and judgement.' The moment the
fighting became fluid, Russian armoured formations were always
likely to be shot up by experienced German units, even when the
latter were heavily outnumbered. A tank crew member from 6th
Panzer Division wrote: 'We had one advantage – mobility. They
were like a herd of buffalo which does not have the freedom of
movement enjoyed by the leopards which prowl around the flanks
of the herd – and we were the leopards.'

Recalling the tank battles of 1942, a German staff officer was
highly critical of the tactical ineptitude and mulishness of Soviet
armoured formations:

> In tight masses they groped around in the main battle; they
> moved hesitantly and without any plan. They got in each oth-
> er's way, they blundered against our anti-tank guns, or, after
> penetrating our front, they did nothing to exploit their advan-
> tage and stood inactive and idle. Those were the days when
> isolated German anti-tank guns . . . would shoot up and knock
> out more than thirty tanks an hour.

The fate which overtook Popov's 'Mobile front group' and
Rybalko's Third Tank Army in February–March 1943 demonstrated how much the Soviet tank arm still had to learn.

It is a paradox that, at the very moment when the Red Army was
painfully forging a new tank doctrine* in the heat of battle, the tank
itself, the principal instrument of Blitzkrieg, was losing the status
it had gained in 1940 and 1941 as an independent war-
winning weapon. In the summer of 1940 rattled French infantry had
fled to the rear at the mere rumour of tanks. Now the experienced

---

* Order No.305, issued by Fedorenko on 16 October 1942, established principles
for the conduct of armoured operations which remained in force until 1944.

infantryman held his ground at the approach of armour. In turn, tanks moved forward supported by artillery and specialized infantry, the panzer grenadiers. Defending infantry who left their positions exposed themselves not only to the fire of enemy tanks but also to that of the panzer grenadiers and artillery. To defeat the advancing armour, they relied on their own anti-tank weapons, air strikes and artillery when available, and the arrival of friendly tanks to do battle with the enemy machines. As John Keegan has observed, the process was well advanced in which the tank 'ceased to be an autonomous instrument of strategy but had taken its place in an elaborate machinery of tactical attrition which achieved its effects by a cumulative wearing-down of resistance rather than by a rapier-like penetration of the enemy's front'.

No soldier was better equipped for anti-tank fighting than the Red Army infantryman. It suited his ability to hug the ground and defend his native soil to his last breath. By June 1943 the Red Army's infantry units had received nearly 1.5 million anti-tank rifles. And the new RPG-43 anti-tank grenade, which fired a hollow-charge projectile from a short steel tube, much like the German *panzerfaust*, was capable of knocking out a medium tank.

In full battle order the Red Army soldier carried 60lb of equipment and ammunition in summer and 77lb in winter. Even when burdened with his own weapons and ammunition, he was often required to carry artillery ammunition to the forward areas. The Red Army's most effective anti-tank gun was the characteristically robust 76mm. Its very high muzzle velocity meant that there was a very short interval between the noise of the gun being fired and the detonation of the shell, prompting the Germans to dub it *Ratsch-boom* (crash-bang).

Like the tank arm, Russian artillery underwent a revolution during the war. The most important development in this field was the creation of an extremely powerful Artillery Reserve of the high command. In the winter of 1941, after the loss of a large percentage of Soviet artillery, Marshal Voronov persuaded Stalin to strip the infantry divisions of much of their remaining organic artillery for the creation of a formidable reserve. By 1943 each division had lost one of its two artillery regiments. The reserve was then built up into regiments, divisions, armies and even corps of eighty battalions, and attached to the fronts by Stavka. This conferred considerable operational flexibility and, aided by Hitler's insistence on holding on to every foot of occupied soil, enabled Stavka to leave some sectors lightly held while concentrating the reserve at key points to deliver systematic massed blows. Implementing this doctrine of the 'artillery offensive'* at Stalingrad, Stavka had achieved a density of 300 guns a kilometre; by the end of the war it was massing 670 guns a kilometre for the assault on Berlin. The lengthy preparation required to bring these masses of artillery into action, and the difficulty of moving forward quickly to consolidate gains, led in late 1942 to the creation of sixteen 'artillery breakthrough' divisions, each of 356 guns, over twice the normal establishment of 168. In April 1943 'artillery breakthrough' corps were formed; anti-tank regiments were also brigaded for breakthrough operations.

Great reliance was also placed on the use of mortars, classed as artillery by the Soviets. In 1941 a separate Commissariat of Mortar Production had been set up to mass-produce mortars as an artillery stop-gap while the reserve was being assembled. In November 1942 Guards mortar brigades were established, equipped with the *Katyusha* (Little Kate) rocket-launcher, dubbed the Stalin Organ by German troops. The scream of the *Katyusha*'s discharge was a sound dreaded by the Germans as its launchers, mounted on a heavy truck, fired volleys of up to forty-eight fin-stablized rockets with a range of up to 3.5 miles. A *Katyusha* division, four of which had been formed by the end of 1942, was capable of firing a barrage of 3840 projectiles (230 tons of high explosive). At Stalingrad the Red Army had deployed 115 *Katyusha* regiments. A German defender recalled their pulverizing effect: 'The Ivans have learned to mass them in whole regiments so as to saturate selected areas of the battlefield. The rocket flames have

---

* In January 1942 Stalin had issued a directive introducing 'for the first time in the history of the military art' the concept of the 'artillery offensive' – the constant support of infantry and armour by massed, active artillery and mortar fire during the entire course of an offensive. Although the cult of personality ensured that this development was credited to Stalin's military genius, it represented not so much a revolution as an increased emphasis on the existing Soviet doctrine of artillery support.

scarcely died before the missiles in hundreds and thousands
crash around us.'

Out of the inferno at Stalingrad rose a new Red Army which, in
John Erickson's words, was 'laden with decorations, loaded with
honours and stiffened with braid'. Having tasted success, the new
Soviet professionals were given tangible evidence of Stalin's confidence in them. On 18 January 1943 Zhukov became a Marshal of
the Soviet Union, the first such promotion of the war. On the same
day Voronov became a Marshal of Artillery, following a Central
Committee decree authorizing branch marshalships; in March
Novikov, the iron man of the air force, became a Marshal of
Aviation. In February, Vasilevsky completed a remarkable twenty-
month journey from major-general to marshal. Three field commanders, Malinovsky, Rokossovsky* and Vatutin, became full
generals. Stalin, too, was upwardly mobile, 'reluctantly' assuming
the title of Marshal of the Soviet Union after a collective appeal
from the Politburo. Stalin now felt sufficiently confident to take the
credit for the Red Army's recovery; it is from this period that
phrases like 'Stalinist strategy', the 'Stalinist military school of
thought' and the 'military genius of Stalin' became commonplace
in the Soviet press and propaganda.

The Red Army's officer corps was invested with new authority.
Saluting was made obligatory and strictly enforced. New decorations, the Orders of Suvorov, Kutuzov and Alexander Nevsky, not
only invoked the pre-revolutionary past but were also exclusive
to officers. With them came the restoration of the badges of rank,
the gold and silver epaulettes – the *pogon* – which, in 1917,
soldiers had ripped contemptuously from the shoulders of Tsarist
officers. Stalin had been pondering this issue since 1942 when a
proposal had been made to provide Guards regiments, their own
name redolent of the Imperial Army, with distinctive uniforms and
formal rank insignia. Wary of the danger of creating 'two armies'
by rewarding the elite Guards with badges of rank and ignoring the
rest, Stalin decided on the universal introduction of the *pogon*, a
move welcomed by formation commanders.

---

* Rokossovsky had been arrested in 1937, during Stalin's purge of the military,
and imprisoned for almost three years.

On 6 January 1943 the Supreme Soviet issued a decree reinstating the *pogon*, and an order was placed with Britain for scarce gold braid. The austerity-conscious British – still fighting for survival in the Battle of the Atlantic – were initially reluctant to meet what they considered a frivolous request, but the braid marked a watershed in the history of the Red Army. A German veteran of the Eastern Front remembered, with some irony, that the smartly uniformed army which had invaded the Soviet Union changed as the war continued, 'reducing our uniforms to basic and simple dress'. Simultaneously, 'the enemy was embellishing his . . . As the officers of our Army became more democratic and comradely, at least in the front-line units on active service, Ivan's officers were acting in a way that can only be described as aristocratic.' He was not wide of the mark. Exclusive officers' clubs and strictly separate messes for junior and senior officers were opened. In 1943 a new 'code of manners' for officers was introduced which stipulated, *inter alia*, that officers above a certain rank could not travel by public transport or carry 'paper parcels', etiquette familiar to veterans of the Tsarist Army.

Stalin's decision to revert from revolutionary egalitarianism to military orthodoxy was as shrewd and pragmatic as his transformation of the struggle against Germany into the 'Great Patriotic War', his enlistment of the Orthodox Church as part of the war effort and his invocation of 'Mother Russia' rather than the Communist Party as a rallying cry.

The Party's influence over the Army had been significantly reduced in October 1942 with the abolition of the 'dual command'* system in which a formation's political officer, the commissar, shared authority with its senior officer. Now redesignated the Deputy Commander for Political Affairs, he still wielded considerable power and reported through separate channels. But his responsibility lay exclusively with political education, propaganda and welfare, the battalion forming the basic unit, and he was no

---

* Political commissars had been introduced during the Civil War to keep an eye on former Tsarist officers whose loyalty to the Soviet regime was considered questionable. First abolished in 1940, the system of 'dual command' was reintroduced in June 1941 until October 1942.

longer able to interfere with a commander's operational decisions. One immediate gain from the reform was the entry into the officer cadre of a large number of former commissars with battlefield experience. 'Army' had bested 'Party' but at the higher levels there remained considerable tension between senior commanders and the political members of the military soviets. Some of the former, notably General Gordov, then commander of Thirty-Third Army, were emboldened to press Stalin for the disbandment of the military soviets and the creation of a purely 'Russian' army on nationalist lines, an innovation too far for the new Marshal of the Soviet Union, who chose to maintain the Communist imprint on the Red Army by the sinister means of the NKVD rather than the Party agencies.

The granting of privileges was balanced by the tightening of a penal code which was already the most savage of any of the combatants in the Western hemisphere. No one could consider himself immune from summary execution, the most notable victim being Colonel-General Dmitri Pavlov, the commander of the Western Front during the first disastrous days of the war. In the autumn of 1942 penal battalions, the *strafblats*, were introduced for both officers and men. Woe betide an officer whose performance fell below the mark when a man like Zhukov was directing a front's operations.

Fear of draconian punishment was a large factor in the Red Army's continuing tactical inflexibility up to army level. After the war the American General Omar Bradley commented that a US lieutenant was granted greater authority on the Elbe than a Russian divisional commander. Only a front commander could, on occasion, exercise personal initiative. At lower levels, armies, corps and divisions were the pawns of Stavka, rigidly bound by plans and instructions from higher commands. Even a general was most reluctant to assume responsibility for an action without a detailed accompanying *dokumenta*.

Even after the great encirclements of 1941, the victories gained in the summer of 1942 and the success of Manstein's counterstroke after the surrender at Stalingrad, Hitler had not come close to destroying the manpower which Stalin remorselessly fed into the

Soviet war machine. Between June 1941 and November 1942 the Red Army's strength at the front grew from 2.9 to 6.1 million men. In March 1943 Hitler was still clutching at straws, declaring exasperatedly that the Soviet Union must run out of manpower 'sooner or later', but, in the fleeting moments when reason prevailed, he had come to recognize that he could not count on it.

Mere manpower, however, would have been meaningless without the Soviet Union's ability to preserve an industrial base to equip, arm and sustain it in the field. The destruction of the Soviet Union's industrial base had figured as a war aim in the plans for Barbarossa drawn up in December 1940; had the campaign reached its planned objective on a line running from Archangel to Astrakhan (the so-called 'A-A' line), 80 per cent of the Soviet Union's productive capacity would have fallen into German hands. But in August 1941 Hitler had fatally switched his main effort from the centre to the south, elevating the seizure of industries of the Donbas to the status of strategic objective. Thus, although partial success in the south had dealt a potentially crippling blow to Soviet coal and steel production, which declined in the winter of 1941 by 63 per cent and 58 per cent respectively, it also placed the central Moscow-Upper Volga region beyond the reach of the Ostheer. After the German retreat from Moscow in December 1941, the Soviet Union retained the central region and this, along with the industrial regions of the Urals and the Kuznets Basin, in western Siberia, was sufficient to provide Stalin with the manufacturing resources that decided the outcome of the war.

It was, nevertheless, a close-run thing. From the moment the panzers rolled off their start lines on 22 June 1941 a special soviet, headed by the economic expert A.I. Mikoyan, began to move heavy industry, lock, stock and barrel, from the western and central areas of European Russia and the Ukraine to the distant rear, beyond the Ural Mountains and the reach not only of the Ostheer's panzers but also the Luftwaffe's medium bombers.

The problems raised by this colossal undertaking were eased somewhat by a pre-war programme for the strategic relocation of heavy industry, aimed at balancing the output of the Soviet Union's traditional industrial centres with that of the raw-material and new manufacturing zones beyond the Urals. As a result it was possible to 'marry' evacuated plants with factories in the eastern regions of the Soviet Union. Thus, at the beginning of July 1941, the armoured-plate mill at Mariupol, in the southern Ukraine, was moved to the new industrial complex at Magnitogorsk, east of the Ural Mountains; and the huge tank plant at Kharkov was transferred to the tractor factory at Chelyabinsk, which also accommodated part of the Kirov plant evacuated from Leningrad; it became popularly known as 'Tankograd'. Ten weeks after the last engineers left the Kharkov works, 'trudging along the railway tracks', the first twenty-five T-34s rolled off the Chelyabinsk production line.

The figures alone can only hint at the magnitude of the effort. In the first three months of the war the Russian railway system moved 2.5 million troops westward and carried 1523 factories eastward: 455 were re-established in the Urals, 210 in western Siberia, 200 in the Volga region and over 250 in Kazakhstan and central Asia. Sometimes the factories were evacuated under fire. Sometimes the Germans overran them before they could be loaded on to the waiting rolling stock. General Guderian recalled that, when 4th Panzer Division took Orel on 3 October 1941,

> our seizure of the town took the enemy so completely by surprise that the electric trams were still running as our tanks drove in. The evacuation of industrial installations, carefully prepared by the Russians, could not be carried out. Along the streets leading from the factories to the station lay dismantled machines and crates filled with tools and raw materials.

There were gigantic bottlenecks and agonizing delays: of the twenty-six chemical plants evacuated to the east, only eight had reached their destinations by the beginning of December and of these only four had started production.

The workers who migrated with their factories suffered immense hardships. Outside Sverdlovsk a factory evacuated from the Ukraine was housed in two enormous buildings erected in a fortnight. According to *Pravda* of 18 September 1942:

> Winter had already come when Sverdlovsk received Comrade Stalin's order to erect two buildings for the plant evacuated from the south. The trains packed with people and machinery were already on their way . . . It was then that the people of

the Urals came to this spot with shovels, bars and pickaxes: students, typists, accountants, shop assistants, housewives, artists, teachers. The earth was like stone, frozen hard by our Siberian frost. Axes and pickaxes could not break the stony soil. In the light of arc-lamps people hacked at the earth all night. They blew up the stones and the frozen earth, and they laid the foundations ... Their feet and hands were swollen with frostbite, but they did not leave work. Over the charts and the blueprints, laid out on the packing cases, the blizzard was raging. Hundreds of trucks kept rolling up with building materials ... On the twelfth day, into the buildings with their glass roofs the machinery, covered with hoar-frost, began to arrive. Braziers were kept alight to unfreeze the machines ... And two days later the war factory began production.

In spite of these heroic efforts there was a sharp fall in war production. By the end of October 1941 steel output had fallen by 58 per cent and total industrial output by 50 per cent. Aircraft production fell by two thirds. Shortages of ferro-alloys, nickel, non-ferrous metals, aluminium, copper and tin, and the loss of the chemical industries in the Donbas, played havoc with ammunition supplies. In the second half of 1941 the fronts were relying on ammunition reserves accumulated in peacetime. These had been consumed by December when current production was falling 40 per cent behind the Red Army's requirements.

Even by 1945 the Soviet Union's overall figures for the production of coal and steel had not returned to those of 1940. In 1944 Germany's coal output exceeded that of the Soviet Union by 160 million tons and that of steel by 23 million tons.* Nevertheless, in 1942 Soviet *armaments* production, exploiting huge stocks of strategic materials accumulated before the war, far surpassed that of Germany: 24,400 Soviet tanks and armoured vehicles to 4800 German; 21,700 aircraft to 14,700; four million rifles to 1.4 million.

As the Soviet Union's pre-war stockpiles ran down, the gap was filled by Lend-Lease supplies from the United States. Stalin was dismissive of the tanks and many of the aircraft shipped to the Soviet Union by the United States and Britain, but the almost lim-

---

* The figures for coal are Germany 281 million tons, Soviet Union 121 million tons; for steel, Germany 35.2 million tons, Soviet Union 12.3 million tons.

itless outpouring of US aid which met his war-industrial needs ensured Soviet survival. By May 1945 the Americans had shipped 16.4 million tons of supplies to the Soviet Union, reaching every aspect of the Soviet war effort: 2000 locomotives and 540,000 tons of rails, with which the Russians laid a greater length of track than they had built in 1928–39; $150 million worth of machine tools and nearly a million tons of steel by the summer of 1943; three quarters of the Soviet Union's copper requirements between 1941–4; 13 million winter boots for the Red Army; high-grade petroleum for aviation fuel.

Food, too, was desperately needed as the land lost in 1941 produced 38 per cent of the Soviet Union's cereals and 40 per cent of its cattle. The mobilization of tractors for the towing of artillery had contributed to a fall in agricultural output in those areas not overrun by the enemy. American agriculture, recovering its strength after the Depression years, provided the Soviet Union with 5 million tons of food, enough to give each Red Army soldier half a pound of concentrated rations every day of the war. To meet a specific request, 12,000 tons of butter were shipped to the Soviet Union for troops convalescing in military hospitals.

As the summer of 1943 approached, Vasilevsky told General (later Marshal) Tolbukhin that, in his opinion, Soviet troops were now superior to the enemy in 'quality and quantity'. He was confident that Stavka was equal to conducting offensive operations on the grand scale and that discipline had displaced the disarray which had overtaken the Red Army in 1941 and the summer of 1942. Military orthodoxy was now the order of the day, and the 'stability of the rear', the most important of the permanent operating principles of war established by Stalin,* was no longer in doubt.

The price of survival and recovery had been a terrible one and was still rising. Great tracts of the Soviet Union had been pillaged by a brutal enemy; the remainder had been stripped by its own

---

* During the Civil War (1918–21) Stalin had propounded the principle of the 'stability of the rear' and its importance to the front 'because it is from the rear, and the rear alone, that the front obtains not only all kinds of supplies, but also its manpower, sentiments and ideas'.

authorities for the waging of war. Old men, women and children had replaced the men who had left farms and factories for the front line, working punishing hours sustained by the most meagre rations. In that characteristically Soviet contradiction between the development of sophisticated technology and the most primitive living conditions, scientists in Moscow were beginning work on an atom bomb while farm workers of collectives were ploughing their fields with implements scarcely changed since the Middle Ages. There was now no doubt in the minds of the Soviet high command that it could not lose the war, while its German counterpart saw the prospect of 'winning' slipping over the horizon. With the onset of the *rasputitsa* in March 1943 and the ending of Manstein's counter-offensive, a lull descended on the Eastern Front. It was, however, the calm that precedes the storm as both sides rested and regrouped, massing millions of men and their most modern weapons for a decisive stroke in the summer.

CHAPTER 5

The Tug of War

Guderian: 'My Führer, why do you want to attack in the East at all this year?'
Hitler: 'You are quite right. Whenever I think of this attack, my stomach turns over.'

IN JUNE 1943 the fighting line on the Eastern Front ran from Leningrad, to which a narrow Russian land corridor had been opened south of Lake Ladoga in January, to the northern shore of the Sea of Azov near Taganrog. From Leningrad the line descended south, across old Russia, to Velikiye Luki, 400 miles west of Moscow. Then it slanted south-east before swelling to fill the northern shoulder of a large salient around Orel. Immediately below the Orel salient a huge chunk was bitten out of the German line by the Kursk bulge which jutted westward for some eighty miles, enclosing an area half the size of England. The southern shoulder of this reverse salient skirted around Belgorod and then ran along the line of the Donets before plunging down to the Sea of Azov. If one includes 200 miles of frontage in northern Finland and Army Group A's front at the Taman bridgehead, covering the crossing of the Kerch Strait to the Crimea, the Eastern Front measured 1700 miles from north to south.

One feature in the line, above all others, absorbed the attention of the German and Soviet high commands; this was the tempting rectangular Kursk salient whose frontage thrust towards the boundary between Army Groups Centre and South. Within the salient the terrain was, for the most part, one of low rolling hills broken by broad shallow valleys. Many small rivers ran through the valleys, their banks dotted with orchards and vast fields of sunflowers, among which nestled small farming communities. On the northern edge of the salient, many of the villages had reassuringly bucolic names:Kusl (Hens), Butlika (Butter) and Sayka (Breadroll). The district seat in this sector, Ponyri, was famous for its apples, known as *Antonovskiye Yabloki*.

In the spring of 1943 this pleasant landscape had been ravaged by war. The withdrawing Germans had left behind their customary calling card, a desert zone of pillaged plant and farms. The workshops of the collective farms had been razed and their machinery plundered. In a region which, in 1940, had boasted 400,000 horses there were now scarcely 20,000, all of them nags fit for nothing. Many collective farms had not a single horse or ox left. The only railway line by which all kinds of supplies could be delivered, running on a single track to Kursk from Kastornoye, had been wrecked. Elsewhere, sixty-two bridges had been blown up and, at the railway junctions, all rolling stock and service facilities were destroyed. The marshalling yards at Kursk had been blown up.

Kursk itself, lying in the centre of the salient, was an important junction on the Moscow–Yalta highway and railway. One of the oldest cities in Russia, first mentioned in documents of 1032, it had been completely destroyed by the Crimean Tartars and not rebuilt until 1586. Its medieval importance as a military outpost had waned as the Russian borders had marched south and the Tartar threat declined, but it remained a regional centre, too small to be of national importance and too big to possess much charm. Now it was scarred by heavy German bombing. Its principal claim to fame was a phenomenon known as the Kursk Magnetic Anomaly (KMA), caused by the deposits of magnetite on which the city was built and which rendered compasses useless.

As the sowing season approached on the southern end of the Russian uplands a magnetic pull of another kind was taking place as military metal, in the form of thousands of tanks, guns and aircraft, was drawn towards the Kursk salient. Crops would be sown as German bombers droned overhead, but the sandy soil would also hide a more deadly planting, millions of mines lacing the landscape in anticipation of a great battle.

To the Ostheer the Kursk salient presented an opportunity and a danger. From the salient, rapidly filling with strong Soviet forces, the Red Army threatened the German position in both the centre and the south. However, if it could be 'pinched out', the Red Army would not only suffer massive losses in men and material but would also become vulnerable to new German offensives aimed either at Moscow or into the steppe lands of the south.

The elimination of the Kursk salient was to dominate the deliberations of the German high command in the spring of 1943 but, with characteristic acuity, Manstein had earlier suggested an alternative solution to the problem posed by the approach of the summer campaigning season. In spite of the success of his counter-offensive and the recapture of Kharkov, it was clear to Manstein that the loss of 'so many major formations' meant that the Ostheer was no longer capable of mounting an offensive on the scale of 1941 and 1942: 'What did seem possible – given proper leadership on the German side – was that the Soviet Union could be worn down to such an extent that it would tire of its already excessive sacrifices* and be ready to accept a stalemate.'

Manstein knew that this aim could not be achieved by adopting a purely static, defensive strategy. There were no longer sufficient forces to hold the line at every point from the Baltic to the Black Sea. Nor was there much time left in which to force a draw in the East. Any initiative taken within the framework of a strategic defensive would have to be launched before the expected Allied landings in Europe forced both the transfer of substantial forces to

---

* According to German sources, 3.35 million Soviet soldiers had fallen into German hands by the end of 1941, of whom over two million were dead by February 1942. By the end of the war some 5.75 million Soviet soldiers had become POWs. By May 1944 the number of deaths among Soviet POWs (from shooting, hunger, cold, forced labour) had reached 3.2 million and may eventually have risen to 4.7 million. Figures issued by the Soviet General Staff in 1989 gave a figure for overall fatalities among the regular forces of 8.6 million killed, died of wounds, illness and accidents, missing and captured and not returned. Eighteen million soldiers were wounded (some more than once), frostbitten or sick. In this context it is worth noting that the remainder of the Soviet war dead was made up of at least 19 million civilians.

meet the threat in the West and, in turn, a renewed Soviet offensive. Manstein concluded that the only hope lay in

> dealing the enemy powerful blows of a localized character which would sap his strength to a decisive degree – first and foremost through loss of prisoners. This pre-supposed an operational elasticity on our part which would give maximum effect to the still-superior quality of the German command staffs and fighting troops.

After the recapture of Kharkov, Manstein presented Hitler with two options. First, he suggested that the Ostheer wait for the Soviet attack which would almost certainly be launched in the southern Ukraine with the aim of rolling up the German front north of the Black Sea. The German response, suggested Manstein, would be to give ground by withdrawing from the entire Donets basin and then launch a smashing counter-blow from the Kiev region against the extended northern flank of the Russian offensive, turning the tables on the enemy and rolling up his front in the south. Manstein laconically called this his 'backhand' stroke, a repeat on a grand scale of the counter-offensive which had recently slewed to a halt in the March mud.

Manstein's 'forehand' stroke involved cutting off the Kursk salient with concentric attacks from north and south, in the process destroying the Soviet armoured reserve which would be fed into the battle and then turning south to deal with the Red Army's front in the southern Ukraine. He emphasized that it was imperative to play the 'forehand' stroke at the earliest opportunity, no later than the beginning of May, before the Red Army could make an effective recovery from the losses it had incurred in the winter campaign.

Hitler, reluctant as ever to yield ground, rejected the 'backhand' stroke. So much for the 'operational elasticity' propounded by Manstein. Hitler was supported by Zeitzler, the OKH Chief of Staff, who judged that an attack at Kursk would involve less risk, entail no preliminary sacrifice of ground and 'would not make such heavy demands on the reserves'.

Colonel-General Kurt Zeitzler now assumed an increasingly important role in the strategic tug-of-war which preceded the launching of the Kursk offensive. He had enjoyed a meteoric rise, succeeding Colonel-General Halder as Chief of Staff in September 1942 and remaining in the post until July 1944 when, on the verge of a nervous breakdown, he was replaced by Guderian. To underline his disgrace, he was forbidden by Hitler to wear a uniform.

The son of a Protestant pastor, Zeitzler had served as an infantry subaltern in the First World War and transferred to the tank arm in 1934. In 1938, as a lieutenant-colonel in the OKW planning staff under Warlimont, he had prepared the draft plans for the occupation of Czechoslovakia. Promoted colonel in 1939, he had served as a staff officer in the Polish and French campaigns in which his assured handling of mechanized logistics led to his appointment as Chief of Staff to Kleist's First Panzer Army with which he served during the invasion of the Soviet Union. Kleist subsequently observed of Zeitzler that there was no one better at maintaining the momentum of panzer formations when whole armies were being 'thrown about' in the sweeping advances which characterized the first six months of the war in the East.

Early in 1942 Zeitzler, now a major-general, was transferred to the West as Chief of Staff to Field Marshal Gerd von Rundstedt, Commander in Chief West. In this military backwater Zeitzler's dynamism and famously short temper earned him the nickname of 'General Fireball', and his role in the repulse of the British–Canadian raid on Dieppe in August 1942 burnished his reputation as a coming man. Zeitzler had long been a favourite of the Führer, granted personal access and cultivating a close friendship with Hitler's adjutant Schmundt. His chance came immediately after the Dieppe raid when Hitler was at loggerheads with Halder after a row over the overstretched state of the Wehrmacht. Hitler remarked that he would like to replace Halder with 'someone like this chap Zeitzler', a disingenuous suggestion which bore fruit on 24 September when Halder departed and Zeitzler, promoted General der Infanterie, arrived as the new Chief of Staff.

On the threshold of office, Zeitzler received some discouraging advice from Keitel: 'Never contradict the Führer. Never remind him that once he may have thought differently on something. Never tell him that subsequent events have proved you right and him wrong. Never report on casualties to him – you have to spare the nerves of the man.' With characteristic candour Zeitzler replied, 'If a man starts a war, he must have the nerve to bear the consequences.'

Zeitzler had to summon up considerable nerve to deal with Hitler and his high command, many of whom were his seniors in age and rank and regarded the forty-seven-year-old 'General Fireball' as the Führer's creature. Nevertheless, Zeitzler's no-nonsense style won the approval of Goebbels who wrote in his diary on 20 December 1942: 'The appointment of Zeitzler has introduced a new method of work at GHQ, clearing away everything except essentials. This has relieved the Führer of a lot of details and everything no longer depends on his decision.'

Unfortunately, at that precise moment a great deal depended on the Führer's decision. On 21 November Manstein had tried and failed to persuade Hitler to order Paulus to break out at Stalingrad. Zeitzler had already clashed with Hitler over Stalingrad, urging the withdrawal of Sixth Army the moment the Soviet counter-offensive north and south of Stalingrad began on 19 November. This merely hardened Hitler's determination to stand fast on the Volga. Zeitzler was also unconvinced by Göring's airy assurances that Sixth Army could be supplied by the Luftwaffe, a scepticism he shared with the Luftwaffe's Chief of Staff, Colonel-General Hans Jeschonnek. On 24 November he told Hitler and Göring that 'the Luftwaffe just can't do it'. Göring began to bluster that, somehow, the Luftwaffe would manage, whereupon Zeitzler lost control and shouted, 'That's a lie!' Hitler intervened to calm things down, loyally siding with Göring. Later, when Zeitzler was proved to have been correct, the Chief of Staff may well have reflected on Keitel's warning. According to General von Blumentritt (then Deputy Chief of General Staff) the Führer thereafter kept Zeitzler 'at arm's length'.

Throughout these tribulations Zeitzler was never afraid to speak his mind to Hitler. On one occasion the Führer sought to amuse himself and his sycophantic entourage with the coarse observation that 'My field marshals' horizon is the size of a lava-tory lid.' The next day Zeitzler asked for a private audience with Hitler, during which he bluntly told him, 'As an Army general I take exception to the language you used about our field marshals. May I ask you not to use expressions like that in my presence again.'

Completely thrown by such forthrightness, Hitler could only offer Zeitzler his hand and say, 'I thank you.'

Ultimately, Zeitzler had to operate as an assistant and learn to roll with the punches. After the war he described his role in rueful terms:

> As the Chief of the General Staff had only an advisory position, he did not have the power of command over the Eastern Front . . . This was exercised by Adolf Hitler himself. He signed the basic orders and instructions himself or copied them out. Occasionally – particularly when he noticed that I was of a different opinion – he even drafted or dictated them himself. In a few cases I refused to countersign orders in the hope of perhaps preventing their being issued. Apart from one single case where, annoyed, he put the draft aside and never returned to the subject again, they were issued all the same via the Adjutant.

In one area Zeitzler was able to assert himself, and in this he proved a great disappointment to OKW (Oberkommando der Wehrmacht). Earlier in his career he had been an apparently enthusiastic supporter of a unified command of the Wehrmacht, and his appointment had encouraged OKW to anticipate a closer cooperation with OKH (Oberkommando des Heeres). However, Zeitzler quickly demonstrated his determination to exclude OKW from the Eastern Front, forbidding members of the Army Operations Section to provide OKW with any information. Thus, as Warlimont observed, Zeitzler 'kept a veil drawn over the Eastern Front and this . . . made it ever more impossible for the OKW Operations Staff to take an overall view of the war situation'.

Zeitzler proved obstructive in other ways, refusing to allow the Intelligence Section – Foreign Armies, West to be transferred from OKH to the OKW Operations Staff in spite of the fact that it was almost exclusively concerned with OKW theatres of war. Zeitzler's appointment had exacerbated rather than ameliorated the divisions within the German high command. Keitel's view was that Zeitzler was 'intent on excluding us to an increasing degree . . . from decision-making on the Eastern Front . . . and it was even more obvious that he feared our influence on the Führer – a very regrettable and narrow-minded point of view'.

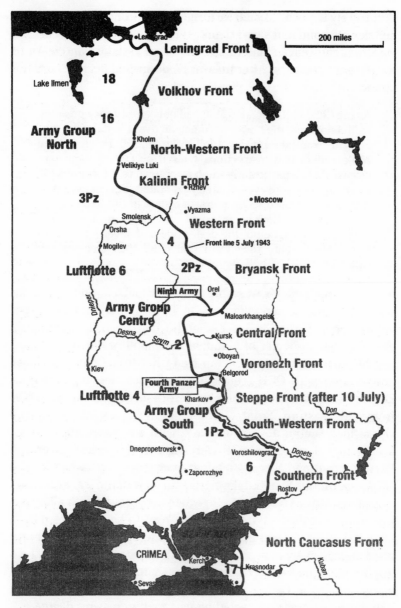

The Eastern Front in the early summer of 1943, with the Kursk salient jutting west south of Orel

In the spring of 1943 Zeitzler also profited from Hitler's continuing loss of confidence after Stalingrad, which had also allowed Manstein to execute his counter-offensive with the minimum of interference from Rastenburg. For the moment, Zeitzler had the opportunity to shape the offensive at Kursk.

At the beginning of April, Major-General von Mellenthin, XLVIII Panzer Corps's Chief of Staff, had a short spell of leave during which he was ordered to report to Zeitzler at OKH headquarters at Lötzen, an hour's drive from Rastenburg in the woods near Angerburg. At Lötzen von Mellenthin 'reported to Zeitzler on the role of XLVIII Corps in the recent battles and learned that he contemplated a great offensive in which we were destined to play a very significant part'.

On 11 April Zeitzler submitted a memorandum to Hitler outlining a pincer attack on the Kursk salient, the tried and trusted formula which had proved so successful against the Red Army since June 1941. On the northern shoulder of the salient, Ninth Army, heavily reinforced by panzer divisions, would strike south of Orel through Ponyri to Kursk; in the south Fourth Panzer Army, screened on its right flank by Army Detachment Kempf, would advance from north of Kharkov through Oboyan to join hands with Ninth Army at Kursk. The Russian forces trapped inside the resulting pocket would then be destroyed piecemeal. The rich haul of prisoners would be transported back to the Reich to work as slave labour in German war industries. With the retaking of Kursk, a shorter line would be established, enabling the Ostheer to redeploy forces to the West.

The plan was calculated to refresh Hitler's memories of past victories. In May 1942 Marshal Timoshenko had used the Izyum salient, surrounded on three sides by German forces, as the launching pad for a major Soviet offensive. The attack had been held and an immediate German counter-offensive, conducted by Field Marshal von Bock's Army Group South and supervised by Hitler and Halder, had cut the Izyum bulge at both shoulders. Paulus's Sixth Army, attacking from the north, and Army Group Kleist, driving from the south, had encircled and destroyed the better part of two Soviet fronts concentrated in the salient for the offensive. The concentration around Kursk offered the chance of a similar success.

Zeitzler was confident that ten to twelve panzer divisions, with supporting infantry, would be sufficient for the operation, code-named Zitadelle (Citadel), but Hitler thought that stronger forces would be needed. Guderian's appointment as Inspector-General of Armoured Troops was proof that the Führer was now fully aware of the deficiencies of the panzer arm and had concluded that only the injection of large numbers of Tiger and Panther tanks would restore the strategic balance in the East. When Zeitzler argued that Manstein had retaken Kharkov with only five divisions, Hitler replied that the clinching factor had been the Tiger, employed in special battalions of about thirty vehicles, each of which was 'worth an ordinary panzer division'. However, only twenty-five Tigers a month were being produced, while the Panther, whose monthly production rate hovered around fifty, was dogged by mechanical teething problems. Its engine and transmission were overstressed to cope with increases in the Panther's weight, cooling was inadequate and the engine had an alarming habit of catching fire. Potentially, the Panther was equal, if not superior, to the T-34 but, in contrast to its Russian rival, its design was both complex and expensive. Such was the Führer's faith in the Panther that he had set an ambitious production target of 600 vehicles a month.

The plan for Zitadelle outlined on 11 April found concrete expression in Operational Order No.6, signed by Hitler on 15 April.

> I have decided to undertake as the first priority offensive of this year the Citadel offensive, as soon as the weather permits. The offensive is of decisive importance. It must be carried out quickly and shatteringly. It must give us the initiative for the spring and summer of this year. Therefore all preparations are to be carried through with the greatest care and energy. The best formations, the best armies, the best leaders and great stocks of ammunition are to be placed at the decisive points. Every officer and every man must be totally convinced of the decisive importance of this offensive. The victory of Kursk must be a beacon to the world.
>
> I therefore order:
> 1. The objective of the offensive is the encirclement of the enemy forces deployed in the Kursk area by means of incisive, coordinated, merciless and fast thrusts by one attacking army each from the regions of Belgorod and south of Orel, and to annihilate them with a concentric attack. In the course of the offen-

sive a shortened front, which will liberate forces for us elsewhere, is to be achieved along the line Nezhega-Korocha (exclusive) – Skorodnoye-Tim – east of Shchigry-Sosna (exclusive).

2a. It is vital to maintain the element of surprise as far as possible, and above all to keep the enemy guessing about the timing of the offensive.

2b. The offensive forces are to be concentrated on the narrowest possible front, so that with the overwhelming support of tanks, artillery, rocket mortars, etc., they can break through the enemy in one blow and destroy him in a 'cauldron battle'.

2c. The front-line forces must be supplied with forces from the rear as quickly as possible to cover their flanks so that the strike forces need only drive forward.

2d. By pushing in quickly from all sides of the cauldron, the enemy must be given no rest and his destruction hastened.

2e. The attack must be executed with sufficient speed to prevent the enemy breaking contact or bringing up strong reserves from other fronts.

2f. The speedy establishment of the new front will liberate forces, particularly mobile formations, for further operations in good time.

3. Army Group South will jump off with strongly concentrated forces from the line Belgorod-Tomarovka, break through along the line Prilepy-Oboyan and link up with the attacking army of Army Group Centre in and east of Kursk. To cover this attack from the east the line Nezhega-Korocha-Skorodnoye-Tim must be reached as quickly as possible . . . To cover the attack from the west, secondary forces will be used to drive into the cauldron with the main force as the cauldron is formed.

4. Army Group Centre will jump off with its attacking army from the line Trosna-north of Maloarchangelsk . . . to break through along the line Fatezh-Vereytenovo, with its main effort on the eastern flank and join up with the attacking army of Army Group South in and east of Kursk. The forces of Army Group Centre operating from west of Trosna to the boundary of Army Group South are to tie up the enemy's strike forces with local attacks from the moment the offensive begins and then push on into the cauldron in good time. Constant air and ground reconnaissance will ensure that any attempt by the enemy to disengage will be detected. In these circumstances, a general offensive is to be mounted immediately along the whole front.

5. The deployment of both Army Groups must exploit all possible means of camouflage, deception and disinformation, so that, from 28 April, an offensive can be launched within six days of

the order from OKH. The earliest date for the offensive will be
3 May. The forward movement to the start line must be carried
out only at night under the strictest camouflage precautions . . .
7. To maintain security, these plans are to be made available
only on a need-to-know basis. Briefing is to be conducted at the
last possible moment and then only phase by phase. We must
ensure that, at all costs, no part of our plans leaks out through
carelessness or negligence. Enemy intelligence activities must
be checked by an enhanced counter-intelligence effort . .
8. Because of the reduced scale compared with earlier operations . . . the attacking forces are to leave behind all vehicles
and impedimenta which are not absolutely necessary . . . every
commander must see that he takes with him only that which is
absolutely necessary for battle. Commanding generals and
divisional commanders must keep a strict control over this.
Strict traffic control is to be established. They must drive forward without a backward glance . . .
10. The air force will concentrate all active forces at the decisive points. Conferences with the command organizations of
the air forces must begin immediately. Special care must be
taken to preserve secrecy.
11. For the success of the offensive, it is of the utmost importance that the enemy does not succeed against other sectors of
Army Groups South and Centre, in nullifying Citadel, or com-
pelling attack formations to be prematurely withdrawn. Both
Army Groups must, in addition to the Citadel offensive battle,
prepare for a defensive battle on the remaining sectors of the
front by the end of the month. In this respect it is crucial that
all means are used to make these sectors safe, that those vulnerable to armoured attack are well supplied with anti-tank
defence, that local reserves be readied and that enemy preparations be discovered through detailed reconnaissance of
strongpoints.
12. The ultimate objectives of the operation are:
a. The movement of the boundary between Army Groups South
and Centre to line Konotop (South) – Kursk (South) – Dolgoye
(Centre).
b. The transfer of Second Army headquarters, with three corps
headquarters and nine infantry divisions, as well as other army
troops yet to be determined, from Army Group Centre to Army
Group South.
c. The deployment of three further infantry divisions from
Army Group Centre, so that they may be available to OKH
north-west of Kursk.

d. The withdrawal of the majority of armoured formations from this front for deployment in other theatres . .
13. The Army Groups will report what steps they have taken for attack and defence on the basis of this order, using 1:300,000 maps . . .
(Signed) Adolf Hitler
Certified authentic: Lieutenant-General Heusinger.*

Operational Order No.6 left the date of Zitadelle to be determined, merely stating that the 'earliest date' for the operation would be 3 May; this lay at the far limit of the time-frame envisaged by Manstein for the launching of the operation. Anxiously awaiting the arrival in force of the Panthers, Hitler could not bring himself to make up his mind. As had happened before in his political and military careers, a long period of hesitation followed before the final, irrevocable decision was made.

While the Führer brooded at the Berghof, contemplating the prospect of Zitadelle, the German high command split between those who supported the plan, with varying degrees of enthusiasm, and those who harboured the gravest doubts about its wisdom. Chief among the latter was Jodl, Chief of Staff at OKW, who was still chafing at OKW's exclusion from effective involvement in the running of the Eastern Front. Jodl opposed Zitadelle on the grounds that it was dangerous to plunder the reserves when so many problems loomed in the Mediterranean.

Zeitzler responded by turning logic on its head with the assertion that the Ostheer was so weak that it could not afford to stand still and 'wait to be hit' but, rather, must take the initiative. In any case, as Warlimont later observed, Zeitzler's anger at his own exclusion from the Western theatre of operations meant that he was not concerned with 'these far-off problems . . . He urged all the more the execution of "his" offensive and complained to Hitler of Jodl's intrusion into the sphere of his responsibility.' Thus the intimate and problematic relationship between the Mediterranean and Eastern theatres was buried beneath a welter of recriminations within the high command.

Almost immediately Hitler fell prey to second thoughts about

---

* General Adolf Heusinger was OKH's Chief of Operations.

the Zitadelle plan. A few days after signing Operational Order No.6 he telephoned Zeitzler at Lötzen, suggesting the substitution of the pincer attack – for which the enemy would almost certainly be well prepared – with a frontal assault on the centre of the Kursk bulge by the combined forces of Army Groups Centre and South.

Zeitzler was sufficiently alarmed by this proposal to fly to Berchtesgaden on 21 April to demonstrate with maps and the tables of statistics, so beloved by the Führer, that such a redeployment would impose an intolerable delay on the launching of Zitadelle.

Others were also having second thoughts. In command of Ninth Army was Colonel-General (later Field Marshal) Walter Model who had led 3rd Panzer Division in the invasion of the Soviet Union and whose energy had earned him quick promotion, first to a panzer corps and then, in the winter of 1942–3, to Ninth Army. Foulmouthed and forceful, Model was a soldier's general and a favourite of Hitler's. He had been studying aerial reconnaissance photographs of the deeply echeloned defensive system the Russians were now building in the Kursk salient. He did not like what he saw. Originally, he had been confident that Ninth Army could break through the Russian defences in two days. Now he was not so sure. He needed a further day and more tanks. Model's anxieties communicated themselves to Hitler who asked the commander of Ninth Army to fly to the Berghof where they studied Model's mosaics in the Great Hall. Twelve months later Hitler remarked that Model's request for an extra day, with the additional heavy loss of assault troops this implied, had given him 'cold feet' about Zitadelle. He decided to postpone the operation, first to 5 May and then to the 9th.

At this point Guderian, exercising the autonomy he enjoyed as Inspector-General of Armoured Troops, joined the fray. Since the end of March he had been on the move: visiting the headquarters of frontline units in the East, among them Leibstandarte and Grossdeutschland, to gain a clear picture of the tactical and technical capabilities of the Tiger; meeting Speer to discuss increased Tiger production; making his first visit to the Berghof; attending a melancholy briefing with the Luftwaffe's Chief of Staff, Colonel-General Hans Jeschonnek, whom Guderian found 'a tired man whose mood was one of outspoken discouragement'; discussing the deteriorating situation in North Africa with Schmundt and unsuccessfully urging the immediate evacuation of experienced tank crews and technicians. After another meeting at the Berghof on 29 April, at which Guderian discussed questions of organization and equipment with Keitel, Speer and General Bühle,* and also argued unsuccessfully for the withdrawal of Tiger units from Sicily to mainland Italy, he travelled to Paris to meet Field Marshal von Rundstedt, Commander in Chief West, and examine the Atlantic Wall. Guderian's French tour of inspection was interrupted by a telegram from Hitler, summoning him to a conference in Munich.

Guderian met Hitler on 3 May 1943, urging a delay in the launching of Zitadelle until the Panther's teething troubles had been ironed out and tank production increased to meet the targets promised by Speer: 1140 in May, 1005 in June and 1071 in July. Meanwhile, May would see the activation of two new battalions each of Panthers, Elefants and Hummel (Bumblebee) self-propelled guns, the last mounting a 150mm howitzer on a PzKw IV chassis. Tanks operating on the Eastern Front were to be reinforced against anti-tank shells by the addition of armoured skirts. In reality, Guderian was temporizing, suggesting the postponement of an operation to which he was already firmly opposed. Germany's armoured strength, he believed, should be conserved in 1943 in readiness for the Allied assault in the West.

Still racked by indecision, Hitler presided over a larger meeting on 4 May at which the principal participants were Manstein, Kluge, Model, Zeitzler, Guderian and Speer. Zitadelle dominated the debate. Hitler opened the conference with a forty-five-minute *tour d'horizon* of the Eastern Front, an outline of Zeitzler's proposal for Zitadelle and Model's reservations. Guderian later wrote of the conclusions which Model had drawn from the aerial reconnaissance:

---

* Bühle's role as Chief of Army Staff attached to the Chief of OKW was another example of the confusion which reigned within the German high command. Bühle used this position to bypass his nominal superior, Keitel, and establish a direct relationship with Hitler.

The Russians were preparing deep and very strong defensive positions in exactly those areas where the attack by the two army groups was to go in. The Russians had already withdrawn the mass of their mobile formations from the forward area of the salient; in anticipation of a pincer attack, as proposed in this plan of ours, they had strengthened the locations of our possible breakthroughs with unusually strong artillery and anti-tank forces. Model drew the correct conclusion from this, namely, that the enemy was counting on our launching this attack and that in order to achieve success we must adopt a fresh tactical approach; the alternative was to abandon the whole idea.

Hitler's initial remarks indicated that he had been impressed by Model's argument and that the implementation of Zeitzler's plan was by no means a foregone conclusion. Manstein was then asked to give his opinion. According to Guderian, whose account is self-serving, Manstein sat on the fence, observing that the offensive would have had a good chance of success had it been launched in April but that it now looked more problematic. It should not be undertaken, he said, without first adding two full-strength infantry divisions to the order of battle. Hitler squashed this, remarking that there were no more divisions available, and then asked Manstein to restate his position to which, Guderian recalled, the Führer 'received no very clear answer'.

Kluge, the next to be interrogated, spoke enthusiastically in favour of Zeitzler's plan. Guderian followed him, declaring that Zitadelle was pointless:

We have only just completed the reorganization and re-equipment of our Eastern Front; if we attacked according to the plan of the Chief of the General Staff, we were certain to suffer heavy tank casualties which we would not be in a position to replace in 1943; on the contrary, we ought to be devoting our new tank production to the Western Front so as to have mobile reserves available for use against the Allied landing which could be expected with certainty in 1944.

Guderian then returned to the theme of the Panthers on which Zeitzler seemed to be placing an undue reliance. Once again he referred to the development problems which inevitably preceded the introduction of a new item of weaponry, and warned that there was no guarantee that these would be rectified in time for the offensive. In this he received the solitary backing of Speer. No one else was inclined to oppose Zeitzler's plan. Rather, they opposed any further delay, arguing that the only beneficiary of a postponement would be the Red Army, hard at work strengthening its already formidable defensive system within the Kursk salient. However, the three-hour conference had the effect of causing another delay. Hitler put off the date of Zitadelle to mid-June.

Six days later Guderian was summoned to Berlin for another wearisome discussion with Hitler on Panther production. After the conference Guderian seized Hitler's hand and begged him to abandon Zitadelle, telling him the commitment which the operation demanded could never yield an equivalent gain and would hold back more pressing defensive preparations in the West. He ended with the plaintive question, 'Why do you want to attack in the East at all this year?' Keitel, hovering anxiously at the Führer's shoulder, replied, 'We must attack for political reasons.' Guderian pressed on, a hint of desperation entering his voice as he asked, 'How many people do you think even know where Kursk is? It's a matter of profound indifference to the world whether we hold Kursk or not . . . Why do we want to attack in the East at all this year?' It was at this point that Hitler remarked that the very thought of Zitadelle made his stomach turn over. Unwilling to let go, Guderian assured him, 'In that case your reaction to the problem is the correct one, leave it alone.' The exchange ended with a confession from Hitler that he had by no means committed himself to Zitadelle.

The 'political reasons' to which Keitel referred had little to do with military reality and everything to do with the need to bolster the flagging morale of Germany's allies. By 10 May the Tunis bridgehead had been written off and three days later the Axis forces in North Africa surrendered. The Mediterranean was now Hitler's main concern as he fretted about Allied intentions, the growing isolation of the Duce and his fellow countrymen's lack of stomach for continuing the fight.

On 8 May Hitler was informed of the discovery off the Spanish coast of the corpse at the centre of the Allies' Mincemeat operation. The German high command was divided about the authenticity of the War Office documents which British intelligence had thoughtfully placed in the briefcase attached to the wrist of the notional Major Martin of the Royal Marines, serving on the staff of Vice-Admiral Lord Louis Mountbatten, Chief of Combined Operations. OKW and Admiral Canaris, head of German military intelligence, were deceived but Hitler was at first sceptical about this fortuitous revelation of Allied intentions. But it was not long before the apparent Allied threat to the Dodecanese and Pelopponese began to play on Hitler's preoccupation with the defence of the Balkans. As the devisers of Mincemeat intended, Hitler's obsession with the Balkans overrode his doubts and gave him added reasons for a redeployment of forces to which he was already disposed. Early in June, Guderian had to step in to prevent OKW despatching 1st Panzer Division, recently brought up to full strength and equipped with the first completed Panther battalion, to the Pelopponese to guard against an Allied landing. After much argument he saved the Panthers, which were too wide to negotiate Greece's narrow mountain tracks and bridges, but not 1st Panzer which, he later wrote, 'we were soon to miss bitterly in Russia'.

Hitler's faltering grip on strategy now found him pulled this way and that as he sought to resolve the contradictions inherent in his conduct of the war. He was depressed by the loss of Tunisia and anxious about the gathering threat to Italy. The loss of the Balkans would deprive him not only of his last wavering allies but also of Romania's oil and the bauxite, chrome and copper which sustained Speer's war factories. As the Führer flitted back and forth between Berlin, Rastenburg and the Obersalzberg, the tension gnawed away at him. In mid-May Hitler's personal physician, Dr Theodor Morell, the corpulent quack dubbed the 'Reich injection-master' by the Führer's entourage, was treating his patient for severe constipation with laxatives of 'increasing savagery'. Lieutenant-General Count von Schwerin has left a description of Hitler's physical appearance at this time:

> I reported in the prescribed manner and Hitler came over to me
> – a man stooping as though under a heavy burden, with slow,
> tired steps . . . Hitler was completely down, and in bewilder-
> ment I looked into his lustreless eyes with their unnaturally
> blue colour . . . There can be no doubt at all that those were a
> sick man's eyes. It may be that he had rehearsed this scene.

On 15 May Hitler presided over a secret conference of his generals. Addressing them, he cited Italy and Hungary as the two critical areas, reaffirmed his faith in the Duce while restating his fears about the Italian dictator's personal safety, and emphasized the importance of preventing the opening of a 'Second Front . . . on the Reich's frontiers'. His audience was left in no doubt that, at the top of his agenda, was the approaching crisis in Italy and the need to transfer at least eight armoured and five infantry divisions from the East to secure the Italian peninsula against an Anglo-American assault. Hungary might also have to be occupied. Hitler concluded with the startling revelation that, in the circumstances, he was prepared to contemplate a strategy of withdrawal in the East, including the evacuation of the Orel bend and the Donets region, to which he had doggedly clung in his February confrontations with Manstein. Only by shortening the line could the Wehrmacht offset the transfer of troops to the West. Speed was of the essence, for the activation of the new 'Stalingrad' divisions would not be completed for another two months.

The meeting on 15 May was significant on at least two counts. First, Hitler had made it clear that, for the moment at least, he had abandoned his fixation with holding ground and was considering a strategic defensive along the lines proposed by Manstein. Secondly, his determination to prop up an ally who could no longer be relied upon had taken precedence over the launching of Zitadelle. The implementation of Zeitzler's plan still hung in the balance.

Had the German high command known the full extent of the Russian preparations to defend the Kursk salient, Model's misgivings might have led to a reassessment of the entire plan for Zitadelle. But German intelligence estimates of what was happening 'on the other side of the hill' remained imprecise if deeply disquieting. The Soviet high command, on the other hand, had been kept informed of every twist and turn in the Zitadelle debate. The true source of this information remained unknown to them, but the Russians came to rely on it as their single most important intelligence asset of the war. For this they were indebted to Ultra, the intelligence source derived from the interception and decryption of German coded signal traffic by the Government Code and

Cypher School at Bletchley Park – one of the outstanding British technical triumphs of the war.

The background to Ultra was the Enigma machine cypher system, adopted as standard equipment by the German armed services by 1935. Outwardly, the Enigma machine resembled a portable typewriter but its innards were rather more complex. When one of its keys was depressed an internal system of gears gave any letter input an alternative letter which was not logically to be repeated before 200 trillion subsequent depressions. The Germans were convinced that Enigma's coded messages, from which no apparent pattern could be discerned, were unbreakable.

In this they were deceived. In the 1930s the Polish and French intelligence services had begun to unravel Enigma's secrets. In July 1939 they shared their knowledge with the British who were given an Enigma machine two weeks before Hitler invaded Poland. At Bletchley Park the British cryptographers concentrated on Enigma's principal weakness, the necessity for the operator to preface each message with a repeated sequence of the same letters. Here they found the pattern which enabled Bletchley's brilliant mathematicians to break into the messages and unlock their meaning. Eventually, many messages in the Enigma code were being read in 'real time'. To the end of the war the Germans remained unaware that their code had been broken.

Maintaining the security of the source of the Ultra information, while disseminating it to appropriate and highly restricted quarters, posed many problems for the British. They shared the Ultra secret with the Americans from the beginning of 1942 but were less forthcoming with the Soviet Union. Ultra-derived intelligence was supplied to Stalin but its source was not revealed. In June 1941 the British used Ultra to give him two clear warnings about the imminence of Barbarossa. On 12 June, Foreign Secretary Anthony Eden and Victor Cavendish-Bentinck, head of the British Joint Intelligence Committee, gave the Soviet Ambassador Ivan Maisky detailed evidence of the German plans and the date of Barbarossa's D-Day – 22 June. This Stalin chose to ignore, as he did the complete Wehrmacht order of battle, breakdown of German objectives and correct D-Day, transmitted to Moscow at about the same time by Alexander Foote, second-in-command of the Soviet spy network in Switzerland.

Foote was, in fact, a double agent, recruited before the war by Lieutenant-Colonel Claude Dansey's shadowy 'Z' organization with the aim of infiltrating and controlling Soviet intelligence operations in Switzerland whose neutrality provided an arena in which espionage flourished and agents of opposing powers could meet. Foote was to play an important role in feeding Stalin with Ultra information which he would eventually deem 'reliable' while continuing to maintain the security of its source.

Foote was not the only conduit for Ultra intelligence. Also working for British intelligence in Switzerland was Rachel Dübendorfer, head of a Communist cell at the International Labour Office, an agency of the League of Nations. Dübendorfer was given selected Ultra information by several British agents in Switzerland, among them Victor Farrell, British Consul in Geneva, and Karel Sedlacek, who worked for the highly efficient intelligence service of the Czech government-in-exile, which was hand-in-glove with its British counterpart.

Both Dübendorfer and Sedlacek passed on the Ultra material to Rudolf Rössler, a German emigré who ran an anti-fascist publishing house in Lucerne. Rössler had left Germany in 1933, the year Hitler came to power, but kept close links with a number of highly placed figures in the German anti-Nazi establishment which enabled him to write lengthy assessments of German political and military developments for Swiss intelligence. Much of this information found its way into the Russians' Swiss network and was forwarded to Moscow. In time Rössler, codenamed Lucy, became the lynchpin of the Soviet network in Switzerland. But he was not the spymaster of postwar legend, in contact with senior figures at Hitler's headquarters or the devious Admiral Canaris. The information which so impressed Moscow Centre came not from Rastenburg but from Hut No.3 at Bletchley Park. Rössler was just one element in an impenetrable maze created by the British through which they laundered Ultra material bound for Moscow. The Germans never discovered Lucy's identity, although it is clear that the Swiss, who took Rössler into protective custody in 1944, were in some measure privy to his activities. The Russians remained unaware that their Swiss operation was controlled by the British in the form of the resourceful Foote.

The stop-go gestation of Zitadelle was ideal for the cryptographers at Bletchley Park. The longer the preparations and the greater the disagreements within the German high command, the more numerous were the signals to be intercepted, deciphered and used. This had not been the case during Manstein's counter-offensive when the key decisions were made by the commander of Army Group South at his Zaporozhye headquarters. Lucy had been unusually silent during these weeks but was now able to keep Moscow informed of the enemy's every move. On 8 April Foote's chief, Sandor Radó, transmitted this message to Moscow: 'The differences in the German high command have been settled by the decision to postpone to the beginning of May . . . the attack against Kursk.' The details of Operational Order No.6, with its deception element, Operation Panther, a dummy drive to the oilfields of the Caucasus, were transmitted to Moscow. While Hitler was celebrating his fifty-fourth birthday on 20 April, Radó reported to Moscow that Zitadelle had again been postponed. Nine days later he informed Moscow that the new date set for the offensive was 12 June. On 7 May Moscow Centre, anxious that Hitler might change his mind again, demanded information on current German plans and intentions. On the 9th Radó sent a long signal of more than 120 cypher groups, giving an assessment of the enemy high command's intentions and an accurate account of Speer's promise to Hitler that 324 new Panthers would be available by 31 May. In the build-up to Zitadelle, Stalin was kept informed of every new development. No other intelligence source could provide such a wealth of accurate information.

Isaac Deutscher observed of Stalin that he was, 'in effect, his own commander in chief, his own minister of defence, his own quartermaster, his own minister of supply, his own foreign minister and even his own chef de protocol'. As commander in chief, minister of defence and supply and quartermaster, he was preoccupied with the strengthening of the Kursk salient. As foreign minister his horizons ranged far beyond the central Russian steppe to the arguments which played around the strategic objectives of the Allies and the opening of a 'second front' in northern Europe.

In his Red Army Day Order of 23 February, Stalin pointedly omitted any reference to the fighting in North Africa and claimed that the Soviet Union was 'bearing the whole brunt of the war'. While paying generous tribute to Soviet war industry, he made no mention of Lend-Lease and other Western war supplies which were now beginning to arrive in bulk, much of it coming through Iran.

Although he had previously endorsed it, Stalin was unimpressed by Churchill's Mediterranean strategy. Nor was he receptive to the British Prime Minister's reassurances about the damage which the Anglo–American combined bomber offensive was inflicting on Germany. He continued to urge an Allied invasion of France by the end of the summer of 1943. On 16 March he told President Roosevelt: 'I consider it my duty to state that the early opening of a second front in France is the most important thing (and) it is . . . particularly essential for us that the blow from the West be no longer delayed, that it be delivered this spring or in early summer.'

On 4 June, however, Stalin was informed through official channels that the cross-Channel invasion over-optimistically mooted for August–September 1943 had been postponed until the spring of 1944. He grumbled that this decision created 'exceptional difficulties for the Soviet Union . . . and leaves the Soviet Army, which is fighting not only for its country but also for its allies, to do the job alone, almost singlehanded.'

Stalin was also fencing with Churchill over the sensitive subject of Poland. In Moscow he had set up a puppet Polish government, the Union of Polish Patriots, in direct opposition to the Poles in London, and had authorized the formation and training on Russian soil of a 10,000-strong Polish fighting force, the Tadeusz Kosciuszko Division. His hand in the poker game which represented Anglo–Russian–Polish relations had been inadvertently strengthened by the Germans. On the morning of 13 April German troops discovered a mass grave near Smolensk, at Kosogory in the forest of Katyn. In a 'great pit' 30 yards long and 17 yards wide they uncovered the mummified bodies of 3000 Polish officers stacked in twelve layers. The corpses were wearing military uniform, with their overcoats pulled over their heads, their hands bound and their mouths stuffed with sawdust. They had been killed by a pistol shot to the back of the neck. According to Berlin radio, which broke the news on the evening of the 13th, further excavation had revealed another 7000 corpses.

Between the Soviet occupation of eastern Poland in September 1939 and the German invasion of the Soviet Union, thousands of Polish soldiers, officers and civilians had been imprisoned by the Russians. About 15,000 of them had disappeared without trace. The German discovery of the mass grave at Katyn seemed to provide an answer to the unresolved question of their fate. Delighted to be able to accuse someone else of atrocities, Goebbels made the most of the affair, accusing the Russians of murdering the Poles. Nearly 3000 bodies were eventually identified, the overwhelming majority of them being members of the Polish officer corps, intelligentsia and professional class. All had last been seen in Russian captivity. Some of the corpses bore the distinctive wounds inflicted by the four-sided Russian bayonet.*

The Soviet Union denied the charges vehemently; the Poles in London believed them implicitly. The British, more concerned with maintaining the common war effort than the susceptibilities of the Poles in London, hovered on the sidelines. The Katyn revelations were briefly embarrassing for Stalin who refused to allow an independent investigation by the Red Cross; but they also enabled him more easily to engineer an 'interruption' of relations with the Poles in London. The latter were now caught between a rock and a hard place – Stalin's agenda for a 'friendly' Poland in postwar Europe and the reluctance, indeed inability, of the Western allies to deny him. Later in 1943, when the Poles in London refused to countenance any postwar alterations to Poland's prewar frontiers, they were cast adrift by Churchill.

Poland was one issue which Stalin was determined to settle in his own way. Nevertheless, in spite of the Katyn revelations and the bickering with Churchill over the second front, Stalin's manoeuvring fell far short of a threat to the alliance in spite of rumours about German efforts to secure a separate peace with the

---

* Goebbels sat on the information that German ammunition had been found on the site, the leaking of which might mean that 'the whole Katyn affair would have to be dropped'.

Soviet Union. In his May Day Order of 1943, Stalin sent a series of reassuring signals to Churchill and Roosevelt. The peace feelers were dismissed as a 'German trap' and praise was heaped on our 'victorious Allies in Tripolitania, Libya and Tunisia' and the 'valiant Anglo-American airmen' who were dealing 'smashing blows on both Germany and Italy, thus foreshadowing the establishment of a second front in Europe'. On 22 May, in a gesture designed solely to impress the British and Americans with Russia's new respectability, Stalin dissolved the Comintern.

Four days later, in a reply to an offer from Roosevelt to meet informally 'on the Russian or American sides of the Bering Straits', Stalin expressed his regret that the military situation required his full attention: 'This summer – possibly as early as June – we would expect the Hitlerites to launch a new offensive.' While Stalin haggled with his allies, Stavka was preparing for the anticipated German offensive. At the end of March Soviet intelligence estimated that, in the Orel, Belgorod and Kharkov areas, the Ostheer fielded some sixty divisions, of which twenty were panzer, and had concentrated an extremely powerful shock group, comprising Grossdeutschland, Leibstandarte, Totenkopf and Das Reich in the Kharkov area. On the northern shoulder of the Kursk salient, Rokossovksy's Central Front faced up to seventeen infantry and eight panzer divisions; on the salient's southern shoulder an estimated thirteen infantry and four panzer divisions were massed in the Belgorod area, facing Voronezh Front, now commanded by Vatutin; moving south, Soviet intelligence placed up to nine infantry and nine panzer divisions opposite Malinovsky's South-Western Front.

Even as Manstein's counter-offensive came to an end in the March *rasputitsa*, Stalin was developing a characteristically ambitious plan for a renewed offensive by Central and Voronezh Fronts. Both were to drive for the Dnieper, Central Front aiming for Gomel as a preliminary to the clearing of Belorussia, Voronezh Front retaking Kharkov before liberating the Donbas. However, the German concentrations to the north and south of the Kursk salient now posed a threat to Central and Voronezh Fronts which made Stalin's plan seem unusually reckless. From the beginning of April, Stalin, Stavka, the General Staff and the front commanders combined to draw up new plans to deal with what was clearly seen as the offensive intention of the Ostheer.

In this process much responsibility fell on the broad shoulders of Zhukov. At the end of March he began an extensive tour of the Kursk salient, 'assisting commanders in assessing the situation, explaining their objectives and how best they could achieve them if the enemy launched an offensive'. He gave special attention to the Voronezh Front, making two visits to the sector held by 52nd Guards Rifle Division, covering Oboyan, which Zhukov anticipated might meet the full weight of an enemy attack. While he concentrated on the strengthening of critical areas on Voronezh Front, all three fronts combined under the overall direction of Vasilevksy to mount a massive ground and aerial reconnaissance to establish the full extent of the enemy's strength and his reserves. This exercise yielded sufficient information for Zhukov to deliver a detailed preliminary strategic report to Stalin on 8 April.

Comrade Vasilyev [Stalin's codename]
5.30am, 8 April 1943

Herewith is my report on possible enemy operations in the spring and summer of 1943 and my conclusions about our defensive operations during the immediate future.
1. Having suffered heavy losses during the winter campaign of 1942–3, the enemy will apparently not be able to assemble sufficiently large reserves by spring to renew his advance in the Caucasus and towards the Volga River in an attempt to outflank Moscow in a deep-ranging manoeuvre.

In view of the lack of large reserves, the enemy will have to limit his offensive in the spring and first half of summer 1943 to a narrower front. He will have to make his plans as he moves, stage by stage, with the ultimate objective of seizing Moscow in 1943.

Given the enemy's present disposition of forces opposite our Central, Voronezh and South-Western Fronts, I hold that he will direct his principal offensive operations against these three fronts, hoping to defeat our forces in this area and thus achieve enough room for manoeuvre to outflank Moscow closer to the city.
2. In the first stage the enemy will apparently attempt to mass maximum force, including up to thirteen to fifteen tank divisions with a great amount of air support, and strike with his

Orel-Kromy group to bypass Kursk on the north-east, and with his Belgorod-Kharkov group to bypass Kursk on the south-east. An auxiliary strike, aimed at cutting up our front, may be expected from the west near Vorozhba, between the Seym and Psel rivers, directed against Kursk from the south-west.

With this attack, the enemy would try to surround our Thirteenth, Seventieth, Sixty-Fifth, Sixtieth, Thirty-Eighth, Fortieth and Twenty-First Armies. The ultimate objective of this stage would be a line running through the Korocha River, the town of Korocha, the town of Tim, the Tim River and Droskovo.

3. In the second stage, the enemy is likely to strike against the flank and rear of the South-Western Front in the general direction of Valuki and Urazovo. He may try to join this drive with another strike from the area of Lisichansk northward towards Svatovo and Urazovo. Elsewhere the enemy may be expected to drive towards a line through Livny, Kastornoye, Stary Oskol and Novy Oskol.

4. In the third stage, after appropriate regrouping, the enemy may attempt to reach a line running through Liski, Voronezh and Yelets and, having covered his south-east flank, he may try to outflank Moscow through Ranenburg, Ryazhsk and Ryazan.

5. We can expect the enemy to put greatest reliance in this year's offensive operations on his tank divisions and air force since his infantry seems to be far less prepared for offensive operations than last year. Opposite the Central and Voronezh Fronts, the enemy now has up to twelve tank divisions so that, by moving three of four additional tank divisions from other sectors, he may throw as many as fifteen or sixteen tank divisions, with a combined strength of 2500 tanks, against our Kursk grouping.

6. In view of this threat, we should strengthen the anti-tank defences of the Central and Voronezh Fronts, assemble as soon as possible thirty anti-tank artillery regiments in the Supreme Headquarters reserve for use in the threatened sectors and concentrate all self-propelled artillery regiments along the line through Livny, Kastornoye and Stary Oskol (in the rear), placing some of the regiments immediately at the disposal of Rokossovsky and Vatutin. As much air strength as possible should be concentrated in the Supreme Headquarters reserve so that massed air attacks in conjunction with tanks and rifle units can strike at the enemy's shock forces and thus disrupt his offensive plans.

I am not familiar with the final disposition of our operational

reserves, but in my view they should be assembled in the areas
of Yefremov, Livny, Kastornoye, Novy Oskol, Valuiki, Rossosh,
Liski, Voronezh and Yelets, with most of the reserves concentrated around Yelets and Voronezh. Deeper reserves should be
positioned at Ryazhsk, Ranenburg, Michurinsk and Tambov.
One reserve army should be stationed in the area of Tula and
Stalinogorsk.

I consider it unwise to launch a preventive attack in the next
few days. It would be better if we wore the enemy down with
our defences and destroyed his tanks, and only then, after
having moved up fresh reserves, went over to a general offensive and finally destroyed his main force.

KONSTANIN [Zhukov's codename]

Here, in brisk outline, was Zhukov's battle plan. The battle was
going to be contested on *his* terms. It was the meticulously
planned offspring of the improvised holding operation and
counterstroke which he had executed in the winter of 1941. He
had correctly gauged the enemy's underlying weakness and had
focused on the Red Army's strengths. The Ostheer was to be worn
down in the Russian defences, his armour destroyed, 'and only
then, after having moved up fresh reserves', would the Red Army
go over to a general offensive to destroy the enemy's main force. It
was the Zhukov doctrine in all its brutal simplicity.

On 10 April Zhukov was joined on the Voronezh Front by
Marshal Vasilevsky. The latter fully supported Zhukov's conclusions; they quickly reached agreement on the disposition of operational and strategic reserves, and 'the character of the impending
operations'. Together they drafted a Stavka directive on reserves
and the creation of a new Steppe Front in the rear of the Kursk
salient, and despatched it to Stalin for signature. Simultaneously
they invited the front commanders and their headquarters staffs
to express their opinions on coming operations.

They received an immediate reply from Central Front whose
Chief of Staff, Lieutenant-General M.S. Malinin, anticipated that, 'in
view of the results of the offensive operations of 1941–2, we can
expect the enemy to limit his offensive in the spring and summer
of 1943 to the Kursk-Voronezh operational direction'. However,
rather than stand on the defensive to meet the enemy attack,
which Malinin estimated would be launched as early as mid-May,

the combined forces of Western, Bryansk and Central Fronts should take the initiative, strike at the enemy groupings around Orel, seize the Mtsensk–Orel–Kursk railway, deprive the Ostheer of the use of the Bryansk rail and road junction and forestall the planned offensive against the northern shoulder of the Kursk salient.

Two days later Stavka received the recommendations of the Voronezh Front, signed by Vatutin, Khrushchev (the political member of the front's military council) and Lieutenant-General F.K. Korzhenevich, Vatutin's Chief of Staff. Summing up, the report stated:

> The enemy's intentions would be to strike concentric blows from the Belgorod area towards the north-east and from the Orel area towards the south-east with the objective of encir- cling our forces west of the Belgorod-Kursk line. Subsequently, we can expect the enemy to strike south-east at the flank and rear of the South-Western Front to be able to move northward later.
>
> However, there is a possibility that the enemy may not move south-eastwards this year and will, instead, adopt another plan calling for an offensive north-eastwards to bypass Moscow after concentric strikes out of the area of Belgorod and Orel. We must keep this possibility in mind and prepare reserves accordingly.

Although there was a substantial measure of agreement among the senior commanders on the spot, their reports had shaken two straws in the wind which were to distract Stalin – the possibility of launching a pre-emptive strike out of the Kursk salient and the cal- culation that a renewed drive on Moscow featured in the German plans. Zhukov, however, was not contemplating an attack out of the salient for the very sound reason that 'our strategic reserves were still in the process of being formed and the Voronezh and Central Fronts, having suffered heavy losses in the previous fight- ing, required reinforcement in manpower, arms and equipment'.

Zhukov was never farther than a telephone call away from Stalin and no sooner had he arrived in the Kursk sector than he was summoned back to Moscow from the headquarters of Voronezh Front. Arriving on the 11th, he was met by Vasilevsky who informed him that Stalin had ordered the preparation of maps and detailed proposals for the spring-summer campaigning season. Zhukov, Vasilevksy and Antonov worked through the 12th on the presentation. It was in this field that Antonov, the General Staff's Chief of Operations, excelled. Composed and controlled, precise in thought and speech, he prepared the situation map while Zhukov and Vasilevsky drafted the report for Stalin. All three were in agreement that the German high command was planning a major offensive against the Kursk salient, striking south from Orel and north from Belgorod while remaining on the defensive along the rest of the Eastern Front. This posture was dictated by the Ostheer's lack of forces for multiple offensive operations. It was at Kursk that OKH was prepared to pay 'any price' to restore the strategic balance in favour of the Ostheer by destroying Central and Voronezh Fronts.

On the evening of the 12th, Zhukov, Vasilevsky and Antonov made their presentation to Stalin who 'listened more attentively than ever before to all we had to say'. Stalin accepted that the principal danger lay in the Kursk sector, but retained his preoccupation with safeguarding the approaches to Moscow. A compromise was reached. Priority was to be given to the construction of a deeply echeloned defensive system within the Kursk salient, but attention was also to be paid to all the 'main axes'. The troops were to dig in, a task for which they were ideally fitted by temperament and experience. At the same time, the Soviet defensive strategy was to be reinforced by the creation of a powerful reserve to the east of Kursk.

Stalin, however, was beset by doubts, his lingering indecision over the shape of the summer offensive providing a mirror image of Hitler's agonizing over Zitadelle. While the Führer sought to put off the final decision on Zitadelle by successive postponements, Stalin seized on a report from Vatutin which, while stressing the defensive nature of the planned operation, suggested that a disruptive strike might be launched on the German concentrations in the Belgorod–Kharkov area. Brooding on the uncomfortable fact that, up to spring 1943, no German strategic offensive had ever failed to achieve immediate tactical and operational success, Stalin was instinctively drawn towards the offensive option suggested by Vatutin. It was not until mid-May, and after much

argument, that Zhukov, Vasilevsky and Antonov were able to neutralize, if not entirely eliminate, Stalin's predilection for jumping
the gun. As Zhukov recalled, the result was that Stalin

> firmly decided to meet the German attack with artillery fire,
> with air strikes and with counter-attacks by our operational
> and strategic reserves. Then, having worn down the enemy, we
> were to launch our own powerful counter-offensive in the
> Belgorod-Kharkov directions, followed by deep-ranging offen-
> sive operations in all major directions. After the defeat of the
> Germans in the Kursk salient, Supreme Headquarters pro-
> posed to liberate the Donets Basin and the entire Ukraine east
> of the Dnieper River, eliminate the enemy bridgehead on the
> Taman Peninsula in the Northern Caucasus, reach the eastern
> part of Belorussia and thus prepare the way for the complete
> expulsion of the enemy from Soviet territory.

CHAPTER 6

Digging In

'Ask anything of me but time.' Napoleon Bonaparte

IN THE EARLY spring of 1943, as Hitler edged crabwise towards a decision on Zitadelle, the German troops massed around the Kursk salient enjoyed the longest lull of the war on the Eastern Front. While OKH and Stavka applied themselves to planning in detail the great battle which summer would bring, there was time for recreation as well as training, and time also to reflect on the dangers which lay ahead.

In April 102nd Infantry Division passed through Svesk on its way to join Ninth Army around Orel. In Svesk they saw for the first time captured American M-4 Sherman tanks and other evidence of Lend-Lease, including preserved meat, chocolate and powdered egg and milk. So much, reflected the men of 102nd Division, for the propaganda line that the Luftwaffe was preventing Allied convoys from getting through.

The division's journey ended twenty miles south of Orel in a sector adjoining that of 7th Infantry Division, a Bavarian formation. The Bavarians had kept themselves well supplied with beer, including fifty-litre barrels of their own brew, which the Silesians of 102nd Division were happy to exchange for their supplies of French cognac. Erich Mende, a junior officer in 102nd Division's 84th Infantry Regiment recalled that the Bavarians had a low opinion of the area, claiming that only large amounts of alcohol made it tolerable. To Mende, however, the rolling countryside, dotted with farms and orchards under a bright blue sky, was close to paradise.

Relations with the local population were good, as many of the Silesians spoke Polish or Russian. The regimental doctor and his orderlies delivered babies and tended serious injuries sustained by farm workers. The regiment's medical staff also had their work cut out dealing with an outbreak of spotted fever, a problem which nagged away at the Ostheer, eating into manpower and morale. The regiment's officers were innoculated against the fever – there was not enough of the newly developed vaccine for the men – but the results were discouraging. Those vaccinated immediately fell ill – only the regimental doctor seemed immune, or unvaccinated – but all survived their ordeal.

A new and equally unwelcome remedy arrived to deal with the perennial campaigning problem of lice and fleas. The regiment took delivery of a lice powder, Lauseto, a pungent brown mixture patented by Hitler's personal physician Dr Morell who saw a quick way of turning his position with the Führer into a large personal profit. Unfortunately, the troops found Lauseto utterly useless. Some of Mende's colleagues made a point of dropping live lice into small piles of Lauseto where they seemed to suffer few ill effects. The only way of dealing with lice was by detailed investigation of the seams of one's shirts and trousers. Some of the men took to boiling their underwear, but this only shrunk them several sizes.

To the south of the salient Gerd Schmückle, a junior officer in the artillery regiment of 7th Panzer Division, part of III Panzer Corps, found quarters in Zirkuni, a small village surrounded by collective farms whose workforce he found friendly and, to his surprise, in no way servile. During a rest period Schmückle went to the opera in Kharkov; he was accompanied by a Hiwi driver, Vladimir, who acted as an interpreter. Schmückle was impressed by the opera's corps de ballet and struck up a friendship with one of them, an eighteen-year-old dancer named Natasha. Soon they were having an affair, meeting in a house in Kharkov. Schmückle was fascinated by the elfin Natasha who apparently believed in demons, wood sprites and witches.

Shortly afterwards 7th Panzer's commander, General Hans von Funck, invited Schmückle to a dinner given in honour of General Hans Speidel who, like Schmückle, was a Swabian. In his memoirs Schmückle recalled that von Funck had often been openly critical of Speidel and that he anticipated, therefore, that a reconciliation was now on the cards. Speidel was entertained under canvas at a simple wooden trestle table which groaned beneath the weight of silver plate 'liberated' by 7th Panzer's commander from a French battleship in Toulon, 'so that Göring didn't get his hands on it'. Jovially, von Funck remarked that he would return the plate to the Commander in Chief of the French fleet when the war was over. Speidel arrived, declaring that the brave display on the table made him feel as if he were at Maxim's in Paris, an impression undone by the simple canteen meal which followed. Von Funck remarked, with pointed irony, that 'We owe it all to the Führer,' and, for a fleeting moment, Schmückle thought he saw a flicker of acknowledgement in Speidel's eyes. During the meal Speidel was critical of Hitler's repeated postponements of Zitadelle. After the table had been cleared there was a surprise for him, a soldiers' choir who sang Swabian songs for the visitor. Schmückle noted that Speidel's eyes were moist when he left.

Speidel's anxiety was also shared by Lieutenant-General von Hünersdorff, commander of III Corps' 6th Panzer Division and an immensely experienced armoured leader. On 22 May he held a meeting of his senior officers in Kharkov, during which they consumed a large meal prepared by Ukrainian cooks. Drink loosened tongues and Hünersdorff ventured the opinion that there were insufficient German forces to break through the Soviet defences in the Kursk salient and that the entire operation 'violated the ground rules of leadership'. At least one member of the company heard Hünersdorff use the word 'idiotic' when referring to Zitadelle.

Both 6th and 7th Panzer took part in manoeuvres near Kharkov laid on for a military delegation from Turkey, a propaganda stunt dreamt up by Franz von Papen, the German ambassador in Ankara. The tank crews were clean shaven for the day and, wearing their best uniforms, were led by the most highly decorated officers. Twelve Turkish officers turned up for this demonstration of German armoured might, accompanied by a distracted-looking

Manstein. Afterwards, the convivial von Funck laid on another tented dinner. Inside, the French plate made a further appearance; outside stood two captured T-34s. The atmosphere was friendly but the Turks were studiously non-committal. Funck made a speech in which he referred to the 'Turkish–German brotherhood in the First World War', but, while the Turks expressed their admiration for the German weaponry on display, they stonewalled on suggestions that Turkey might abandon its neutrality in favour of the Axis. As one Turkish officer politely observed, the Wehrmacht seemed so powerful that it would not need any Turkish help to beat the Red Army. Schmückle was once again in attendance and, after the meal, Funck told him that, with or without Turkey, the war was lost. The Germans had over-reached themselves and could no longer control their conquests.

During the quiet weeks which followed Manstein's recapture of Kharkov the struggle for air supremacy continued unabated. Fierce air battles were fought in the south on the Kuban front, and there was increasing air activity over the Kursk salient as German and Russian bombers attempted to disrupt the enemy's preparations for the summer fighting.

In the summer and autumn of 1941 the Soviet aviation had taken a terrible hammering at the hands of the Luftwaffe. By 5 October 1941 the Russians themselves admitted that they had lost 5316 aircraft, many of them on the ground. Like the Red Army, the Army Air Force (VVS) had been caught by Barbarossa in the middle of a major reorganization; its officer corps was diminished and demoralized by the purges of the late 1930s in which as many as 70 per cent of its senior commanders had been killed.

After the débâcle of the opening weeks of Barbarossa, the Commander in Chief of the VVS, Smushkevich, a veteran of the Spanish Civil War, shared the fate of General Pavlov and was summarily executed.

However, in the depths of defeat lay the seeds of recovery. The large numbers of obsolete Soviet aircraft destroyed on the ground in 1941 did not entail the loss of aircrew, who were retrained on the new types which the VVS was bringing into service. The loss of thousands of obsolescent aircraft, although spectacular, was not fatal, as they were replaced by potent new types capable of meet-

ing the challenges of a rapidly changing air environment. Air warfare hinges on the establishment of small but crucial technical
advantages over the enemy. By 1943 the VVS had gained a significant edge over the Luftwaffe in that the best aircraft it fielded had
been designed in the late 1930s and early 1940s, in contrast to
their German rivals whose history stretched back to the early
1930s. Thus the Lavochkin La-5FN fighter, which entered service in
the autumn of 1942, possessed a superior all-round performance
to that of its most formidable German opponent, the
Messerschmitt Bf109G, the last major production model of a
classic fighter designed in 1933. Similarly, the sleek Soviet
Petlyakov Pe-2FT dive-bomber, developed in 1939 from a design
for a twin-engined fighter, was a superb instrument of close-
support operations with an impressive top speed of 361 mph at
16,400 feet. Its German opposite number, the Junkers Ju87, which
had entered production in 1936, was now entering obsolescence
although, in its G version, it was to enjoy a spectacular swansong
in the summer of 1943.

In 1941 the eastward evacuation of more than 100 aircraft factories ensured the survival and subsequent expansion of a production infrastructure which, throughout the war, functioned without
German interference. Moreover, the factories had only one front to
supply while the Luftwaffe had to devote large numbers of aircraft
to the defence of the Reich and operations in the Mediterranean.
In 1942 the Soviet Union produced 25,000 aircraft for one main
front while Germany produced only 15,000 for three fronts. This
led to a haemorrhage of aircraft from the Eastern Front which
could not be staunched: between February 1943 and February
1944 the ratio of fighters between the West and East rose from
2:1 to 3.5:1. The dispersal of effort meant that, although German
aircraft production rose to 25,000 in 1943, it was not possible
to redress the balance in favour of the Eastern Front. It was only
a matter of time before the Red Air Force gained, first, air superiority and, then, air supremacy over wide areas of the East.

The Luftwaffe's problems were compounded by the inadequa-
cies of its high command. Göring elevated technical ignorance
almost to an art form, while his Chief of Staff, Jeschonnek, had
only a limited grasp of the tactical and technical demands of the

air war and was undermined by the political infighting within his command. Obsessed with operational thinking, Jeschonnek* failed to make adequate provision for the replacement of aircrew and obsolescent aircraft. His observation that 'First we have to beat the Russians, then we can continue training,' might well have served as his own epitaph.

In contrast the VVS had its own Zhukov in Marshal A.A. Novikov, its Commander in Chief from April 1942. Within a month of his appointment he had activated the first of seventeen air armies, each with its own internal chain of command. As a rule each front was supported by one air army. The closest cooperation was ensured by placing the air army's deputy commander and staff at the front where they either shared or were near the headquarters of army units with whom they were in constant direct contact. The front and air army commanders jointly worked out operational plans. The front commander determined the priority of missions and, with the advice of the air army commander, decided on the overall plan for missions flown by the air forces in support of ground operations.

In addition to the reorganization of the tactical air forces, Stavka created three strategic forces and a service maintenance command directly subordinate to the central command. Like the artillery arm, the Red Air Force amassed a formidable strategic reserve comprising corps equipped with one type of aircraft (fighter, ground-attack, etc.) which could be transferred swiftly from front to front or, within a front, from one critical area to another. By the end of the war the reserve contained about 43 per cent of all tactical air forces available to the VVS. The formation of the air armies was accompanied by the creation of a long-range bomber arm (ADD) and a new fighter defence force (PVO) which took as its model RAF Fighter Command as it functioned during the Battle of Britain.

---

* On 17 August 1943 the demoralized Jeschonnek was forced to endure a tongue-lashing from Hitler after the US Eighth Air Force's raids of Schweinfurt and Regensburg. Early next morning he received news that RAF Bomber Command had made a heavy raid on the rocket research establishment at Peenemunde. On Jeschonnek's orders his night fighters had mistakenly assembled over Berlin where they had been fired on by their own anti-aircraft batteries. Jeschonnek shot himself on the same day.

The British and Americans, with their heavy investment in the strategic bomber, saw the ground and air forces as independent and co-equal, neither being the auxiliary of the other. In contrast, the VVS undertook very little strategic bombing during the war, devoting only 5 per cent of its effort to long-range bombing operations. The mission of the VVS was the tactical support of the ground forces with light and attack bombing, reconnaissance and fighter operations – an auxiliary function, termed the 'air offensive', which cast the VVS in the role of airborne artillery.

The air offensive was planned to unroll in two phases. In the first, the VVS paved the way for the ground forces with heavy strikes against enemy airfields and supply lines. In the second, it provided close support while continuing to attack tactical targets in the enemy's rear. As a result, the air fighting on the Eastern Front was overwhelmingly concentrated within its relatively shallow combat zones, and even the ADD was used principally in a battlefield role while also flying important transport missions and supporting the partisans operating behind German lines.

The doctrine of the air offensive attached great importance to attack aviation, the 'flying artillery' which accounted for about a quarter of all missions flown and suffered proportionate losses. The prime weapon of attack aviation was the Ilyushin Il-2 Shturmovik ground-attack aircraft which was built in larger numbers than any other aircraft in the Second World War. Constructed around an armoured steel 'bath' which housed the engine and the cockpit, the Shturmovik was almost impervious to light ground fire. Originally built as a single-seater, the early Il-2s lacked power and manoeuvrability and were vulnerable to attack from the rear. By the summer of 1943 they had been replaced by the Il-2m3 with a more powerful engine and a second seat for a rear gunner firing a 12.7mm machine-gun on a flexible mounting. The Il-2m3 also carried two 37mm cannon in its wings; these were capable of penetrating the armour of most German tanks. RS-82 and RS-132 rocket-propelled missiles could also be carried under the wings and anti-personnel or the new PTAB hollow-charge anti-tank bombs could be accommodated internally in a number of small bomb bays.

German aircrew dubbed this businesslike aircraft the *Zementer* ('cement bomber') and, as its nickname suggests, it was a difficult opponent to shoot down. Erich Hartmann, in the spring of 1943 a flight lieutenant with the crack fighter unit Jagdsgeschwader 52 (JG52), has described the disposal of a tough customer:

> Our position was behind and above our enemies. We . . . attacked in a steep dive, firing through the fighters and attacking the bombers. I attacked the aircraft on the extreme left, closing in very fast and opening fire at about two or three hundred feet. I saw numerous hits but the bullets ricocheted off the Il-2. The heavy armour plating in those Il-2s resisted even 20mm cannon-shell hits.
>
> I began my second attack on the same machine, starting with a steep dive and coming up on him from behind and below. This time I closed in even closer before opening fire. A hit in the oil-cooling system! Black smoke belched from the Il-2 followed by rapidly lengthening tongues of flame. The fire swept back under the fuselage. I was alone at the time because the aircraft I had attacked had pulled out of formation and was trying to escape to the east. I was still sitting behind him and we were both in a shallow dive. Then there was an explosion under his wing and, simultaneously, a heavy explosion in my own aircraft. Smoke billowed back into the cockpit and I could see fire glowing redly under the engine cowlings. There was no time to lose.
>
> Quickly I went through the drill. Altitude: low level and still on the German side of the lines. Fast – power back, fuel master switch off and ignition switch off in quick order. None too soon. I bellied into a field, raising a huge shower of dirt and dust which quickly extinguished the fire. Just as I clambered out of the cockpit, my first kill crashed thunderously three kilometres away.

Stalingrad had marked a turning point in the air war. At that time the VVS had gained a numerical superiority over the Luftwaffe which it was able to exploit to establish local air superiority over the battlefield. The Luftwaffe's heavy losses – nearly 500 aircraft – had not only laid to rest the aura of invincibility it had previously enjoyed but had also taken a huge toll of experienced aircrew. When the Red Army launched the counter-offensive which created the Kursk salient it was able to mass 2000 aircraft against 400 German.

Nevertheless, the Luftwaffe, like the panzer arm, was able to level the odds with superior flying skills and tactical flexibility, qualities which were sorely needed when, as frequently happened, German fighter pilots were faced with odds of 30:1. In the air, as on the ground, the VVS displayed a dogged determination to maintain formation, the result of the general Soviet curb on initiative at all levels. As another member of JG52, Günther Rall, recalled:

Tactics were different in Russia. The Russian pilots liked to fly in large masses. And at the beginning of the war, we had experience and it was easy. Later, it became much more difficult. They didn't have the individual initiative of pilots we fought on the Western Front, but the Red Banner Guard Regiments were very good.

Experten like Hartmann, Gerhard Barkhorn and Günther Rall – all of JG52 – were able to run up victory tallies in the East which were unrivalled in any other theatre: Hartmann finished the war with 352 victories, the highest achieved by any fighter pilot, followed by Barkhorn with 301 and Rall with 275.

Not all the Luftwaffe's teeth had been drawn. In the Focke-Wulf FW190A, which entered service in 1941, it had one of the best fighters of the war, armed with two 7.9mm MG17 machine-guns in the nose, two 20mm MG151 cannon in the wing roots and two 20mm MG/FF cannon in the wings. Capable of 413mph at 20,400ft and with a service ceiling of 36,800ft and range of 565 miles, the FW190A had the edge over the La-5FN. In its fighter-bomber, or Shlacht version, the FW190A had its outer cannon removed to accommodate underwing bomb racks, while an additional rack was fitted under the fuselage. As a fighter-bomber, and particularly as a dive-bomber, the FW190A had its limitations. It had not been designed for these roles and its poor visibility and high speed made it difficult for pilots to linger over the target to achieve precision results.

No such problems were suffered by the Henschel Hs129B, the Luftwaffe's first and only specialist anti-tank aircraft whose full complement of 'tank-busting' weapons comprised two 7.9mm MG17 machine-guns and two 20mm MG151 cannon in the fuselage and a 30mm MK101 gun in a 'gondola' fairing fitted beneath the fuselage. Designed to loiter over its targets, the twin-engined Hs129B had a top speed of 199mph at 9845 feet when fully loaded, a service ceiling of 24,600ft and a range of 384 miles.

Also packing a big punch was the anti-tank version of the Stuka, the Ju87G, which carried a 37mm Flak 18 (or BK37) cannon beneath each wing in addition to its basic machine-gun armament. Each cannon was fitted with a six-round magazine of 1.36kg wolfram-cored armour-piercing shells.

To establish whether the Ju87G could perform successfully in operational conditions, the *Versuchsverband fur Panzerkampfung* (Anti-Tank Experimental Unit) was formed at Bryansk in February 1943, under the command of Lieutenant-Colonel Otto Weiss, Inspector-General of Ground-Attack Forces. Many of the unit's pilots were sceptical about the Flak 18's ability to deal with the 45mm sloped frontal armour of the T-34 and the 75mm protection of the KV-1. One of them, however, Flight Lieutenant Hans-Ulrich Rudel, a brilliant pilot seconded for the trials from Stukageschwader (StG2), recognized in the cannon's excellent ballistics a chance to defeat the Soviet armour. He wrote:

> What impresses me is the possibility of being able to shoot with an accuracy of within 20 to 30cm. If this is attainable, one should be able to hit vulnerable parts of the tank, provided one could get within close enough range – that is my conviction. From models we learn how to identify the various types of Russian tank and are taught where the most vulnerable parts are located: engine, petrol tank, ammunition chamber.

The Ju87G was combat tested in the Bryansk sector in March 1943. In May Rudel went south to the Crimea to continue trials on the Kuban front. The Ju87G's cannon reduced its speed and manoeuvrability, making it vulnerable to anti-aircraft fire. Subsequently, it was accompanied on operations by the standard dive-bombing Ju87Ds which suppressed anti-aircraft fire while the Ju87G dealt with enemy armour.

Hitler was never 'air-minded', but Stalin took a close interest in all matters relating to aviation, often intervening on points of technical detail. Lieutenant-General A.S. Yakovlev, the designer who served throughout the war as the minister responsible for research and development, recalled a stormy meeting in March 1943 at which Stalin confronted him with evidence of faulty wing-covering fabric on his own Yak-9 fighter which had entered service at the time of Stalingrad. Brandishing a piece of cracked wing fabric, Stalin reminded Yakovlev and his deputy, P.V. Dement'ev, that this defect was threatening the preparations for 'serious fighting' in the Orel–Kursk area, operations which 'cannot be carried out without fighter participation . . . after all, you know that fighters at this point are as vital to us as the air we breathe'. Working himself into a towering rage while Yakovlev and Dement'ev attempted to exculpate themselves, Stalin repeated time and again, 'This is working for Hitler!'

Finally, Stalin accused them both of being 'Hitlerites'. Yakovlev recalled: 'It is difficult to imagine our condition at that moment. I felt that I was shivering. And Dement'ev stood there, completely flushed, nervously twirling a piece of the ill-fated covering in his fingers.' Several minutes of 'tomb-like' silence followed, during which Yakovlev and Dement'ev might well have pondered the fate of Pavlov and Smushkevich. Finally, Dement'ev secured their release by promising to remedy the defect in two weeks, a task which normally would have taken two months.

The Yak-9's teething troubles did not significantly affect the air build-up in the Kursk sector: in the north Central Front was supported by Sixteenth Air Army, commanded by Colonel-General S.I. Rudenko; in the south, Voronezh Front was supported by Second Air Army, led by Colonel-General S.A. Krasovsky and based in the Oboyan area, in addition to Seventeenth Air Army, commanded by Colonel-General V.A. Sudets and based in the Korocha area. These air armies were in turn supported by substantial elements of Stavka's reserve (AFLRO) and Fifteenth Air Army, on the Bryansk Front, which could be called in if necessary. The total number of aircraft available to Stavka in the Kursk sector was approximately 2900 – some 500 day bombers, 400 night bombers, 1060 fighters and 940 ground-attack aircraft.

On the northern shoulder of the Kursk salient the VVS was opposed by Luftflotte 6, based around Orel and commanded by General Ritter von Greim; in the south was Luftflotte 4, supported by II Hungarian Air Corps and based around Belgorod and Kharkov. In mid-June of 1943 Luftflotte 4's dynamic commander, Field Marshal Wolfram von Richthofen, Hitler's favourite airman, had been transferred to Italy to take over Luftflotte 2, further proof of the importance Hitler attached to the Mediterranean theatre. He was replaced by General Otto Dessloch.

The combined strength of the two Luftflotten was approximately 2050 aircraft – 1200 bombers, 600 fighters, 100 ground-attack and 150 reconnaissance aircraft. The concentration represented nearly 70 per cent of the Luftwaffe's available operational strength on the Eastern Front. Only in the north around Leningrad and the Arctic regions were substantial elements of air strength left in Luftflotten 1 and 5. The rest of the Eastern Front had been stripped almost bare for the Kursk offensive. More than a dozen Kampfgruppen were operating in the Mediterranean, as well as three Stukagruppen, but there were few such units left in Western Europe and the Reich whose forces had been drained to give the Luftwaffe a significant numerical superiority over the VVS in bomber aircraft in the Kursk sector. In contrast, the Soviets fielded nearly three times as many fighters and ground-attack aircraft as the enemy.

Throughout May and June the VVS mounted an interdiction campaign against the Luftwaffe's airfields in an effort to blunt the edge of the forces accumulating in the Kursk sector. According to Soviet sources a particularly heavy effort was put in between 8 and 10 June when three air armies (First, Second and Fifteenth, supported by long-range bombers of the ADD) attacked twenty-eight enemy airfields, destroying over 220 aircraft. German sources claim, however, that it was the Red Air Force which came off worst in these raids in which they incurred serious losses while inflicting little damage on their targets. During this period the Germans claimed to have destroyed some 2300 aircraft, against Luftwaffe losses of approximately 250.*

On occasion the Russians stayed their hand. Writing about the Kursk campaign after the war, Marshal Rudenko recalled an incident which took place in mid-June. Sixteenth Air Army's intelligence chief, Colonel G.R.Prussakov, had presented him with aerial reconnaissance photographs of two small woods near Kromy, south-west of Orel, which concealed a large number of tanks. Traces of tank tracks and other evidence suggested that the

---

* The air war in the East was characterized by some extravagant over-claiming by both sides.

woods were playing host to two panzer divisions. Rudenko wrote: 'Tank concentrations are always tempting targets for an air force. And so I immediately decided to bomb these two small woods and knock out two large panzer units.' However, he was overruled by Central Front's commander, Colonel-General K.K. Rokossovsky who, after listening to Rudenko's proposal, said:

> Well, say we shake up these two divisions, and so tell the ene-
> my we know much about him. He'll restore their combat power
> and hide them so that our reconnaissance will never find them.
> What we want now is to make him believe we know nothing
> and, at the same time, discover his strength and his plans. We
> shouldn't alarm the Germans. Let them attack and then, if you
> want to, take a smack at those woods. Only it's hardly likely
> that you find any tanks there. You have to watch their move-
> ment and then shower them with bombs.

Rudenko concluded that there was 'nothing for me to do but agree'.

The Luftwaffe was less circumspect about attacking the Voronezh–Kastornoye–Kursk and Kursk–Yelets railway lines (both heavily damaged during the German retreat), along which rolled the bulk of supplies to Central and Voronezh Fronts. In March– April the Luftwaffe flew about 1500 sorties against railway installa- tions in the Kursk salient, and in May–June the figure rose to 4300. The Liski station and bridge on the River Don was bombed on at least fifteen occasions by a total of 600 aircraft; Yelets was bombed twelve times, Kastornoye sixteen times and Kursk fifteen times by over 1300 aircraft. Even small bridges and facilities, of which there were a large number near the front line, were subjected to repeated attacks. Anti-aircraft batteries were deployed by the bridges, 'duty brigades' with spare rail and equipment stood by at the points most at risk and 'ambushes' were laid by mobile anti- aircraft groups. These groups, equipped with cross-country vehi- cles and tractors, took up camouflaged positions by likely targets under the cover of darkness and then waited for the German bombers. After two or three engagements they moved on.

Under a steel-blue sky flecked with the vapour trails of fierce aerial clashes, Central and Voronezh Fronts completed their basic deployments for a defensive battle. Stalin might well have toyed with the idea of a pre-emptive strike, but in the Kursk salient the troops were digging in and their commanders evaluating the 'variants' presented to them by their intelligence staffs. On the Central Front, Rokossovsky anticipated that his right wing would bear the brunt of the German attack, running along the Orel-Kursk axis and driving south or south-east through Ponyri and Zolutkhino to Kursk. Confident that an assault in any other sectors could be held, Rokossovsky deployed his main strength along a fifty-mile front covering the northern curve of the Kursk salient.

The deployments were in two echelons. In the first echelon were three armies, Forty-Eighth, Thirteenth and Seventieth. Thirteenth was in the middle of the line, with Seventieth on its left and Forty-Eighth on its right. Each of the armies was deployed in two echelons. Thus, in Thirteenth's first echelon were two rifle corps, 29th and 15th, whose own first echelon – responsible for the defence of the 'main field' of its designated tactical zone – comprised four rifle divisions,* 15th, 81st, 148th and 8th. In the second echelon, covering the 'second field', were two divisions, 307th and 74th. In the second echelon of Thirteenth Army were two Guards rifle corps, 17th and 18th, six rifle divisions and a tank regiment. At Fetezh, fifty miles south-west of Ponyri, Rokossovsky placed Second Tank Army, commanded by Lieutenant-General A.G. Rodin, as a reserve echelon. Covering the face of the salient, along a front of 100 miles, were Sixty-Fifth and Sixtieth Armies. The Front's reserve consisted of 18th Guards Rifle Corps, 9th and 19th Tank Corps and anti-tank artillery regiments.

On Voronezh Front, Vatutin's dispositions provided a mirror image of the situation in the north. He placed his main strength in the centre and on the left of the shoulder, paying particular attention to covering the Kharkov–Oboyan–Kursk highway, the shortest route to Kursk. Barring the Germans' way to Oboyan was Sixth Guards Army, formerly Don Front's Twenty-First Army, a battle-hardened formation commanded by Colonel-General I.M. Chistyakov, which had been in the thick of the fighting at

---

* On average, Rokossovsky's divisions were approximately 5–6000 strong. A huge effort was underway to comb hospitals at the front and in the rear for troops sufficiently fit to bolster Central Front's strength.

Stalingrad. The first echelon in its thirty-mile front comprised four rifle divisions, 71st, 67th, 52nd Guards and 375th, reinforced by a tank brigade and two tank regiments. In the second echelon were three Guards rifle divisions, 90th, 51st and 89th, supported by a tank brigade. On Chistyakov's left was another Stalingrad army, Seventh Guards, formerly Sixty-Fourth Army, commanded by Colonel-General M.S. Shumilov. In the first echelon of its twenty-five-mile front were four Guards divisions, 81st, 78th, 72nd and 36th, with a tank regiment. In the second were 73rd, 15th Guards and 213th Rifle Divisions, reinforced by two tank brigades and two tank regiments.

Immediately behind Sixth Guards, forming part of the second echelon and covering the approaches to Oboyan, was Katukov's First Tank Army, consisting of 31st and 6th Tank Corps and 3rd Mechanized Corps. Commanding 3rd Mechanized Corps was Lieutenant-General S.M. Krivoshein who knew many of his German opposite numbers personally, having led a Soviet armoured brigade which had linked up with Guderian's XIX Corps at Brest-Litovsk in Poland in September 1939. At a party held after a joint parade of German and Soviet troops, Krivoshein had toasted the 'eternal friendship' of the two nations then carving up Poland. Now Krivoshein and his corps were about to be locked into a different kind of embrace.

On the left of First Tank Army and also forming part of the second echelon, were the five divisions of Sixty-Ninth Army, covering the Belgorod–Korocha and Volchansk–Novy Oskol axes. The face of the Voronezh Front and Vatutin's right were held by Fortieth and Thirty-Eighth Armies. In the Front reserve were 35th Guards Rifle Corps and 5th and 2nd Guards Tank Corps. Thirty-five divisions were eventually available to Vatutin, of which seventeen formed the first echelon and eighteen were assigned to the second echelon or army and front reserve. Behind Vatutin, Rokossovsky and the Kursk salient, along a line between Livny and Stary Oskol, Stavka assembled a powerful strategic reserve, created out of the Steppe Military District and designated Steppe Front in May. Popov, the hapless commander of South-Western Front's 'mobile group', was briefly in command before being replaced by Colonel-General (later Marshal) Ivan S. Konev. It was intended to use

Steppe Front to counter a deep German penetration and to reinforce the counter-offensive when the Wehrmacht's assault on the
salient had been brought to a halt.

Steppe Front comprised five rifle armies, Fourth and Fifth
Guards, Twenty-Seventh, Fifty-Third and Fifty-Seventh, Rotmistrov's Fifth Guards Tank Army and six reserve corps – 4th Guards
and 10th Tank, 1st Guards Mechanized and 5th, 7th and 3rd
Cavalry Corps. Air support was provided by Fifth Air Army. In
short, Steppe Front represented nothing less than Stavka's entire
strategic reserve.

It was powerful enough on paper but, in mid-April 1943, many of
its formations were exhausted by winter fighting and were seriously under strength. This presented no problem to Fifth Guards
Army, an elite formation which was given priority in reinforcements and equipment, and was irrelevant to Fourth Guards, made
up of parachute troops, who had seen little action. Both these
armies were relatively well up to strength, as was Fifth Guards
Tank Army. However, the divisional strengths of the three remaining rifle armies were as low as 1000–1500, and they lacked motor
transport and artillery. The cavalry corps, which had been in
action throughout the winter, were in need of immediate rest and
replenishment. Throughout April and May the task of the Chief
Directorate for Formation and Equipment of Forces was to turn
Steppe Front into the strongest strategic reserve assembled by
Stavka at any time during the war.

Here was proof of the principal strength of Stalin's leadership
which lay not in the operational area, where he was still liable to
make serious errors of judgement, but in his ability to organize the
mobilization of manpower and material resources. Now both were
being fed into the Kursk salient on a massive scale.

Ninety-two artillery regiments from the Stavka reserve raised
the combined gun and mortar strength of Central and Voronezh
Fronts from 10,000 to 20,000, including 6000 anti-tank guns. In
addition there were 920 *Katyusha* multiple-rocket launchers.
Artillery was to be the key to the battle, and in the salient artillery
regiments outnumbered the infantry by 3:2. Thirteenth Army, covering the Kursk–Orel railway and commanded by Colonel-General
N.P. Pukhov, received a particularly heavy artillery reinforcement

in the shape of 4th Artillery Breakthrough Corps which had a complement of 700 guns and mortars and half the artillery reserve regiments allocated to Central Front.

When the German Ninth and Fourth Armies withdrew from the Rzhev salient, they left behind them a 'devil's garden' of booby-traps and minefields. The minefields laid by Soviet engineers in the Kursk salient were to prove equally deadly. As the German armour lumbered into the Russian defences, like a plague of giant beetles, it was to be entangled in a web of anti-tank ditches, scarps and counter-scarps, hedgehogs, road blocks and minefields. The laying of minefields was the principal task of the engineers in the salient; they planted over a million anti-personnel and anti-tank mines, erected 500 miles of barbed-wire entanglements and built myriad other anti-tank obstructions. Soviet sources estimated that, on average, the minefield density was 2400 anti-tank and 2700 anti-personnel mines per mile of front, about one every foot. In the anti-tank fields the mines were planted in two layers and sur-rounded by flame-throwing devices consisting of a mine and a number of petrol bombs. The great density of mines in key areas would win vital time for the defenders when rushing reinforce-ments to sectors most threatened by a German breakthrough.

Thirteenth Army's sector received special attention from the sappers. The Army's first echelon had about 100 sapper compa-nies in its battle formations, nearly 40 per cent of the total number of engineers at work on Central Front. Even this proved insuffi-cient, and infantry, gun and tank crews were given crash courses in the laying and removal of mines which the Soviets now consid-ered 'a mass and indispensable weapon for all ground troops . . .'.

Inside the salient each rifle army was assigned three defence zones: the first two – 'main' and 'second line' – formed the tactical defence zone with a depth of up to three miles, while the third con-stituted the 'army defensive field'. Overlaying the defence zones of the rifle armies were the three defence lines of the front of which the armies were constituent parts. These front positions stretched up to fifty miles to the rear where they were reinforced by two more defence lines built by Steppe Front. Thus the Russian defence rested on eight echeloned defence lines reaching over 100 miles into the rear.

The heaviest fortifications were built in the 'main' defence sector whose five trench lines, linked by a network of communication passages, were studded with interconnected strongpoints and anti-tank positions provided with underground bunkers as a protection against German artillery. Battalion and fire-support positions were laid out in circular fashion, giving all-round fire, and particular care was given to siting them at the junction of units. The trenches significantly increased the flexibility of the Soviet fire system, creating conditions for extensive battlefield manoeuvre unobserved by the enemy. And, like the trenches on the Western Front in the First World War, their bunkers gave a healthy measure of protection to the defenders of the salient. As the Germans had ridden out the British bombardment on the Somme at the end of June 1916, so the Russians at Kursk would sustain relatively few casualties during the initial German barrage. The destruction of the trench system in the preparatory phase of the battle would have required the expenditure by the German artillery of mountains of shells.

The Russian anti-tank defences were organized in a system of strongpoints guarded by ditches and minefields designed to channel the attackers into their fields of fire; defences were reinforced by machine-gun nests and mortars whose task it was to deal with the German infantry. Termed 'anti-tank resistance points' (*protivotankovye opornye punkty*, or PTOPs) they were placed in chequerboard style across the salient at half-mile intervals; clusters of PTOPs were sited in depth up to five miles. Here the Russians had absorbed a valuable lesson from the Ostheer which had discovered, early in Barbarossa, that a single anti-tank gun, or a cluster of them operating independently, were ineffective against massed armoured attacks. Once their position had been located, each could be put out of action in turn. The German solution was the *Pakfront* in which up to ten anti-tank guns were placed under a single commander who was responsible for concentrating their fire on a single target at a time. As Major-General von Mellenthin recalled:

> Groups of anti-tank guns were thus welded into one unit, the groups were organized in depth and strewn all over the defended area. The idea was to draw the attacking armour into a web

of enfilade fire. Fire discipline was of the first importance and to open fire too early was the gravest mistake that could be made.

The Russians adopted these tactics with a vengeance. Each of their PTOPs contained a standard complement of five 76mm anti-tank guns, five anti-tank rifles, a section of sappers and a squad of troops armed with PPSH sub-machine-guns; some PTOPs were supported by tanks and self-propelled guns. By consolidating PTOPs with regimental sections, 'anti-tank areas' could be created. Threatened sectors could be shored up with 'mobile blocking squads' – engineers in motorized units up to battalion strength, supported by infantry – which stood ready to move along the axis of an enemy attack, laying mines as they went.

The PTOPs and their associated minefields, mortar and machine-gun positions were camouflaged with great skill. When the battle began, neither the minefields nor the PTOPs could be detected until the leading tank blew up or the first '*Ratsch-boom*' opened fire.

The Russians have long enjoyed a reputation as masters of military deception (*maskirovka*) as newspaper readers were constantly reminded during the build-up to the Gulf War in the winter of 1990–91 when Saddam Hussein was widely believed to have employed a range of deception measures learned during the years of Iraq's military cooperation with the Soviet Union. Forty-seven years earlier, Stavka formulated for the first time a general strategic defensive plan which incorporated broad *maskirovka* measures in its implementation and also concealed preparations for the launching of a counter-offensive when the enemy had been brought to a halt.

Within the salient the front and army commanders went to considerable lengths to hide from the enemy the strength and depth of the defences they were preparing. The detailed *maskirovka* plans drawn up by Central and Voronezh Fronts included the concealment of preparations, the creation of false troop concentrations, the simulation of radio nets and communications centres and the construction of dummy armoured concentrations, airfields and aircraft.

On Voronezh Front radio security was maintained, and the

movement of Seventh Guards Army to the area east of Belgorod concealed, by the prohibition of all radio transmissions. Sets on the front could receive transmissions but these were sent in short ten-second bursts. Acknowledgement was by wire communication. Daily changes were made to all call signs and frequencies changed four or five times a month. In June, while Seventh Guards Army was deployed in Sixty-Ninth Army's sector, all orders to Seventh Guards were passed through Sixty-Ninth's communications. On both fronts the flow of all written correspondence to the army and corps staffs was controlled by the front chief of staff.

To deceive German aerial reconnaissance during the build-up, at least forty false airfields were created, complete with dummy aircraft, runways, control towers and blast pens. These were repeatedly bombed by the Luftwaffe. Dummy tanks were assembled on both fronts to simulate armoured assembly areas; on Voronezh Front there were 829. Special *maskirovka* units and combat troops were used to give the fake airfields and armoured laagers every appearance of activity. Along both fronts the defence lines were dotted with false gun positions. And on some sectors the main defence line lay behind a complete dummy defence line in the expectation that the latter would draw heavy enemy fire in the preparatory phase of the battle. Sixth Guards Army sought further to confuse the enemy by building a network of dummy observation posts which were manned by experienced reconnaissance troops.

Troops were moved up to the front line and regrouped at night under strict blackout conditions, the routes having been staked out and guides placed in position during daylight hours. All movements by foot near command posts during the day were forbidden and vehicle traffic at night was carefully controlled under blackout conditions. Fighter squadrons moved up to their forward bases in small groups at dusk, flying as low as 300ft; only the day bombers were held back on airfields dispersed in the rear.

Rail movements were also made at night and stepped up when bad weather grounded German bombers. Troops and equipment were detrained on the approaches to railheads rather than at stations. Army supply services sited their depots in the many small gullies and ravines which broke the bland folds of the landscape and where they were concealed from the prying eyes of enemy aerial reconnaissance.

Command and observation posts were expertly camouflaged and heavily strengthened. The number of visitors to important points was closely controlled. On the Central Front, Lieutenant-General P.I. Batov, commanding Sixty-Fifth Army, instructed his staff to receive only subordinate division commanders, their deputies or their chiefs of staff; there was a ban on all other visitors. The heads of all other army departments quartered liaison officers in nearby villages where necessary business was conducted.

Of this phase of the Kursk build-up Marshal Konev later wrote:

> Did the enemy know about the organization of a firm defence in the rear of our fronts? He knew. And that played a positive role. The enemy thought that *we were preparing only for a defensive battle* [author's italics]. Possessing a large number of tanks and self-propelled guns of a new type, the Germans hoped that it was not possible to stop them.
>
> Thus, as the enemy prepared, we prepared. The main thing was not to conceal the fact of our preparation, but rather the force and means, the concept of battle, the time of our counter-offensive, and the nature of our defences. It is very likely that it was the only . . . occasion in military history when the stronger side, having the capability for offensive action, went over to the defence. The future course of events affirmed that, in the given instance, the correct decision was made.

The civilian population of the region played an important part in turning the Kursk salient into a huge *place d'armes*. Men and women of military age were drafted into the armies on both fronts. (The recapture of large tracts of Soviet territory was by now an important factor in meeting the manpower demands of the Red Army.) Others were set to work on Steppe Front's defence lines and the rehabilitation of the railway system. On 9 February 1943, the day after the liberation of Kursk, there were over 1000 people working on the repair of the city's rail station. Eventually, 50,000 collective farm workers were working flat out to restore the Kastornoye–Kursk rail link and maintain it under heavy aerial attack. On 17 April thousands of civilians responded to an order issued by the Central Committee for the construction of a fighter

airfield near Kastornoye within three days. On 24 May the
Secretary of the Kastornoye District Party Committee reported
that the first fighters had touched down at 9am. From mid-June
25,000 peasants were employed on the construction of a new rail
line running parallel to the Kastornoye–Kursk track and based on
a prewar plan to link the Moscow–Donbas and Southern track
lines which had been discovered in the local archives. The building of the line, which involved the laying of sixty miles of track, the
erection of ten bridges and many huge earthworks, was completed in thirty-two days. It was to play an important part in the preparations for the Red Army's counter-offensive. By June there were
300,000 civilians at work in the salient.

While the civilians bent their backs, the troops trained. Such
was Stavka's confidence in the stream of reports from Lucy that,
by the end of April, most formations in the salient and the Reserve
Front had been given their assignments and were training for
defensive or offensive operations. Infantry commanders reconnoitred the ground to establish their 'variants' and confirm their
assumptions about the axes of projected enemy attacks. Tank
officers rehearsed their movements and gunners wrestled
their artillery pieces into place. In mid-May 97th Guards Rifle
Division, part of the newly created Steppe Front's Fifth Guards
Army, reached its assembly area along the Oskol river on a line
Zalomonoye–Yutkovo–Istobnoye. It was intended to employ the
division in Zhukov's counter-blow, and it immediately embarked
upon a training programme which emphasized offensive operations, particularly attacks against echeloned fortifications. Much
time was also devoted to methods of dealing with the new German
tanks and self-propelled guns.

In June the division's regiments were put through a rigorous
series of exercises conducted by the regimental commanders and
their staffs: the platoon in attack, attack by a rifle company on a
strongpoint and attack by a reinforced rifle battalion behind a
creeping barrage. On 15 June the divisional chief of staff presided
over a demonstration of an 'attack by a reinforced rifle company
on a support point'. For this exercise the division received special
praise from the commander of Fifth Guards Army, General
A.S.Zhadov, and at the end of June it was awarded its Guards

regimental banners in a series of official ceremonies. Solemn oaths were sworn on these occasions. The commander of 289th Guards Rifle Regiment, Lieutenant-Colonel P.R.Pansky, and his men swore to the CPSU and the government that they would carry their banner all the way to Berlin.*

Staff officers were not exempt from training, particularly those in Steppe Front's headquarters during the brief interregnum between Popov and Konev which was filled by Lieutenant-General M.A.Reiter, commander of Bryansk Front, who had exchanged commands with Popov. Reiter had a bee in his bonnet about licking his staff officers into shape with physically punishing arms drill and field craft, in both of which he deemed himself a great expert. On the day after his arrival the bemused officers of his headquarters operations and intelligence sections were given a personal demonstration by Reiter who performed a series of seemingly impossible exercises with a rifle before swarming snake-like over the surrounding terrain on all fours. Invited to imitate this virtuoso display, none of Reiter's subordinates could emulate his agility or hand-eye coordination, which was probably just as well. Warming to his task, Reiter then proposed to extend the programme to the staff officers of Fifty-Third Army, all of whom went into strict but fruitless training for a test to be conducted personally by their army commander. On the evening before they were to submit themselves to this ordeal, word came through that Reiter had been replaced by Konev, a commander with a formidable reputation for 'persistence' but one who would not waste the time of his overworked staff with ill-considered callisthenics.

The strengthening of the Soviet defences within the Kursk salient was complemented by partisan operations behind the German lines aimed at disrupting the enemy's build-up for the offensive. In his radio broadcast of 3 July 1941, Stalin had called for a vast partisan movement to spring up in the enemy rear and, two weeks later, the Central Committee issued a decree on 'The Organization of the Struggle in the Enemy Rear'. It was some time,

---

* As part of First Ukrainian Front, Fifth Guards Army ended the war at Torgau, on the Elbe, where it joined hands with US First Army.

however, before the partisans became a thorn in the German side. A year later they were tying down twenty-five special security divisions, as well as thirty regiments and over 100 police battalions. In 1943 the ranks of the anti-partisan forces were swelled by nearly half a million Russian auxiliaries.

It was after Stalingrad that the partisans – now well supplied by air with arms, food and medical supplies, and centrally directed from Moscow – became a broad mass movement. 'Partisan regions' were carved out of areas where there were no Germans and in which a semblance of Soviet normality was restored. Postwar Soviet sources estimated that, in the winter of 1942–3, some 60 per cent of Belorussia was under the effective control of partisans. Other 'partisan regions' included the Porkhov area south of Leningrad, the wooded northern part of the Ukraine and the forests of Bryansk. In the Orel region some 18,000 partisans controlled an area containing nearly 500 villages. The 'partisan regions' had their own airstrips into which supplies could be flown and from which wounded could be evacuated.

It was not until 14 July 1943 that Stavka ordered the partisans to launch an all-out 'Rail War' against the enemy; nevertheless, the battle of the rails had been gathering pace for several months in the rear of Army Group Centre where many rail lines converged in territory ideal for partisan warfare. In January 1943 German reports logged 397 attacks on railways in the region, with damage to 112 locomotives. In February the number of attacks rose to about 500, then 1045 in May and 1092 in June when, in the rear of Army Group Centre, forty-four bridges were blown up and 298 locomotives damaged.

In May the Ostheer mounted five major anti-partisan operations in the region, the first of which – 'Gypsy King' – involved 18th Panzer Division. It was claimed that, in this campaign, 3152 partisans were killed and twenty-four guns, three tanks, fourteen anti-tank guns, fifty-five mortars, two aircraft, 124 machine-guns and 1130 small arms destroyed – a relatively disappointing rate of return for the diversion of substantial forces from front-line duties. As soon as the last anti-partisan operation, 'Neighbour Help 2', came to an end on 6 June, there was a renewed upsurge in partisan activity.

One effect of the disruption of rail movement was the creation of bottlenecks at important junctions where crowded troop trains and ammunition wagons provided tempting targets for the VVS. In a night raid on the marshalling yards at Orsha on 4 May, Soviet bombers hit three ammunition wagons and, in the resulting inferno, another 300 were burnt out. The short distances involved in flying these raids meant that Soviet night bombers could fly two or three sorties in the hours of darkness. German reports indicate that they represented more of an irritant than a serious threat to the logistic build-up around Orel and Belgorod, but the psychological effect was considerable.

So, too, was the sapping effect on morale of the battle of the rails. To counter the partisans, trees were felled and undergrowth cleared for a distance of up to 250 yards on either side of the track. Block houses were set up at regular intervals. Infantry patrols swept the ground by day but the night was left to the partisans to lay more mines and destroy ever longer sections of track. Captured letters home revealed the weary resignation which had settled over German troops in the East. A corporal wrote to his wife: 'With us trains move for one day and three days have to be spent repairing the track, since the partisans blow everything up. The night before last they arranged a collision between an express train and a leave train, so that the trains aren't running . . . that's how we live in Russia.'

Stavka's planning for the summer fighting flowed from the decision, taken as early as 12 April, to fight a defensive battle. This was three days before Hitler signed Operational Order No.6 which, thanks to Lucy, was probably in Stalin's hands before it reached the Führer's front-line generals. Notwithstanding the intermittent consideration given to the launching of a pre-emptive offensive, the preparations went ahead in measured fashion. There was a flurry at the beginning of May when a German attack was thought to be imminent and Stalin ordered a full state of readiness. But he was the beneficiary of another of Hitler's postponements and the alert in no way disrupted the build-up or dispelled the growing feeling of confidence in the Red Army. As a company commander put it, 'At the beginning of the war everything was always done in a hurry, and time was always lacking. Now we go calmly into action.'

Everything was in place. Defending the salient were 1.3 million men, including seventy-five infantry divisions, 40 per cent of the Red Army's rifle formations. As many as 150 guns a mile were massed along the likely German axes of advance. And Stavka had concentrated some 3500 tanks and self-propelled guns, of which 2000 were integrated with Central and Voronezh Fronts for close support and the bulk of the remainder held in reserve in Steppe Front's Fifth Guards Tank Army.

Although the emphasis was laid on the strategic defensive to be fought at Kursk, this was linked with the counter-offensive to be launched once German power had been spent in the salient's defences. In the exploitation phase two groups would attack in different directions: the left flank of Western Front, Bryansk Front and Central Front would strike at Orel; Steppe and Voronezh Fronts would launch an attack on the Belgorod–Kharkov axis. Planning for the drive north of the salient was to be 'coordinated' by Voronov and Vasilevsky, that in the south by Zhukov. As the pleasant spring days turned into the broiling heat of summer on the steppe, the Red Army only awaited the decision of the Germans.

In the early summer of 1943 Hitler immersed himself in literature about Verdun, the terrible 'mincing machine' of 1916 in which the German Chief of Staff, von Falkenhayn, had attempted to 'bleed France white'. The parallel between Verdun and Zitadelle was hardly reassuring, for the planned assault on the deep defences of the Russian salient was beginning to assume the shape of the doomed slogging matches on the Western Front. Even the notion of 'pinching off' a salient had a ring about it which recalled the château generals of the Great War. Intelligence of the trench system which the Russians were building at Kursk must have reminded Hitler of his own experiences as a runner on the Western Front where he was wounded and gassed. And the runner-turned-*Feldherr* had engineered his own Verdun at Stalingrad. At Verdun the Germans had lost almost as much blood as the French while, at Stalingrad, they had bled the most. Neither precedent was encouraging as Hitler steeled himself to make the final decision on Zitadelle.

The plans for the offensive, stiff with textbook formalism, marked the death of Blitzkrieg. Here the German armour could not be used in rapid, slashing, narrow thrusts against the rear of a disorganized enemy. Rather, it was reduced to the role of bludgeon, beating at strong defences across fronts of sixty miles. The Red Army's tenacity in clinging to the sides of a breach, and the multiplication of its firepower on the ground and in the air, had ruled out independent action by the panzers in the early stages of the battle. This battle threatened to resemble the positional warfare of 1917 rather than the scything advance of 1940–42.

Even if the German armour could punch its way through the Russian defences, the details of which lay frustratingly beyond the grasp of OKH intelligence, would they not be so weakened by the time pincers closed around Kursk itself that keeping the pocket sealed would be immensely difficult, clearing it even more so, and mounting rolling-up operations to the north or south impossible? Grievous though the Russian losses might be, would they not cauterize the wound and then hold on for another three or four months, by which time their war industries and Lend-Lease would have restored the material balance?

These thoughts troubled Hitler, as they did capable commanders like Funck and Model who remained sceptical about Zitadelle's chances of success. Nevertheless, misgivings about Zitadelle tended to increase in direct proportion to the distance between the doubter and the front line. The generals with active commands on the front, most notably Kluge, were strong supporters of the offensive. Opponents were thicker on the ground at Rastenburg, but it appeared that they had been argued into the ground by Zeitzler's relentless advocacy of 'his' offensive.

The commanders in the Kursk sector, and the men who advised Hitler on military, political and economic matters, had but a partial knowledge of the strategic picture. Hitler alone possessed this knowledge and bore the self-imposed burden of decision on Zitadelle. In no small measure this accounts for the operation's long and agonizing gestation. That, and the faith he placed in his new weapons to tip the balance. At Zaporozhye on 18 April the Führer had told Manstein, 'We can't achieve much with men, because we don't have enough. However, with a massing of our

best and heaviest weapons . . . (a breakthough can be achieved).'
The Führer was placing his trust in machines rather than men.

The first week of June found him at the Berghof, editing a long
speech which Goebbels planned to deliver to munitions workers in
Berlin. Belief in ultimate victory was ebbing away. In one passage
Goebbels had promised to compensate the German people for
their sacrifices 'when victory is ours'. In his spidery hand Hitler
altered the passage to read 'when this struggle is over'. A few days
later, on 11 June, the Italian–German garrison on Pantelleria, the
small island sixty miles south of Sicily, surrendered after a month-
long aerial bombardment and a seaborne assault by the British 1st
Division. The British had met little or no opposition. This did not
augur well for the coming campaign in the Mediterranean.

The situation in Italy occupied much of Hitler's time. He was
fearful that, once his panzers were locked in the minefields of the
Kursk salient, the Allies would invade Sardinia and the Duce would
be toppled by his scheming generals.* The machines on which he
was relying were proving as troublesome. On 16 June, Guderian
reported to Hitler that he was most reluctant to see the Panther
committed to action in the East. The tank's track suspension and
drive were still giving trouble and there were problems with the
optics. Three days later, flying to another conference with Hitler at
Berchtesgaden, Guderian diverted to Grafenwöhr to inspect 51st
and 52nd Panther Battalions so that he could make a first-hand
report to the Fuhrer. He recalled: 'Apart from the technical weak-
nesses of the not yet perfected tanks, neither the crews nor the
commanders were by then sufficiently experienced in their handling, while some of them even lacked battle experience.'

On the same day OKW operations staff submitted an appraisal
to Hitler which concluded that, 'until the situation had been clari-
fied', Zitadelle should be cancelled. The report also recommended
that a strong operational reserve, at the disposal of the Supreme
Command, be constituted both in the East and in Germany, the latter by the formation of new units. It was even thought that Zeitzler,

---

* Top-secret plans for the occupation of Italy, codenamed Alarich, had been
drawn up on Hitler's instructions at the end of March. A similar plan, codenamed
Konstantin, was prepared to deal with Italian withdrawal from Greece and
Croatia.

the 'onlie true begetter' of Zitadelle, was now wavering and reverting to a version of Manstein's 'backhand' option. None of this cut any ice with Hitler who had finally committed himself to the launching of Zitadelle.

On 21 June he set 3 July as the date for D-Day and then, after listening to representations from Model and consulting Kluge and Manstein, he authorized the final postponement to 5 July. There could be no turning back but, even with the clock standing at five minutes to midnight, and in full knowledge of the massive confrontation which was about to erupt on the steppe, Hitler strove to minimize the importance of the operation as if, by doing so, he could calm the inner voices which tormented him. Conducting a strategic *tour d'horizon* with Goebbels at the Berghof on 24 June, Hitler confessed that the grand designs which had underpinned his Eastern strategy in 1942 were now lost dreams. The great pincer movements which he had envisaged arcing out from the Caucasus, Egypt and the Balkans, to swallow the oilfields of the Middle East, were no longer capable of achievement. The major task in hand was the holding of the Italian mainland, even if the Italians defected. In the East the Ostheer's mission was to conserve its strength until 1944, ensuring that the front was spared the crises which had gripped it in the previous two winters. The aim of Zitadelle was merely to produce 'a minor correction of the line'.

Five days later Hitler decided to return to Rastenburg. He was confident that Zitadelle could proceed on schedule and he was heartened by intelligence reports which suggested that the Allies were planning to postpone their invasion plans in the Mediterranean; he also drew comfort from Stalin's ritual grumblings about foot-dragging by the Western Allies over the opening of a 'second front'. Perhaps the Russians were now getting 'cold feet' about the summer campaign.

On 1 July, Hitler addressed his senior commanders at Zeitzler's headquarters near Rastenburg. According to General Johannes Friessner, a corps commander in Ninth Army who attended the conference and kept notes, the Führer spoke in 'a grave, clear and confident voice', blaming the Italians, Hungarians and Romanians for the difficulties he now faced. However, there would be no more withdrawals – 'Where we are – we stay.' The German hegemony over Europe could only be preserved by mounting a defence far from Germany's frontiers. On the Eastern Front, Hitler declared that nothing would be yielded without a fight. He averred that the Red Army was marking time, gathering strength for another winter offensive. It was vital to 'disrupt' these plans now to forestall the kind of crisis from which Army Group South had so recently recovered.

The details of the operation, around which so much argument had flowed since March, received perfunctory attention. Hitler pored over the map, examining Ninth Army's dispositions and listening for the last time to Model's misgivings. The meeting briefly burst into life when Manstein tactlessly urged the recall of von Richthofen to the Eastern Front to ginger up the Luftwaffe, distressing his replacement, Dessloch, and prompting much huffing and puffing from Göring who was smarting at the prestige now attached to the commander of Luftflotte 2. On the surface, at least, the mood was one of optimism. Jodl, however, warned that an offensive based on hopes of gaining victory 'in one bound' might degenerate into a battle of attrition. Jodl had already hedged his bets on the outcome, instructing OKW propaganda to paint Zitadelle as a counter-offensive to create the impression of a strong defensive capability and to establish a ready-made alibi if Zitadelle failed.

The die was now cast. In the north, on Kluge's front, Ninth Army was to break through the Russian defences between the Orel–Kursk highway and railway, advancing on Kursk on both sides of the latter. It was to drive its spearheads across the Orel-Kursk railway sufficiently far east to establish a new front which would guarantee use of the railway and throw back any counter-thrust by the Red Army reserve. Contact with the right wing of Second Panzer Army was to be maintained by taking Maloarkhangelsk, on the extreme left of Ninth Army's attack frontage. After securing this objective, Ninth Army and elements of Second Panzer Army would be committed in a concentric attack to close the salient.

In the south, on Manstein's front, Fourth Panzer Army was to attack on both sides of Tomarovka, breaking though the enemy positions in the sector south of a line Belgorod–Gertsovka (ten miles north-east of Borisovka) and driving a sharp wedge through Oboyan to link with Ninth Army north of Kursk and close the salient. Army Detachment Kempf was given the task of screening the right flank of Fourth Panzer Army, pushing its own right wing to the Koren river to pivot north around Toplinka. In the event of a rapid breakthrough, the advance was to be extended to the Korocha river. The enemy's reserve, which had been identified in the rear of the salient, was to be met and destroyed by III Panzer Corps driving on Korocha. As the situation developed, and freedom of manoeuvre was gained, III Corps was to advance north or north-east on the right wing of Fourth Panzer Army.

The months of waiting were over. On Manstein's front a preliminary attack was to be made on the afternoon of 4 July to seize observation posts needed to bring artillery into action against the 'main field' of Sixth Guards Army. The chief of staff of XLVIII Panzer Corps reflected on the timing of the attack: 'Independence Day for the United States, the beginning of the end for Germany.'

CHAPTER 7

The Dogfight

'Guns yes, prisoners yes, territory yes, but all at an outrageous cost and without strategic results.' General Messimy on the eve of the Nivelle offensive, April 1917

'. . . the campaigning of 1941 and 1942 had proved that our panzers were virtually invincible if they were allowed to manoeuvre freely across the great plains of Russia. Instead of seeking to create conditions in which manoeuvre would be possible – by strategic withdrawals or surprise attacks in quiet sectors – the German Supreme Command could think of nothing better than to fling our magnificent panzer divisions against Kursk, which had now become the strongest fortress in the world.' Major-General F.W. von Mellenthin

'And now to work – prepare to welcome the fascists.' Nikita Khrushchev, First Tank Army headquarters, 2 July 1943

THROUGHOUT MAY AND June the prospect of Zitadelle hung over the Eastern Front like the heavy thunderclouds now massing in the skies over Kursk. A Ninth Army report described the coming offensive as a 'collision between armies at the point of readiness on both sides' in which the skill of German soldiers would tip the balance. There were no illusions, however, about the magnitude of the task facing the Ostheer. The time for exploiting the enemy's weakness had long since passed. As Hoth, the commander of

Fourth Panzer Army, warned on 26 June, the chances of success declined with every day that passed.

For Hitler, victory at Kursk was, above all, vital to 'dispel the gloom of our allies and crush any silent hopes still lingering within our subjugated peoples'. But he entertained little hope that a successful outcome would, as Operational Order No.6 had portentously put it, 'shine like a beacon to the world'. On 24 June he had confessed to Goebbels that success at Kursk would not be sufficient to swing neutral opinion behind a revitalized and victorious Germany.

Zitadelle had acquired a horrible life of it own, dragging Hitler and his high command behind it. Launched in the spring, as Manstein had urged, it might well have secured a 'minor correction' in the line as part of a series of limited offensives, including a renewed assault on Leningrad,* which would have strengthened the German position in the East. But repeated postponements encouraged the growth of Zitadelle so that it became the only option available to Hitler. Cancellation was also increasingly unthinkable to OKH, as this would have released the substantial reserves which OKW was seeking to have transferred to its own theatres of operations.

Far from conserving German strength in the East, as he had told Goebbels, Hitler was preparing to throw two armies, containing a high proportion of his finest armoured divisions, against a defensive system which he had given his enemy three months to strengthen. Success would involve bloody losses which he could ill afford. Failure would not only result in an even greater loss in men and materials but would also expose Army Groups South and Centre to the inevitable Russian counter-blow to retake the Ukraine and central Russia.

If the Ostheer did not attack at all, but transferred troops to the West to meet the anticipated Allied invasion, Stalin, stronger than ever, would launch an offensive against army groups weakened by withdrawal rather than the minefields and guns of the Kursk

---

* The taking of Leningrad would have heartened the war-weary Finns and served as a warning to neutral Sweden whose attitude towards Germany was becoming increasingly hostile.

Men and maps:

top left Hitler confers with Colonel-General Kurt Zeitzler (*right*) the driving force behind *Zitadelle*

above Marshal Georgi K. Zhukov, photographed in 1944, architect of Soviet victory

left Marshal Konstantin Rokossovsky (*left*), commander of Central Front

below Marshal P.A. Rotmistrov (*left*), commander of Fifth Guards Tank Army and General A.S. Zhadov, commander of Fifth Guards Army, photographed near Prokhorovka, July 1943

above Field Marshal Erich von Manstein, commander of Army Group South, attends manoeuvres staged for a Turkish military delegation near Kharkov in the weeks before *Zitadelle*

right Colonel-General Hermann Hoth, commander of Fourth Panzer Army. After the fall of Kiev in November 1943 he was removed by Hitler and retired from active service

above Field Marshal Walter
Model, commander of Ninth
Army on the first day of
Zitadelle, 5 July 1943

left General Paul Hausser,
commander of II SS Panzer
Corps, a tough customer
who in February 1943 defied
Hitler's orders to hold
Kharkov

above Flight Lieutenant
Erich Hartmann of JG52,
highest-scoring fighter
ace of all time with 352
victories, who shot down
seven Soviet aircraft on
7 July, the third day of
Zitadelle

left Flight Lieutenant
Hans-Ulrich Rudel (*left*),
the Luftwaffe's undisputed
Stuka ace, with his
radio-operator/gunner
Erwin Hentschel

above right A tank-driver's
view of the fighting at Kursk
as T-34s move into action

right MkVI Tigers move
forward in the Belgorod
sector

Two German failures at Kursk:

above The MkV Panther, whose combat debut at Kursk was dogged by mechanical failures. When these were rectified, the Panther became one of the most effective tanks of the war. Note the skirt armour plates on the sides of both tanks. These were 5mm thick and designed to detonate high-explosive anti-tank (HEAT) projectiles prematurely

right The Goliath miniature tank which carried a 220lb charge detonated by remote control. Goliath was extremely vulnerable to small arms fire

top MkIV panzers at Kursk. The MkIV was the mainstay of the German tank fleet throughout the war. These are equipped with a powerful 75mm gun which enabled the MkIV to give a good account of itself against the T-34

above Soviet gunners in action against a StuG III assault gun

overleaf T-34s and infantry race past a 76mm anti-tank gun whose crew carry their personal weapons for close-in defence against German mechanized infantry. The 76mm gun had a range of about 14,000 yards

left A German 'Bison' 150mm assault gun

below German assault troops go over the top on the first day of *Zitadelle*, covered by an MG34 machine gun, used with a bipod as a squad weapon. It could also be used on a tripod in a sustained-fire support role

right A Soviet *Katyusha* rocket battery opens up. German troops called this much-feared weapon the 'Stalin Organ'

below right The god of war: Soviet artillery in action at Kursk

Above Soviet firepower in the Kursk cauldron. T-34s of Fifth Guards Tank Army move up at Prokhorovka

Right Air power: a column of German trucks is set ablaze by Soviet aircraft on Voronezh Front at the height of the battle

Left Ilyushin II–2 ground attack aircraft fly over Berlin in 1945. The *Shturmovik* was built in greater numbers than any other aircraft in World War II

left Mother Russia:
Red Army soldiers escort
peasants back to their
homes in 1943

right Undaunted by severe
headwounds, a Red Army
commissar (political office
urges on his men. The
weapon in the foreground
a PPSH sub-machine gun

above **Victory:** 'Ivan', the archetypal Red Army infantryman, an opponent not to be underestimated

right **Defeat:** A German gunner in the Orel salient

salient. Hindsight suggests that Manstein's 'backhand' strategy, which he had outlined to Hitler after the battle of Kharkov, was the only practical solution to the problems facing the Ostheer after the conclusion of the winter fighting in 1942–3 – but the chance had passed. Hitler, the inveterate gambler, was now staking everything on a single throw of the dice, risking the working capital of two armies which, in the event of defeat, could not be replaced. There would be no second chance. There were no reserves. And there was no alternative plan.

On the north of the salient, along the thirty-five miles of Ninth Army's attack front, between Trosna and Krasnaya Slobodka, were three panzer and one infantry corps. Screening Model's left flank was General Friessner's XXIII Corps whose sector was separated from that of General Harpe's XLI Panzer Corps by the Orel–Kursk railway. On Harpe's right was General Lemelsen's XLVII Panzer Corps, then General Zorn's XLVI Panzer Corps. West of Trosna and the Orel–Kursk highway, on Model's right,was General Freiherr von Roman's XX Corps. Including his army reserve, designated Group von Esbeck, Model had under his command a total of twenty-two divisions: two panzer grenadier, six panzer and fourteen infantry. Of the infantry divisions, seven had been allocated to Zitadelle. Air support for the attack was to be provided by 1st Fliegerdivision of Luftflotte 6, commanded by General Deichmann. Model's left flank to the east and north of Orel was protected by Second Panzer Army.

On the south of the salient Manstein's main striking force was Fourth Panzer Army, commanded by Colonel-General Hermann Hoth. An experienced armoured commander, Hoth had led Panzer Group 3 during the invasion of the Soviet Union and, operating in conjunction with Guderian, closed the Bialystock pocket, taking at least 300,000 prisoners and an immense amount of equipment. He had escaped the wave of dismissals which had followed the withdrawal from Moscow and was appointed commander of Fourth Panzer Army in the drive on Stalingrad, leading the last desperate attempt to relieve Sixth Army which was stopped and then turned back thirty miles short of its goal.

Hoth stood ready to launch his panzers against Sixth Guards and Sixty-Ninth Armies towards the highway running through Oboyan to Kursk, the principal 'variant' selected by Vatutin. On

Hoth's left flank was General Ott's LII Corps; in the centre von Knobelsdorff's XLVIII Panzer Corps; and, on the right, Hausser's II SS Panzer Corps.* South of Belgorod, on the right wing of the German front and facing Seventh Guards Army, was Army Detachment Kempf, with General Breith's III Panzer Corps on the left, Lieutenant-General Raus's XI Corps in the centre and General Mattenklott's XLII Corps on the right. Under Hoth's command, squeezed into a frontage of twenty-eight miles, were nine of the finest divisions in the German Army: running west from south of Belgorod were 7th, 19th and 6th Panzer (III Panzer Corps), SS Totenkopf, SS Das Reich, SS Leibstandarte (II SS Panzer Corps), and 11th Panzer, Grossdeutschland and 3rd Panzer (XLVIII Panzer Corps) – the most powerful striking force ever assembled under a single German commander.

For Zitadelle, Manstein had at his disposal twenty-two divisions: four panzer grenadier, seven panzer and eleven infantry, including his army group reserve, General Nehring's XXIV Panzer Corps. Of the infantry divisions he allocated seven to the offensive. Charged with providing air support was VIII Fliegerkorps of Luftflotte 4, commanded by General Seidemann. Covering the face of the salient, between the two offensive arms of Zitadelle, were the seven infantry divisions of Second Army.

Around the Kursk salient the Ostheer had concentrated 10,000 guns and mortars, and nearly 2400 tanks** and assault guns, the latter representing over 70 per cent of the total armoured strength on the Eastern Front and 46 per cent of Germany's *total* front-line panzer strength. To achieve this concentration, the rest of the Eastern Front had been ruthlessly pillaged. Second Panzer Army, to the north in the Orel salient, had lost all its armoured formations to Model, and along the rest of the front there were only 890 tanks.

The infantry had been in their attack positions for several weeks, reconnoitring the Russian defences and noting the details of the terrain. Officers leading the assault forces, down to com-

---

* Hausser's Panzer Corps had been redesignated after the retaking of Kharkov when Hitler agreed to the creation of an additional SS Corps built around Leibstandarte.

** Of these, about 500 were obsolete types.

pany commander, spent days in these positions, familiarizing themselves with the ground and the enemy. Panzer officers discarded their black uniforms before visiting these forward positions to make their reconnaissance. In XLVIII Panzer Corps's sector they gazed out on a

> far-flung plain, broken by numerous valleys, small copses, irregularly laid-out villages, and some rivers and brooks; of these the Pena ran with a swift current between steep banks. The ground rose slightly to the north, thus favouring the defender. Roads consisted of tracks through the sand and became impassable for all motor transport during rain. Large cornfields covered the landscape and made visibility difficult. All in all, it was not good 'tank country', but it was by no means 'tank proof'.

The panzer and panzer grenadier divisions which were to spearhead Zitadelle had all been rested, refitted and brought up to strength. Nevertheless, the loss of battle-tried personnel and experienced leaders during the winter fighting was keenly felt. The majority of Leibstandarte's replacements were Luftwaffe ground crew who had received a few days' infantry training in Germany before transferring to the East. Grossdeutschland's veterans cast a cynical eye over the pristine uniforms of their new tank crews and worried about their ignorance of Red Army tactics.

Grossdeutschland was the most powerful of the armoured divisions at Kursk. It was equipped with 163 tanks and thirty-five assault guns, including a company of fourteen Tigers and the 104 mission-capable Panthers of Panzer Regiment 39 which arrived at the front at the end of June. The other divisions in XLVIII Panzer Corps, 11th and 3rd Panzer, each had an armoured regiment of eighty tanks and full-strength artillery. In all, the Corps fielded over 300 tanks and sixty assault guns, a striking power it was never to enjoy again.

The strength of each of II SS Panzer Corps's three divisions hovered around 130 tanks and thirty-five assault guns, including Tiger companies of thirteen (Leibstandarte), fourteen (Das Reich) and fifteen (Totenkopf). In common with Grossdeutschland the three SS divisions had six panzer grenadier battalions rather than the normal panzer division's establishment of four. This not only increased their hitting power but also gave them the ability to absorb heavy punishment and remain in the field.*

Perhaps the most significant statistic to be teased from the German order of battle at Kursk is that, of the 902 operational tanks and assault guns available to Fourth Panzer Army on 3 July, only fifty-six were Tigers and 104 Panthers. An additional forty-five Tigers of Heavy Panzer Battalion 503 were assigned to Army Group Kempf, bringing Army Group South's combined total of operational Tigers and Panthers to 205.

During the conference he held with Manstein on 18 February, Hitler had estimated that 300–400 of the new tanks would be needed to ensure a breakthrough. Great hopes were placed in the Panther with its well-sloped armour and powerful 75mm gun. But the mechanical problems which had plagued the Panther's development pursued it to the front. As they moved up to their start lines, the panzer grenadiers of Grossdeutschland saw jets of flame belching from the exhausts of the division's Panthers. Several of them caught fire while rolling slowly down the road and their crews were extricated with some difficulty as the new 'wonder weapons' were reduced to blackened hulks.

In the north Model had only the thirty Tigers of the 1st and 2nd Companies of Heavy Panzer Battalion 505, which had moved into the Orel area early in May and been placed under the command of 2nd Panzer Division in XLI Corps. To offset Ninth Army's weakness in heavy tanks, Model's armour was reinforced by Jagdpanzer Regiment 656, comprising two battalions, 653rd and 654th, with ninety of the sixty-eight-ton Elefant tank-destroyers.

In the weeks preceding Zitadelle, Model and Manstein evolved different tactics to break open the Red Army's defences. Model, calculating that he had an adequate ratio of infantry to armour, decided to use infantry, combat engineers and artillery to make breaches in the Russian lines into which he would feed his panzers. Montgomery had adopted a similar tactic in November

---

* At full strength a panzer grenadier battalion contained 850 men organized into three rifle companies and a support company which was lavishly equipped with mortars and heavy machine-guns. At Kursk, Das Reich had eight Panzer grenadier batallions.

1942 at the second Battle of El Alamein and had prevailed, but at Kursk the enemy not only enjoyed a significant numerical and material edge but was also holding back a powerful armoured reserve to commit at a later stage in the battle. Moreover, Model's decision to forego the initial punch of massed armour placed a heavy burden on Ninth Army's artillery which lacked the towing vehicles necessary for the quick exploitation of success.

In contrast, Manstein was concerned that he did not have enough infantry to sustain these conventional but inevitably costly tactics. Thus he planned to use his stronger armoured forces to punch a hole in the Russian lines. The tool for the job was the *panzerkeil* ('armoured wedge'), with Tigers at its tip and Panthers and MkIVs fanning out behind, followed by infantry armed with automatic weapons and grenades. At the base of the wedge were more heavily armed panzer grenadiers carried in tracked personnel carriers. Once they had broken into the Russian trench system, the momentum of the panzers had to be maintained at all costs. Tank crews were given strict orders that, in no circumstances, should they stop to assist disabled vehicles. 'Recovery is the responsibility of engineer units only. Tank commanders are to press on to their objectives as long as they retain mobility. When a tank is immobilized (e.g., from mechanical failure or track damage) but the gun is in working order, the crew will continue to give fire support.' When the battle began, these orders were to sound the death knell of the crews in many disabled panzers.

In the June sunshine Grossdeutschland had trained in the rear, conducting exercises against dummy positions resembling the Russian defence lines in its sector. The atmosphere was relaxed, almost one of peacetime training. Some old hands recalled the mood of confidence which had prevailed in the balmy summer of 1940 when, as a regiment, Grossdeutschland, crossed the Meuse and helped to secure the bridgehead at Sedan which sealed the fate of France. Others, mindful of more recent fighting, were sceptical of Fourth Panzer Army's chances. And yet this massive assembly of armour had only to fight its way thirty-five miles through the Kursk salient to link with Ninth Army; in June 1941 Manstein's LVI Panzer Corps in Army Group North had advanced

270 miles from Brest Litovsk to Bobryusk in the first seven days of Barbarossa, covering over seventy miles in the last day. But there lay the rub. As Alan Clark has written: 'Once again the old Blitzkrieg formula – Stukas, short, intense artillery bombardment, massed tanks and infantry in close contact – were fed into the computer, with little regard for the changed conditions save a simple arithmetical increase in the strength of the respective components.'

On 22 June 11th Panzer Division celebrated the second anniversary of the launching of Barbarossa. The campaign which, at one point, seemed set to end in victory within two months, had now lasted twenty-four, with no end in sight. Busloads of Russian women driven in from Poltava took some men's minds off this sobering thought for an hour or two, but the party mood was dispelled late that night when aircraft droned overhead and, shortly afterwards, parachutes were seen descending in the moonlight. The partisans were receiving supplies.

On 2 July, within twenty-four hours of the battle conference held at Rastenburg, Lucy was relaying the details of the German high command's final decision on Zitadelle to Moscow. Stalin immediately despatched a signal to Rokossovsky and Vatutin:

> According to information at our disposal, the Germans may go over to the offensive on our front between 3–6 July.
>
> The Stavka of the Supreme Command orders:
>
> 1. Intensification of reconnaissance and observation of the enemy in order to ensure timely discovery of his intentions.
>
> 2. Ground troops and aircraft to be at readiness to repel possible enemy blow.

With equal speed the information was conveyed to the army commanders in the front line. Late in the afternoon of 2 July, Vatutin and Nikita Khrushchev, now the political member of Voronezh Front's military council, paid a visit to Lieutenant-General Katukov's command post, concealed in a wooded ravine, or *balka*, near the village of Zorinskoye Dvory, between Oboyan and Prokhorovka. The commander of First Tank Army was at the ready, standing over maps of his front sectors. Outside an aged *babushka* chivvied a herd of cows, a *maskirovka* touch designed to fool German aerial reconnaissance.

Khrushchev came straight to the point, telling Katukov: 'The fascists are attacking between 3 and 5 July. This isn't a guess, but a fact. We know it.' Lieutenant-General N.K. Popel, the political member of First Tank Army's political council, who had listened to Khrushchev's dramatic announcement, later recalled the last days of preparation in the Kursk salient:

> The roads at night were loud with the noise of engines. Convoys of tanks and guns, covered with dust, were rumbling into the sector where we expected the German onslaught. While German officers were reading out the Führer's Order of the Day, our defences made the final preparations for the reception of the enemy. We thickened our foremost line, moved more guns into position, once more coordinated and completed our firing tables and concerted our plans. We moved two artillery regiments of our Army into the strip held by Sixth Guards Army. One armoured brigade strengthened the order of battle of our infantry.

On the shoulders of the Kursk salient an ominous silence descended over the German concentrations west of Belgorod and south of Orel. The night-time movement of vehicles and equipment had ceased. South of Kharkov, however, columns of vehicles were reported to be moving away from the salient, another element in the German deception plan for Zitadelle. German radio was also devoting much airtime to Manstein's visit to Bucharest where he decorated Marshal Antonescu with the Gold Crimea Shield to mark the anniversary of the capture of Sebastopol. In fact, Manstein had flown to Bucharest immediately after the 1 July meeting at Rastenburg. Having presented Antonescu with his medal, he had flown straight back to the front to take up quarters in a train parked in a wood behind Fourth Panzer Army's start lines.

Everything pointed towards an imminent German attack. The air fighting in the salient had become increasingly ferocious as the Luftwaffe's bombers and their escorts battled their way to and from their targets, harried all the way by Russian fighters. A significant tonnage of bombs was still falling on the dummy airfields so expertly sprinkled around the salient, but at the end of June the bombers missed a more important target. In a night raid a stick of bombs had found Rokossovsky's headquarters, but the commander of Central Front was not at home, having decided, apparently on a whim, to establish his signals group in the officers' mess. The next morning Rokossovsky removed himself to the greater safety of a bunker in the grounds of a nearby monastery.

At the beginning of July the interrogation of the pilot of a downed He111 bomber on Voronezh Front produced the information that many Luftwaffe formations were moving up to Kharkov from the Crimea. On 4 July, in the Belgorod sector, a Slovene sapper deserted from the German lines and informed his Russian captors that the opening of the offensive had been set for 3am on 5 July. That night, after a firefight in no-man's land in 13th Army's sector on Central Front, a Red Army patrol captured an enemy sapper, one Private Fermello from the sapper battalion of 6th Infantry Division. Fermello confirmed that the attack was to open at 3am on the 5th and that the units were already in their starting positions.

On the night of 3 July German sappers had been at work in the dead zone between the two lines. On the Southern Front sector opposite Butovo they cleared and taped paths through the minefields which barred the way to the high ground beyond no-man's land. These low hills overlooked the German assembly areas and provided perfect positions from which Russian forward observers could call down artillery fire on the assault forces at their jumping-off points. At the same time the hills concealed the enemy's artillery and main defences from German gunners. Aerial reconnaissance had provided a wealth of photographs, but the Russian genius for camouflage and deception meant that it was almost impossible to distinguish between genuine and dummy positions. The success of the main attack in Zitadelle hinged on the swift seizure of these ridges from which German observers could then direct intense and accurate fire on the previously 'invisible' enemy artillery and main defence lines.

Mine clearing was the difficult and extremely dangerous preliminary to the seizing of the ridges facing Fourth Panzer Army. So much fighting had washed back and forth over this part of the Soviet Union since 1941 that detectors were useless. The ground was full of metal which meant that the instruments were driven into a meaningless frenzy of readings. The mines had to be located by gentle probing with metal rods and then dug out by hand. Sweating in the sultry heat, and constantly in fear of illumination by the enemy flares which arched over no-man's land, the engineers went about their business with grim efficiency. In five hours on the night of 3 July ten men of Grossdeutschland's 2nd Engineer Company successfully lifted some 2700 mines in the Butovo sector – a rate of a mine a minute by each man.

The fourth of July dawned hot and sticky. Throughout the morning bursts of thundery rain sent troops under their ground sheets and wrapped the landscape in a steamy haze. West of Belgorod an expectant silence fell over the front line. The assault forces of XLVIII Panzer and II SS Panzer Corps waited tensely in their trenches for the signal to attack. SS Obergrenadier (Lance-Corporal) Günther Borchers found time to write in his diary: 'I am in a flamethrowing team, and we are to lead the company attack. This is a real suicide mission. We have to get within 30m of the Russians before we open fire. It's time to write the Last Will and Testament.'

At 2.45pm both sides heard the drone of approaching aircraft, the five Ju87D Gruppen* of Luftflotte 4 and their escorts which crossed the German lines five minutes later to pulverize a box around Butovo two miles long and 500 yards deep. The attack lasted ten minutes and then, as the dive-bombers turned for home, the German artillery opened up. To the roar of conventional artillery was added the howl of *Nebelwerfer* rocket batteries** – the German equivalent of the Russian *Katyushas* – each of which

---

* Within the Luftwaffe the largest flying unit was the Geschwader, designated and numbered according to its function, for example, Stukageschwader 77 or Jagdgeschwader 52 (operating single-engine fighters). A Geschwader was divided into three, four or sometimes five *Gruppen*, each with a nominal strength of thirty aircraft. The *Gruppe* was the basic unit, a little larger than an RAF squadron, and its three component flights were known as *Staffeln*.

** The multi-barrelled Nebelwerfer ('smoke thrower') had originally been intended for use in connection with smokescreens and gas warfare but the latter was never implemented and Nebelwerfers were increasingly put to use firing high-explosive projectiles.

could saturate an area 2,200 yards long by 110 yards deep with 108 rockets in ten seconds. As they fired, great gouts of flame belched from the Nebelwerfers' barrels, followed by clouds of billowing smoke from which emerged a skein of red streaks as the rocket projectiles hurtled through the sky towards their targets. In the Russian trenches the troops braced themselves for the shattering impact of a Nebelwerfer bombardment, the blast effect of which could destroy the nerve of even the most seasoned troops.

As the artillery bombardment reached a climax, the main attack was launched by XLVIII Panzer Corps, in the centre of Hoth's front, against the Russian forward positions running three miles south of the villages of Savidovka, Alekseyevka and Luchanino. Panzer grenadiers and riflemen, supported by assault guns and engineers, pushed up the lanes cleared through the minefields. Behind them came the armoured observation and signals vehicles of the artillery, zig-zagging their way across no-man's land as the Russian gunners, recovering from the initial surprise of the attack, opened up with a counter-barrage.

Simultaneously the heavens opened with a thunderstorm of almost tropical intensity. At Butovo the Soviet 199th Guards Rifle Regiment was slow to react and its outpost lines were stormed by 3 Battalion of Grossdeutschland's Panzer Grenadier Regiment. The high ground to the east of Butovo was taken by 11th Panzer Division whose meticulous preparations were unaffected by the

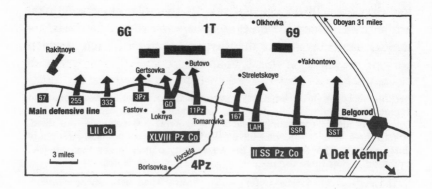

Fourth Panzer Army's preliminary assault on 4 July 1943, aimed at taking the hills in front of the German lines

curtain of rain driving across the battlefield. By 4.45pm German artillery observers were in position on the high ground, taking in their first unobstructed view of the enemy's main defensive lines.

West of Butovo, near Gertsovka, the going proved tougher for the Panzer Fusilier Regiment of Grossdeutschland and the 394th Panzer Grenadier Regiment of 3rd Panzer Division, both of which encountered stiff resistance from the Soviet 71st Guards Rifle Division. Under heavy flanking fire from the Sybino heights, 3rd Panzer did not secure its objectives, including the village of Gertsovka, until midnight. The Russians threw in fierce counter-attacks throughout the night as the artillery was moved up and signallers worked frantically to establish communications between observation posts and batteries.

While LII Corps made a pinning attack on the left of XLVIII Corps, II SS Panzer Corps on the right launched subsidiary attacks to secure observation posts for the next day's fighting. Here the rain was less heavy, but there was bitter fighting before the enemy's combat outposts were cleared by assault troops equipped with flamethrowers. In the captured Russian trenches the stench of burning flesh mingled with that of wet grass, sodden battledress, cordite and *mahorka*, the coarse Russian tobacco whose rank odour permeated dug-outs and command posts.

At 10.30pm, with rockets and flares lighting up the sky between Belgorod and Tomarovka, Vatutin hit back with a counter-bombardment delivered on the front of Sixth Guards Army and directed at the German artillery and assembly areas. Judging that the activity on his front was the preliminary to Zitadelle, he issued orders activating No.1 Variant, readying Sixth Guards Army to absorb the brunt of the German attack towards Oboyan while Seventh Guards Army took the secondary thrust. As his orders went out, the tanks of XLVIII Panzer Corps were slewing through a sea of mud on the approaches to the stream running between Savidovka and Sertsev. The rain had significantly strengthened the second line of Russian defences to the north of the stream. Mud, the constant factor of the *rasputitsa*, was about to play a baleful role in the summer fighting.

On the night of 4 July, Zhukov was at Rokossovsky's head-quarters, in the office of the latter's Chief of Staff, Lieutenant-

General M.S. Malinin, whom Zhukov had known since the defence of Moscow when he had served as Chief of Staff of Sixteenth Army. Over a high-security telephone line he was briefed by Vasilevsky, who was at Vatutin's headquarters, on the fighting west of Belgorod. Intelligence was piling up. First, Zhukov learned that a prisoner from 168th Division had revealed that the main offensive would begin the next day. At approximately 2am the commander of Thirteenth Army, Pukhov, came through on the telephone to report the capture of Private Fermello and the information he had given his interrogators.

Turning to Zhukov, Rokossovsky asked, 'What shall we do? Inform Supreme Headquarters or issue orders for the preliminary ourselves?' Zhukov replied, 'We can't waste time. Give the order according to plan, and I will call Stalin and report the information.' He was immediately put through to Stalin who had just finished talking to Vasilevsky. Zhukov told Stalin about the information gleaned from prisoners and the decision to order a counter-bombardment. Stalin approved the decision and asked that Zhukov keep him informed. He would remain at Stavka, waiting for events to unfold.

Stalin was clearly very tense – and he was not alone in this. Zhukov later confessed that 'all of us, despite our long-prepared defences in depth, despite our powerful striking potential, were in a state of high excitement. It was night, but none of us felt like sleeping.'

The decision to launch the counter-bombardment was of critical importance as it would consume more than half the artillery's initial allocation of ammunition. Central Front's artillery Chief of Staff, Colonel G.S. Nadsyev, was now busy on the telephone, talking to the commanders of the artillery units from the reserve and with General M.I. Kazakov, the front's artillery commander who was with 4th Artillery Corps. At 2.20am, ten minutes before the German bombardment was planned to begin, Rokossovsky's command post shook to its foundations as 600 guns and mortars of Central Front's artillery opened up. As heavy guns boomed away in the background and *Katyusha* rockets slashed off their launching ramps in sheets of flame, Stalin came back on the line to Zhukov. 'Well, have you begun?' he demanded.

'Yes, we have', was the deadpan reply. 'What's the enemy doing?' Zhukov told Stalin that the Germans were attempting to reply with fire from a few independent batteries. Reassured, Stalin said that he would ring again later.

Rokossovsky's counter-bombardment lasted for about thirty minutes, temporarily engaging 100 enemy batteries,* of which about half were suppressed, and sowing confusion in the infantry assembly areas. The German response was initially ragged but, by 4.45am, had gathered powerful momentum as more guns were brought back into action. Overhead, bombers from Luftflotte 6 flew in to pound Thirteenth Army's positions around Ponyri.

Both sides were like blindfolded heavyweight boxers striving to land knock-out blows in the dark. Neither could gauge how much damage it was inflicting. The Russian artillery, dispersed, well dug-in, concealed and camouflaged, was relatively untroubled by German guns still rolling with the punch delivered at 2.20am. Rokossovsky decided to hammer the enemy with a second thirty-minute bombardment, this time with 1000 guns. However, he had no clear picture of the German assembly and jumping-off areas and thus could concentrate only on area bombardment in the hope that his boxes would contain specific targets. The German timetable was disrupted but losses were not heavy. Analysing the battle after the war, Zhukov concluded that both fronts had opened up too early when the enemy's infantry was sheltering in their dug-outs and his armour was under cover in the waiting areas. He also admitted that, at the start of the battle, the VVS had been notable by its absence:

> Because the preliminary bombardment took place at night, aerial support was insignificant and, to be frank, ineffective. Our strikes at the enemy's airfields at dawn were too late; by that time German planes were already in the air in support of their ground forces. Our air strikes were much more effective against tactical military units and enemy columns attempting to regroup in the course of the battle.

---

* The German artillery *abteilung*, or detachment, normally contained twelve to sixteen guns; a British battery contained six to eight guns.

By 5.30am both Russian fronts were reporting heavy infantry and tank attacks aimed at Thirteenth Army and the right flank of Seventieth on Central Front and Sixth Guards on Voronezh Front. In the north an aerial bombardment of Thirteenth Army by Luftflotte 6, beginning at 5.10am, was followed twenty minutes later by an attack along a thirty-mile front between Trosna and Maloarkhangelsk by one panzer and nine infantry divisions.

In the opening phase of the battle, Model had planned to use his infantry to clear paths through the minefields. During the weeks of waiting Ninth Army's infantry formations had been rotated back to the rear areas to train on old Russian minefields. In their day these had been daunting obstacles, but they were as nothing compared with the minefields the assault engineers encountered as they moved out under heavy fire through the long summer grass into the fields of rye, corn, clover and sunflowers which lay between the lines. The cover they offered from mortar and machine-gun fire was illusory as, in the spring, they had been seeded with a second planting of wooden 'cigar box' anti-personnel mines whose fine web of tripwires was now hidden by the lush summer growth. Sharp explosions and showers of earth soon revealed their presence.

In open ground and taking heavy casualties from well-sited Russian strongpoints which had survived the initial bombardment, assault engineers worked feverishly to clear the way for the waiting armour. Steady hands and calm nerves were needed for the job. After scraping away the earth around an anti-tank mine, the mine had to be grasped, lifted a little way and then held to ascertain if it was additionally secured with a short length of wire anchored to a peg. The mine-clearing parties inched their way forward, probing, clearing the earth, lifting the mines, removing their detonators and then placing them aside. Mortar shells rained down among them while, overhead, shells screeched from their own tanks lined up for the attack and firing into the Russian positions to keep the enemy gunners' heads down.

Model's initial probing attacks were beaten back with a hail of artillery fire at short range. The main blow struck the left flank of Thirteenth Army at 8.30am after a renewed hour-long bombardment. On a fifteen-mile sector held by 15th and 81st Rifle Divisions,

Model threw in 31st, 6th, 292nd, 86th and 78th Divisions and 20th Panzer Division, supported by Tiger and Elefant units charged with smashing their way through the Russian defences.

By 9.30am 20th Panzer had fought its way through to Bobrik. On its left the 58th Grenadier Regiment of Lieutenant-General Grossmann's 6th Division had crossed the River Oka to seize the village of Novy-Chutor. Grossmann now decided to order forward the Tigers of Heavy Panzer Battalion 505 whose two combat companies were in their assembly areas in a forest a mile west of Vesselik-Posselok. Attached to the battalion was a platoon equipped with a new weapon, the 'Goliath' a miniature, unmanned demolition tank, some four feet long, two feet high and two feet wide. Driven by a small electric or petrol motor and steered by radio or trailing wires which unreeled for a distance of 1000 yards, 'Goliath' was designed to detonate mines or neutralize strong-points by remote control with a 200lb high-explosive charge. In addition 505 Battalion was reinforced by platoons from 6th Division's 38th Pioneer Battalion and 37th Grenadier Regiment.

The Tigers' engines coughed into life and the tanks moved forward, closely followed by the infantry. Brushing aside resistance from scattered T-34s and silencing anti-tank guns firing from a cornfield, 505 Battalion's Tigers rolled forward through Oka river to strike at the open flank of the Soviet 676th Rifle Regiment and send a shiver of apprehension rippling through the lines of 81st Rifle Division. At this point, as 6th Division halted to stagger its left wing to the rear against a flanking attack from the Oserki forest, which was still in Russian hands, a break-through beckoned. With the Tigers pushing on ahead of the grenadiers towards Butyrki, and firing at Soviet troops on the move, Grossmann could see far ahead of 6th Division a massif 'on which we could observe movements by the Russians. If the tanks had rolled through then, we could perhaps have reached the objective of Kursk because the enemy was completely surprised and still weak. Valuable time was lost which the enemy used to rush in his reserves.' Heavy Panzer Battalion 505 had advanced farther and faster than the sceptical Model had anticipated, but its penetration could not be enlarged into a break-through because 2nd, 9th and 18th Panzer Divisions were held in reserve and would not be committed for another twenty-four hours.

Behind the Tigers, the MkIVs of 20th Panzer Division were now biting into the first line of Russian defences. Soviet anti-tank batteries fought to the last man, firing over open sights, while 'anti-tank squads' moved in to tackle German armour with petrol bombs and satchel charges. By noon Rokossovsky was facing a crisis. The junction of 15th and 81st Rifle Divisions was being prised apart, threatening the entire right wing of Seventieth Army. It appeared that the main German thrust was not aimed down the railway line to Ponyri, as Rokossovsky had originally calculated, but was directed further west towards Olkhovatka. His plans had envisaged a holding operation by Thirteenth Army while Second Tank Army concentrated in the rear of the defensive field to deliver a counter-blow against the German drive on Ponyri on the second day of the battle. Now a rapid redeployment was put in hand. While 3rd Tank Corps moved to the south of Ponyri, 16th Tank Corps shifted to the north-west and 19th Tank Corps to the west of Olkhovatka. The rear of Thirteenth Army's defensive zone was strengthened by 17th Guards Rifle Corps, and 18th Guards Rifle Corps was moved to the right of the line, south of Maloarkhangelsk, to prevent a flank breakthrough by Ninth Army's 216th and 383rd Divisions.

Momentarily, Rokossovsky found himself in the position of a gambler discovering that his unbeatable hand may not be enough to take the pot. Ponyri was now under threat from Harpe's XLI Panzer Corps, which attacked with 86th and 292nd Divisions and 101st Panzer Grenadier Regiment of 18th Panzer Division. In the sectors held by the Soviet 81st Rifle Division and 294th Rifle Division, Harpe committed the Elefants of Jagdpanzer Regiment 656, commanded by Lieutenant-Colonel von Jugenfeld. To clear a way for the Elefants through the dense minefields, Ninth Army had devised another new weapon, the B-IV, a low tracked vehicle weighing two tons and resembling a British ammunition carrier; it carried a 1000lb high-explosive charge which was jettisoned and then touched off by remote control. The B-IV's driver edged the vehicle into position, switched on a remote-control drive and then legged it for his own lines, a procedure which guaranteed a short life expectancy. On the approaches to Maloarkhangelsk eight B-IVs were used to clear a wide lane through a minefield 400 yards deep. Only four of the drivers made it back.

The Elefants were also running into trouble. The Jagdpanzers were essentially 'mobile pillboxes', formidable in defence but less suited to a mobile offensive role. At first all went well. The Elefants' brutal firepower and heavy armour plating, up to 200mm thick, enabled them to break into the Russian lines with little difficulty; in the attack sector of 292nd Division, Regiment 656's 653 Battalion, commanded by Major Steinwachs, advanced over two miles into the enemy's tactical defence zone to make contact with 6th Division at Butyrki; on the left of Harpe's sector, the Elefants of 654 Battalion, commanded by Major Noak, spearheaded 78th Division's drive on the commanding Hill 253.5 to the east of Ponyri. The Elefants were soon marooned in a maze of slit trenches, however, where they were separated from the lighter tanks needed to cover their flanks, like a screen of destroyers protecting a capital ship. Lacking secondary armament, they fell victim to Soviet infantry who emerged from their foxholes, boarded them on the move and played flamethrowers over the engine ventilation slats. Model's monsters had feet of clay. Reviewing the performance of the Elefants at Kursk, Guderian judged that they were

> incapable of close-range fighting since they lacked sufficient ammunition (armour-piercing and high-explosive) for their guns and this defect was aggravated by the fact that they had no machine-gun. Once (they) had broken into the enemy's infantry zone, they literally had to go quail shooting with cannon. They did not manage to neutralize, let alone destroy, the enemy infantry and machine-guns, so that our infantry was unable to follow up behind them. By the time they reached the Russian artillery they were on their own.

Model's plans were beginning to unravel. As fast as paths were opened up through the minefields, Russian engineers went to work to lay new belts: on 5 July they laid at least 6000 mines in critical sectors. By the end of the day Model had lost about 100 tanks and self-propelled guns to mines. More were knocked out by anti-tank artillery as they were channelled through the minefields on to the guns of the 'anti-tank resistance points', leaving the

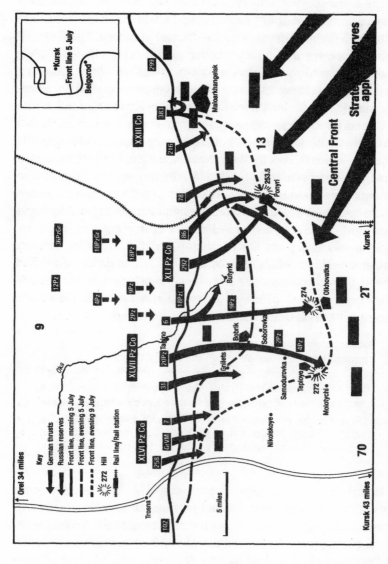

Model's attack in the north of the Kursk salient secured a foothold near Olkhovatka but was halted within sight of success

supporting infantry exposed to the machine-gun nests which formed an integral part of the defensive system.

Ninth Army's attack ground on like the revolving teeth of a giant tunnelling machine, tearing great hunks out of the Russian tactical zone. On Seventieth Army's front, 20th Panzer Division had battered its way to Gnilets, at the junction of 15th and 132nd Rifle Divisions, four miles from the German start-line. In XLI Panzer Corps's sector, 86th Division was in the third line of Russian trenches, and 184th Grenadier Regiment had penetrated to the northern outskirts of Ponyri. On 292nd Division's attack sector six of Steinwachs's Elefants had also ground some three miles into Rokossovsky's defences by late afternoon. But the Russian infantry had not succumbed to 'tank panic'. They remained in their well-camouflaged positions while the German armour rumbled past and then moved out to engage the grenadiers who came in their wake. Fierce fighting erupted in areas which the advancing tank crews believed had passed into German hands.

On Model's left wing there was growing cause for concern. The attack on Maloarkhangelsk by XXIII Corps's 216th and 383rd Divisions had achieved initial success, breaking into the tactical defensive zone of 254th and 148th Rifle Divisions, but then had been thrown back by determined counter-attacks. A deep penetration at this point was vital to protect Model's armour from attack by Rokossovsky's operational reserves to the east. Aerial reconnaissance was now indicating the movement of major enemy forces towards the Ponyri and Olkhovatka areas.

At midnight Model conferred with his Chief of Staff, Colonel von Elverfeldt. His fears about the strength and depth of the Russian defences had been confirmed. The greater part of Ninth Army's assault force was entangled in the enemy's tactical defence zone, while isolated groups of Tigers lay stranded further on with no infantry to protect them. Under cover of darkness panzer grenadier units struggled across a wilderness of wire and trenches to reach the Tigers, clashing with Red Army patrols as they went. Even more serious was the failure to secure Ninth Army's left wing at Maloarkhangelsk; this failure would expose Model's deeply echeloned armour (until now held back) to attack on the 6th by the Soviet strategic reserve now moving into the salient.

Luftflotte 6 had been operating over Ninth Army since first light on the 5th when Stukas of III/StG1, led by their Kommandeur, Major Friedrich Lang, had howled down to attack gun emplacements in the Russian tactical defence zone. While other Stuka units hit strongpoints and supply routes, tank-busting Panzerjager units, equipped with Hs129Bs and twin-engined Me110Gs, roamed the battlefield in search of prey. Above them flew the FW190As of JG51 and JG54 which were soon locked in battle with the La-5s and Yak-9s of General Yerlykhin's 6th Fighter Air Corps and 1st Guards Fighter Air Division as they rose to meet the Luftwaffe above Central Front.

In heavy fighting over the northern shoulder of the Kursk salient on the 5th, the Russians claimed 106 victories in seventy-six different engagements for an admitted loss of ninety-eight aircraft. The leading Soviet pilot of the day was Lieutenant S.K. Kolesnichenko of the 519th Fighter Regiment who claimed three victories. Lieutenant V.K. Polyakov of 54th Guards Fighter Regiment shot down at least one aircraft and rammed a second – the first of at least six deliberate ramming attacks made by Russian pilots during the battle.

These figures were modest when compared with the claims of the Luftwaffe *experten*. Flying from dawn to dusk, Warrant Officer Hubert Strassl of III/JG51 claimed fifteen aircraft shot down, a figure consistent with the the inflated claims which characterized the air war in the East.

Nevertheless, there was no shortage of targets for Strassl and his fellow pilots. As the day wore on, the Soviet Sixteenth Army put all its major units into battle, including the 3rd Bomber and 6th Composite Air Corps and 2nd Guards and 299th Ground Attack Divisions. Flying over the battlefield in formations of six to eight aircraft, the Russian pilots sought targets of opportunity along Model's attack frontage. Tactical naivety, however, drew many of the Air Army's fighters into combat with the enemy's FW190As, allowing the Luftwaffe's bomber and panzerjager units to operate without fighter interference and exposing Russian ground-attack forces to heavy losses.

In the south on 5 July the day opened with an air battle which dwarfed the clashes over Central Front. After the heavy overnight rain the dawn, which arrives at about 2.30am on the steppe, heralded a day of clear blue skies. As the minutes ticked away to 3.30am, H-hour for the main attack on Hoth's front, the atmosphere at VIII Air Corps's headquarters at Mikoyanovka was heavy with tension. When the artillery barrage lifted and the *panzerkeil* rolled forward, General Seidemann planned to have the maximum number of operational aircraft aloft, attacking enemy airfields, fortifications, trench systems and artillery positions. On the Corps's seven principal airfields around Kharkov – Mikoyanovka, Sokoniki, Pomerki, Osnova, Rogan, Barvenkuro and Kramatorskaya – 800 Stukas, bombers and their escorting fighters were preparing for take-off, taxiing wingtip to wingtip. The bomber Geschwader were to take off first, formate over the bases while their fighter escorts took station, and then head for their targets.

Seidemann had no expectation of achieving anything more than initial tactical surprise with this massive strike. It was impossible to conceal such a concentration of air power from the enemy, even by holding back the bulk of the aircraft from the forward air bases until the night before the attack. What Seidemann was about to discover, however, was that the Soviet Seventeenth Air Army was already in the air, heading towards the congested German bases to launch a pre-emptive strike of its own. As the countdown to H-hour continued, the German radio listening service reported a tremendous surge in radio traffic between the enemy's air regiments, a sure sign that a major operation was imminent. Shortly afterwards the chain of German Freya early-warning radars ranged along the front picked up several hundred approaching Russian aircraft. Seidemann's Air Corps was within minutes of destruction on the ground, a dramatic reversal of the fate suffered by Soviet aviation in June 1941.

The survival of Seidemann's command and, with it, the air support vital for the success of Zitadelle, now depended on the ability of the German fighter aircraft to take off and clear the area of the forward bases before the arrival of Seventeenth Air Army. Pell-mell, the fighters from JG3 and JG52 were scrambled while the bombers waited, their engines turning over. Then they took off and climbed heavily away. Seidemann, accompanied by the

Luftwaffe's Chief of Staff, Jeschonnek, spent more anxious minutes as the Soviet formations passed over Mikoyanovka and flew on towards Kharkov, but the target airfields were now empty of all but a handful of unserviceable aircraft.

Instead, the 450 Soviet raiders, some 285 of which were fighters, ran into a swarm of Bf109Gs. Later, Seideman wrote: 'It was a rare spectacle. Everywhere planes were burning and crashing. In no time at all 120 Soviet aircraft were downed. Our own losses were so small as to represent total victory, for the consequence was complete air control in the VIII Air Corps sector.'

The Soviet formations were broken up by the German fighters and battered by anti-aircraft fire. Only a few bombers reached their targets to scatter bombs on empty runways. The sixty German aircraft subsequently claimed by the VVS could not offset a crushing reverse which enabled VIII Air Corps to operate at will over the battlefield for the next five hours.

On Hoth's front the battle was to assume a different shape to Model's offensive against Central Front. OKH had ordered Fourth Panzer Army to 'seek contact with Ninth Army' by a push along the direct route to Kursk through Oboyan. Hoth, well served by aerial reconnaissance, was keenly aware that the direct route was blocked by Katukov's First Tank Army which had been reinforced by two tank corps and fielded 1300 armoured fighting vehicles. He also knew that several tank corps were deployed south-east of Kursk while, behind the south-eastern edge of the salient, lurked Fifth Guards Tank Army. Strict adherence to OKH's orders would not only meet strong resistance from First Tank Army but would also expose Hoth's right flank, still locked in the middle of the Soviet defensive system, to counter-attack by Vatutin's armoured reserves and the heaviest armoured hitter in the enemy's order of battle – Fifth Guards Tank Army.

Studying the map, Hoth noted that any Soviet armoured reserves moving against him from the east would have to pass through the neck of land between the Donets and the Psel at the centre of which lay the village of Prokhorovka. Hoth decided to drive north and then swing north-east, sidestepping a head-on collision with First Tank Army. He told his staff: 'It is better to dispose of the enemy, who is to be expected at Prokhorovka, before the thrust northwards towards Kursk is set in motion.' This would also make it easier for Army Detachment Kempf to keep pace with Fourth Panzer Army's advance after crossing the Donets south of Belgorod and before wheeling north to cover Hoth's right flank.

In making this decision on his own initiative, without reference to OKH, Hoth had denied Lucy crucial information about German intentions and had wrongfooted Vatutin who knew, via Lucy, of OKH's instructions to Fourth Panzer Army. On the morning of 5 July, Vatutin's problems were exacerbated by the absence of air support as Hoth committed all his armour to the assault. The armoured blows were designed to smash open the Soviet defensive system with the maximum speed, enabling the subsequent battle with the enemy's reserve to be conducted on terrain where freedom of manoeuvre and superior German tactical flexibility could be brought to bear.

Hoth's attack was preceded by an artillery bombardment which, in fifty minutes, expended more shells between Gertsovka and Belgorod than the combined total fired by German guns in the Polish and French campaigns. At 5.00am the armour moved forward while Seidemann's dive-bombers and ground-attack aircraft flew overhead to blast a highway down which the *panzerkeil* and infantry began to push into the Russian lines. Among the ground-attack aircraft were the FW190Fs of I/SchG1 armed with the new SD-1 and SD-2 anti-personnel containers. As the containers opened during their descent, hundreds of small fragmentation bombs were scattered over a wide area. The Soviet gunners who did not duck for cover died in a blizzard of metal.

Nevertheless, the Russian artillery did not waste its chance to pound the unprecedented concentrations of armour packed into Hoth's attack frontage. In XLVIII Panzer Corps's sector, Grossdeutschland, assembling in dense formation on the edge of the swampy ground in front of Alekseyevka, came under heavy fire while the engineers struggled to make crossings over the swollen stream. As Seventeenth Air Army recovered from the mauling it had received at the beginning of the day, its attack aviation re-appeared over the battlefield.

Almost immediately Grossdeutschland's Panthers, commanded by Lieutenant-Colonel von Lauchert, ran straight into an undetected minefield in front of the first line of Soviet defences. Other armoured units sank up to their tracks in the mud caused by the overnight rain. Grossdeutschland's fusiliers pressed on without armoured support, only to suffer heavy casualties at the hands of Russian fighter-bombers. The engineers were called up. It was not until well into the afternoon that the 2nd Company of Grossdeutschland's Panzer Assault Engineer Battalion cleared a path through which the division's tanks and self-propelled artillery could move to rejoin the infantry. But, once again, the advance was held up by swampy ground and, this time, the engineers could not bring up the equipment needed to provide immediate assistance. In the Cherkasskoye sector alone, thirty-six German tanks were stuck fast in the minefields.

On Grossdeutschland's right wing progress was more encouraging. By 9.15am the division's panzer grenadiers, supported by assault guns, MkIVs of the Panzer Regiment's 2 Battalion, the fourteen MkVIs of Captain Wallroth's Tiger company and a combat group from 11th Panzer Division, had skirted the swampy ground which had enmired Grossdeutschland's armour and were closing on Cherkasskoye, five miles inside the Soviet tactical defence zone. To hold Cherkasskoye, Colonel-General Chistyakov fed in two regiments of anti-tank guns to fight alongside units of 67th Guards Rifle Division. By mid-afternoon the Tigers were on the scene, nosing their way through a graveyard of smashed and mined tanks and the twisted remains of Soviet anti-tank guns as the village was remorselessly encircled. Finally, all that was left was a rearguard of fifteen Guardsmen covering the withdrawal from the village. By nightfall Cherkasskoye was in German hands and 11th Panzer, on Grossdeutschland's right, was pushing on another five miles along the road to Oboyan.

On XLVIII Panzer Corps's left 3rd Panzer Division fought its way towards the village of Korovino and the important high ground of Hill 220. Korovino was stormed at dusk by the division's 394th Panzer Grenadier Regiment while a light platoon from the division's 6th Panzer Regiment drove on to Krasny Pochinok, the last major Russian defensive position before the River Pena. During the night 255th and 332nd Divisions moved up to the left of 3rd Panzer whose initial thrust had carried it six miles inside the

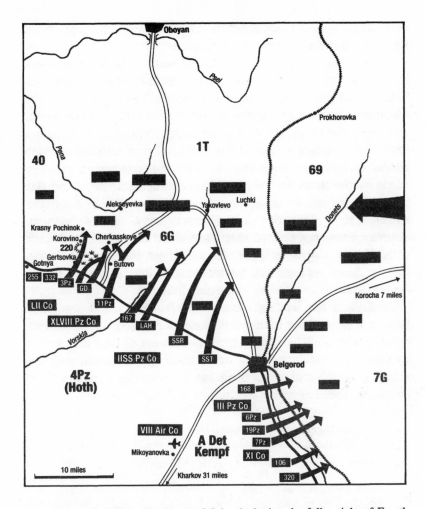

Hoth opened his main offensive on 5 July, deploying the full weight of Fourth Panzer Army against Soviet Sixth Guards Army

enemy's tactical defence zone, the objective it had been given for its operations on the first day of Zitadelle.

It was on XLVIII Panzer Corps's right, on the attack frontage of II SS Panzer Corps, that Chistyakov had anticipated that Hoth's main blow would fall. He was not disappointed. Hausser's corps, the ideological battering ram of Nazism, was poised to strike with over 400 armoured fighting vehicles, including forty-two Tigers, and a Nebelwerfer brigade. Hausser planned to break into the Russian defences on a narrow sector, the point of maximum effort being made by the units on the inner flanks of Leibstandarte and Das Reich Divisions. Totenkopf occupied the crucial slot on the extreme right flank of Fourth Panzer Army. In this position, Totenkopf was not only to keep pace with the northerly advance of SS Panzer Corps but was also to screen the flank of Fourth Panzer Army, against any Soviet penetration from east of the Donets, until the arrival of supporting infantry.

By 8.15am the leading elements of Das Reich's Deutschland Regiment were about to take the village of Beresov. As Stukas softened up the objective, the panzer grenadiers of Deutschland's 3 Battalion, led by flame-throwing units, fought their way into the village. A member of one of the flame-throwing detachments, Hans Huber, recalled the fight:

> The enemy artillery forced us to take cover. One might almost add, 'Thank God,' because the equipment was damnably heavy . . . Soon we knew from the Very lights being fired that our No.2 Platoon had gained a foothold in the village. Section commander Kiesel grew impatient. He ordered me to get the flame-thrower ready and we worked our way forward into the trenches ahead of us. I fired a burst of flame as we approached every zig-zag in the trench and at every enemy strongpoint. It was a strange feeling to serve this destructive weapon and it was terrifying to see the flames eat their way forward and envelop the Russian defenders. Soon I was coloured black from head to foot from the fuel oil and my face was burnt from the flames which bounced back off the trench walls or which were blown back at us by the strong wind. I could hardly see. The enemy could not fight against flame-throwers and so we made good progress, taking many prisoners.

On Das Reich's left, Leibstandarte's armour had advanced in wedge formation with the Tigers of the division's heavy panzer company, commanded by Captain Kling, at the tip. In the Tiger companies of the SS panzer grenadier divisions were concentrated a high number of the panzer arm's 'tank aces' – commanders with a special ability to destroy enemy armour. These armour-clad *experten* relied on the speed with which they read the immediate tactical situation, a sixth sense for the likely movements of enemy vehicles, a coolness under attack which enabled them to hold their fire until the last possible moment and, perhaps, most important of all, highly trained and experienced crews who were able to anticipate their commanders' orders.

These elements were combined in the Tiger commanded by Lieutenant Michael Wittmann who had joined Leibstandarte in 1937 and, in 1941, had been awarded the Iron Cross First Class after destroying six enemy tanks in a single action during the advance on Rostov. Above all, Wittmann possessed in Balthasar Woll a gunner who had an almost supernatural ability to fire accurately while on the move.

As the German artillery bombardment crashed down on the Russian lines, Wittmann's platoon of five Tigers moved forward, anti-tank fire whipping around them. In Wittmann's Tiger, Woll targeted and destroyed his first anti-tank gun of the day. The advance carried Wittmann's platoon to an enemy strongpoint and a gaggle of T-34s, several of which were knocked out while the rest turned tail. Followed by the panzer grenadiers, the Tigers ground on towards the next line of anti-tank guns. Leibstandarte's commander, Major-General Theodor Wisch, appeared near the Tigers, one of whose commanders called out to him, 'Lunch in Kursk!'

An hour later, as Wittmann's Tiger engaged more anti-tank guns, his radio crackled with the information that the company's Wendorff platoon had run into trouble. A swift change of direction plunged Wittmann's Tigers through a copse from which they emerged to find themselves in the rear of another Soviet anti-tank strongpoint. In a nearby hollow Wendorff's tanks were surrounded by T-34s which had already set one of the Tigers on fire. Wittmann moved into action. Two of his tanks engaged the anti-tank guns while Wittmann went to the aid of Wendorff. Within five minutes he had knocked out three T-34s while sustaining heavy damage to his own tank's tracks as the enemy returned fire. The advance was resumed and, by the end of the day, Wittmann had claimed eight enemy tanks knocked out and seven anti-tank guns destroyed.*

Within three hours II SS Panzer Corps was gouging great chunks out of the tactical defence zone of Sixth Guards Army. At 8.00am, Colonel-General Chistyakov, unaware of impending crisis, received Katukov and the latter's military council member, Lieutenant-General N.K. Popel, at Sixth Guards Army's battle headquarters. Katukov and Popel found Chistyakov taking a second breakfast in an orchard. Popel acidly recalled: 'On the table were cold mutton, scrambled eggs, a carafe of chilled vodka, to judge by the condensation on the glass, and finely sliced white bread – Chistyakov was doing himself well.'

Sixth Guards Army was not doing so well. Chistyakov had no time to invite his visitors to join him. No sooner had they set foot in the orchard than its tranquillity was shattered by shells bursting overhead. Shrapnel pinged about the trees. Chistyakov's Chief of Staff hurried over with the news that enemy forces had broken through the tactical defence zone. As Katukov and Popel raced for their car to return to First Tank Army's battle headquarters, echeloned columns of German tanks appeared on the horizon, unmistakable in their tan-and-mottled-green camouflage. The sky swarmed with enemy aircraft and not a single Soviet fighter was to be seen.

In the build-up to Zitadelle, Stavka had placed a relatively greater emphasis on the danger posed in the north by Ninth Army than that presented in the south by Fourth Panzer Army. The difference was small but significant, leading to a slightly looser and more evenly spread defensive system in the south; this allowed both XLVIII and II SS Panzer Corps to make deeper penetrations into the tactical defensive zone than had been achieved in

---

* Wittmann's career ended in Normandy on 9 August 1944 when he was killed in action leading SS Panzer Abteilung 101. His victory tally, achieved in less than three years, stood at 138 tanks and assault guns and 132 anti-tank guns, an unparalleled achievement.

the north by Model. The southern shoulder of the Kursk salient was now buckling alarmingly. At 4.30pm Vatutin personally ordered Katukov to move 6th Tank and 3rd Mechanized Corps to cover Oboyan and to prepare to launch a counter-attack towards Tomarovka at dawn on the 6th. Two more reserve tank formations, 5th Guards and 2nd Guards Tank Corps, were to concentrate to the east of Luchki to attack in the direction of Belgorod.

Vatutin was also watching the situation south of Belgorod where Army Detachment Kempf had attacked across the Donets at 2.25am on the morning of the 5th. Attacking with III Panzer Corps was Heavy Panzer Battalion 503. Gerhard Niemann, a gunner in the battalion's Tigers, has left a vivid account of the opening blows of Zitadelle against Soviet Seventh Guards Army.

Our company rolls through a narrow forest clearing into the Donets plain. As gunner, I sit in my position at the commander's feet, headset and throat microphone in place. Nervously, I once again check the triggers for the cannon and the machine-gun and the handwheels for the elevating and traversing mechanisms.* My hand trembles a little as I quickly set the various ranges on the range scale.

The Russian artillery opens fire. We drive through a village. We are to cross a river via a ford near Solomino, seven kilometres south-east of Belgorod. The leading tank has reached the ford. The others remain under cover. All around shells burst from the enemy artillery. 'Stalin Organs' also join in. It's a hellish concert.

The lead Tiger, number 321, disappears to above its fenders. Slowly it pushes through the water. Then it becomes stuck on the far bank. Its attempts to get free fail. The marshy terrain is impassable for the sixty-ton tank. Widely spaced, the Tigers take up position on the open plain before the Donets. The Russian artillery is concentrating on the crossing point. The bridge which we are not permitted to use because of its load-bearing limit of thirty tons receives a direct hit.

The *Pioniere* [engineers] make superhuman efforts. The first wounded infantry are coming back. They can't comprehend that the Tigers are still here standing around inactive.

---

* The Tiger's turret had a full traverse powered by the main engine. If the engine was stopped, the turret had to be traversed by hand.

'Drive up! Drive up ! Your comrades are waiting for you!' they cry desperately. But we stand on this side, the infantry on the other, and between us rushes the Donets.

It is midday. The sun burns down on the tanks mercilessly. It's like being in an incubator. Then, finally! The *Pioniere* have done it ! They have erected a crossing.

'Company – advance!'

After a few hundred metres the heavy tanks are in the lines of the pinned-down grenadiers. Then come the first orders.

'*Achtung*, two o'clock bunker, high explosive.'

My foot presses forward on the pedal of the turret-traversing mechanism. The turret swings to the right. With my left hand I set the range on the telescopic sight; my right hand cranks the elevation handwheel. The target appears in my sight. Ready, release safety – fire!

The target is shrouded in a cloud of smoke.

'Driver, advance!' A slight jolt and already another picture presents itself. The first Red Army soldiers appear ahead of the tank. Masses of brown-clad forms rise up. Standing and kneeling, they fire against the tank's steel armour. The machine-gun opens fire. One after another, high-explosive shells detonate among them. They throw their arms in the air and fall. Only a few find cover in a depression in the earth. They are overrun by the following infantry . . .

Fire, fire! A wheat field appears to the right of the company. 'Cannon one o'clock – fifty metres – safety off!'

With great caution we feel our way forward. My forehead is pressed firmly against the headrest of the telescopic sight. My eyes ache from the strain of continuous searching. There, ahead, an enemy anti-tank gun. A fountain of earth explodes in front of the tank. We fire. The anti-tank gun is hit and put out of action. More hits on our Tiger. Crashes from all sides. At least four anti-tank guns are firing on us. The driver yells something like, 'We're hit.'

Our radio operator is wounded. The loader heaves shell after shell into the breech and loads fresh belts into the machine-gun while I fire.

The commander stands in the turret and gives the driver directions. We reach one anti-tank gun. It crunches beneath our tracks. The gun is torn to pieces under the weight of our Tiger.

Again, a hit in front. The lights go out. The gun's electrical firing mechanism fails. But still the tank drives on!

Another anti-tank gun – not fifty metres ahead of us. The

gun crew flees except for one man. He crouches behind
the shield and fires. A terrible crash echoes through the fighting compartment. The driver turns on the spot and another
gun is crushed beneath our tracks. Again, a heavy blow,
this time against the rear of the tank. The motor coughs but
runs on.
   'Cease firing,' calls our Lieutenant.
   'But the anti-tank gun?' I call back.
   'Someone else has destroyed it!'
   We move on. Our Tiger jolts forward over trenches and shell
holes. Behind a rise is a collective farm. In front of it are enemy
tanks. One of them burns after our second shot. The next T-34
moves into our field of fire. Twice we miss. The third shot
strikes precisely between turret and hull. The T-34 is
destroyed. Then the engagement is over. For security the company draws itself together for the night.'

Gerd Schmückle had also been in action on the first day of
Zitadelle, commanding an assault gun in 7th Panzer's artillery
regiment as the division established a bridgehead west of
Dorogobushino near Solomino. Engaging a line of anti-tank guns,
Schmückle saw a massive shaven-headed Russian officer rallying
the troops around him and acting as a centre point of resistance.
This display of bravado eventually attracted the fire of all eighteen
guns in Schmückle's *abteilung* – 'an execution somewhat out of
proportion', as Schmückle reflected.
   Soon Schmückle's assault gun was under fire. The two tanks
ahead of him 'brewed up' and, seconds later, his *Sturmgeschutz*
shuddered from stem to stern as it took a direct hit. Schmückle
blacked out for a few seconds. He came round to find the turret
awash with the blood of his crew. The driver was dead in his seat,
the gunner also lifeless and slumped halfway out of the hatch and
the radio operator standing upright but beyond recall.
   Schmückle scrambled out and ran for cover in a nearby wood.
Lying in the undergrowth, he watched his own tanks withdraw
behind a ridge while all around him crashed Soviet troops, leaderless and disorientated by the German attack. After an anxious fifteen minutes the panzers returned. Schmückle broke cover and
hitched a ride on the MkIV commanded by Lieutenant-Colonel
Adalbert Schulz, an immensely experienced officer whose courage

and legendary luck had earned him the nickname 'Panzer' Schulz. The Colonel immediately gave Schmückle some Pervitin benzedrine pills.*

By the end of the day III Panzer Corps had established itself in a bridgehead seven miles across and five miles deep on the east bank of the Donets. To the south, 106th and 320th Divisions had created a slightly smaller bridgehead. At 7.40pm Vatutin reinforced Seventh Guards Army with three rifle divisions of 35th Guards Rifle Corps which were moved in to cover the Korocha axis.

North-west of III Corps, II SS Panzer Corps had broken through the tactical defence zone of Sixth Guards Army, nearly capturing Colonel-General Chistyakov in the process. Leibstandarte, supported on its left by 167th Division, had penetrated some ten miles along the line of the Vorskla river. On Leibstandarte's right Das Reich and Totenkopf had advanced twelve miles, breaking through 52nd Guards Rifle Division to reach the Belgorod–Oboyan highway.

Darkness fell over the battlefield, broken by the flare of star shells and Very lights, streams of tracer shells and the sudden, livid stab of flame-throwers as patrols clashed in the trench system. The exhausted survivors of the German assault battalions huddled in their slit trenches eating their hard tack and snatching fitful sleep after the strain of battle. Around them lay the dead and dying, strewn among a nightmarish scrapyard of shattered tanks, gutted trucks and smouldering armoured personnel carriers. In the rear the field hospitals were already swollen with wounded.

At the end of the first day's fighting the Red Army communiqué reported no fewer than 586 enemy tanks destroyed or put out of action, an exaggeration to place alongside the over-claiming in the

---

* Schmückle wrote of the effects of Pervitin after the fighting around Zhitomir in November 1943:

> I could not sleep. During the attack I had taken too much Pervitin. We had all been dependent on it for a long time. Everyone swallowed the stuff, more frequently and in greater doses. The pills seemed to remove the sense of agitation. I slid into a world of bright indifference. Danger lost its edge. One's own power seemed to increase. After the battle one hovered in a strange state of intoxication in which a deep need for sleep fought with a clear alertness.

air battle At this point in the battle German losses on the south of the salient were still measured in tens rather than hundreds. Fourth Panzer Army had gone into action on 4 July with 916 mission-capable tanks, a figure now reduced to 865. More revealing of the Soviet appreciation of the situation in the south on the evening of the 5th was the exhortation delivered by Nikita Khrushchev at Vatutin's headquarters: 'The next two or three days will be terrible. Either we hold or the Germans take Kursk. They are putting everything on one card. It's a matter of life and death for them. We must ensure that they break their necks.' Vatutin issued the categorical order, 'The Germans must not break through to Oboyan under any circumstances.'

At the headquarters of Fourth Panzer Army there was also cause for concern. II SS and XLVIII Panzer Corps had broken through the first line of Russian defences, but had nevertheless fallen short of the objectives laid down in their schedules for Zitadelle – and a fast breakthrough had been central to the planning of the operation. Calculations that a blitzkrieg on the 1941 pattern could be achieved at Kursk were proving unrealistic, as von Hünersdorff, front-line commander of 6th Panzer Division, had feared. The 'wonder weapons' at the tip of the *panzerkeil* had displayed a worrying vulnerability. Guderian's doubts that the Panther was ready for combat had been confirmed. By the morning of 8 July mechanical failure was to remove seventy-six of the Panthers to the repair shops, leaving Lauchert with barely forty mission-capable vehicles.

Questions were also asked about the tactical wisdom of placing the Tigers at the head of the *panzerkeil*. The relatively slow-moving Tiger was at its most potent when standing off the T-34 and pounding the lighter tank at long range with its 88mm gun, a battleship against a cruiser. The Tiger lost this advantage in close-quarter combat where the T-34's manoeuvrability and strength in numbers offset the formidable armour and armament of Tigers separated from the main body of the *panzerkeil*.

Enemy resistance was also proving stronger than had been expected. The Russians had not cracked at the first onslaught as they had done so often before. As Paul Carell observed:

The first detailed reports which Colonel-General Hoth received
from his Army Intelligence Officer towards midday contained
an interesting and significant statement. In all earlier German
offensives the tank wireless operators and those at advanced
headquarters had invariably intercepted the excited questions
of Soviet commanders to their superiors: 'Am under attack.
What am I to do?' On 5 July this usually characteristic symptom
of confusion and surprise was not heard even once.

In contrast the air battle in the south on the 5th seemed like a
re-run of the drubbings regularly inflicted by the Luftwaffe on
Soviet aviation. It had yielded German claims of 432 Soviet aircraft
destroyed, seventy-seven by II/JG3 alone. Flight Lieutenant
Johannes Wiesse of JG52 claimed twelve victims, in spite of having
force-landed five times during the course of the day's fighting.
Close behind was the claim for eleven kills made by the ebullient
Flying Officer Walter Krupinski, also of JG52, whose penchant for
high living had prompted his comrades to dub him 'The Count'.
Admitted German losses were no more than twenty-six aircraft.
Seen solely in terms of aircraft claimed shot down, 5 July 1943 was
the greatest single day of air combat in the Second World War,
unequalled even by the air fighting at the height of the 'Marianas
Turkey Shoot' in the Pacific in June–July 1944.

The Luftwaffe, however, was already anxiously watching its fuel
supplies. Shortage of fuel had been a constant problem for the two
Luftflotten in the Kursk sector. In the build-up to Zitadelle both
had been stretched to maintain the rate of preparatory sorties. It
had also been impossible to store sufficient fuel for an estimated
five days of intensive and continuous air combat after the launching of Zitadelle (two sorties a day for bombers, three to four for
ground-attack aircraft and six or more for fighters). Here the partisan attacks on fuel trains had played an important role. The need
to husband fuel placed strict limits on planning . As the battle progressed, and the VVS recovered its balance, fuel would come to
dictate operations. 'Fuel tactics' were introduced and many operations were, to a large degree, influenced by the quantity of fuel
required rather then the number of flying formations needed to do
the job. The longer the battle continued, the more sorties were
sanctioned or withheld on the basis of calculations of the fuel

expenditure involved. Moreover, no matter how high the ratio of kills was in favour of the Luftwaffe, the VVS was still able to respond by putting powerful formations in the air at any given time. And although local air superiority could still be gained by the Luftwaffe, even against markedly superior numbers, the mechanical attrition caused by continuous combat rapidly made inroads into aircraft availability. Holes would soon appear in the German air umbrella and these were rapidly filled by Soviet aircraft.

Dawn broke on the morning of the 6th to reveal a tableau reminiscent of the fighting on the Western Front in 1917. If the Second World War was truly the last great battle of the First, then the scene at Kursk would have been familiar to a veteran of Arras or Cambrai, with only the weaponry on both sides betraying the passage of time. Over the wire entanglements and trenches drifted clouds of smoke from burning cornfields and the thatched roofs of the villages in the battle zone. They mingled with the black, oily plumes rising like so many exclamation marks from burning tanks and were carried westward by a gentle wind.

The incessant chatter of small arms and machine-guns was regularly drowned out by the eruption of *Katyusha* batteries, like great sheets being ripped apart in the heavens, and the sharp crack of the Russians' 76mm anti-tank guns. In the distance the unmistakable bark of an 88mm gun signalled a Tiger defending itself.

At dawn on the Central Front, Rokossovsky put in a counter-attack on the Olkhovatka axis. During the afternoon of the 5th the Front's operational reserves had received orders 'to move off in accordance with the prepared plan into the jumping-off areas for the counter-attack'. Immediately, 3rd, 16th and 19th Tank Corps moved up to their concentration areas, but even the best-laid plans go awry in the friction of battle. The short summer night prevented their making an adequate reconnaissance of the terrain over which the attack was to be launched. German minefields could not be reconnoitred and the corps's engineers were defeated by the density of the Russian minefields through which it proved impossible to clear safe avenues during the hours of darkness.

When the attack went in, it broke down on the Russian mine-fields – which had been strengthened by the Germans after they had passed through them – and was then rolled back by German armour. Rokossovsky responded by ordering Second Tank Army to dig its tanks in, hull-down, as a breakwater against renewed assaults by the German MkIVs and MkVIs. The use of Russian armour in open country was sanctioned only against enemy infantry and light tanks.

Model was now ready to commit the major elements of his armoured forces against the centre of the Russian line. These he had originally planned to hold in reserve for the drive on Kursk after his infantry had broken through Central Front's defences. In the sector running east from Soborovka to Ponyri he committed 2nd, 9th and 18th Panzer Divisions which had been ordered to take the dominating heights of Hills 272, south-west of Teploye, 274, north-east of Olkhovatka, and 253.5, east of Ponyri. The chain of ridges running along a curving line for some fifteen miles in the heart of the Russian defences held the key to the northern half of Zitadelle. From these hilltops Kursk could be seen across more open terrain in which Rokossovsky's armour would be at a great disadvantage against Model's panzer divisions. The prize beckoned.

In the centre of the Russian line, however, were concentrated over 3000 guns and mortars, 5000 machine-guns and more than 1000 tanks. Rokossovsky was also feeding in reinforcements from 'quiet' sectors: a division from Lieutenant-General Chernyakhov-sky's Sixtieth Army, guarding the face of the salient, was loaded on to trucks and moved eastwards into Thirteenth Army's sector; and two tank regiments from Sixtieth's neighbour, Sixty-Fifth Army, commanded by General Batov, were also transferred to the furious battle building up on the northern shoulder of the salient.

Rodin's Second Tank Army and Pukhov's Thirteenth Army had now locked horns with seven German infantry and four panzer divisions attacking on a frontage of twenty miles. Between Soborovka and Ponyri a huge four-day tank battle boiled up. At its peak over 2000 armoured fighting vehicles on both sides were drawn into the slogging match for the high ground in the heart of Central Front's defences.

In the forefront of the drive were the Tigers of Major Sauvant's Heavy Panzer Battalion 505 whose secondment to 6th Division ended at 10.30pm on 5 July, whereupon the battalion was transferred to 2nd Panzer Division. Soborovka fell to Sauvant's Tigers on the morning of the 6th. As strong Russian armoured forces appeared between Soborovka and Ponyri, 2nd Panzer Division moved up to join Heavy Panzer Battalion 505, led by 2 Battalion 3rd Panzer Regiment, under Major von Boxberg, and followed by 1 Battalion and an assault gun battalion. From the afternoon of 6 July to the late evening of the 7th Sauvant's two Tiger companies, already depleted by heavy fighting, fought their way, yard by bloody yard, through clumps of dug-in T-34s, anti-tank guns and special squads of 'tank busters'.

By the evening of the 7th breakdowns and battle damage had blunted the offensive power of Sauvant's battalion. On the morning of the 8th it was joined by its third company which had arrived at its loading station in the small hours, disembarked and rolled straight into battle. Almost immediately the company commander's tank was knocked out and the formation left temporarily leaderless. On the 9th, Heavy Panzer Battalion 505 was withdrawn from the battle to act as corps reserve for XLVII Panzer Corps. On Model's front the Tigers had not broken through.

On 8 July, Model's armour developed three major thrusts into Rokossovsky's defences, towards Teploye, Olkhovatka and Ponyri. The way to Teploye had been cleared by 20th Panzer Division, which had fought a fierce action for the village of Samodurovka; during this action all the officers of 5th Company 112th Panzer Grenadier Regiment had been killed in the space of sixty minutes. From the positions won by 20th Panzer, Lieutenant-General D. von Saucken's 4th Panzer Division moved off against Teploye and the commanding height of Hill 272. Overhead attack formations of Ju87s circled, stepped up in echelon as they spotted their targets. On a signal from their flight leaders, the Stukas peeled away into their attack dives, sirens howling, to release their 550lb bombs on Russian artillery positions. A pall of black smoke and dust billowed up, beneath which the anti-tank batteries sat out the storm in their well-prepared gunpits. Escorting FW190 fighters buzzed protectively around the dive-bombers while Hs129s flew low and slow over the battlefield, seeking out concentrations of troops and armour.

Rokossovsky had grasped the importance of this sector and, on the night of the 7th, had inserted two rifle divisions, an artillery division, two armoured brigades and a mechanized rifle brigade. The three days of fighting which followed 4th Panzer's first assault on Teploye were to confirm Model's worst fears about the impenetrability of the Russian defence system in the Kursk salient.

The attack was opened by 2 Battalion of the 33rd Panzer Grenadier Regiment which advanced through a wall of artillery and machine-gun fire, losing 100 men in the process. The defenders of Teploye were driven out of the village but regrouped on the last crest of high ground before the hills around Teploye fell away to the open terrain below.

Saucken was determined to give the enemy no breathing space in which to organize a defence of their new position or to launch a counter-attack. His division's spearheads, 3rd and 35th Panzer Regiments, with accompanying infantry and panzer grenadiers in half-tracks, were ordered to clear the ridge. They ran straight into the Soviet 3rd Anti-Tank Artillery Brigade, commanded by Colonel V.N. Rukosuyev. The brigade was well camouflaged and supported by dug-in T-34s whose flanks were covered by infantry armed with anti-tank rifles which were effective at close range against MkIIIs and MkIVs. One battery took the brunt of what became a massed tank attack. John Erickson has described the action:

> At a little over 700 yards the Soviet anti-tank guns opened fire; in a little while, the battery was left with one gun and three men alive, who managed to knock out two more tanks. This remaining gun was destroyed along with its crew by a direct hit from a bomb, and the battery was totally wiped out. Just before noon Lieutenant Gerasimov's battery, with its remaining anti-tank gun – its shield blown away and its trail shattered – propped up on ammunition boxes and aimed by the barrel, was also pounded to pieces. The brigade commander finally signalled Rokossovsky: 'Brigade under attack by up to 300 tanks. No.1 and No.7 batteries wiped out, bringing last reserve, No.2 battery, into action. Request ammunition. I either hold on or will be wiped out. *Rukosuyev.*'

The brigade held on but was destroyed in forty-eight hours of bitter fighting. Twice the Germans took Hill 272 and twice they were thrown back by Soviet counter-attacks. The third attack, launched by 2 Battalion 33rd Panzer Grenadier Regiment and led by the battalion's last remaining officer, Captain Diesener, retook the ridge before being driven back for the last time.

At Olkhovatka 6th Division fought its way to the lower slope of Hill 274 where it was halted by a hail of fire directed from the heights. At Ponyri, the straggling village on whose outskirts lay Hill 253.5, the fighting reached an intensity which prompted the military historian Paul Carell to describe it as the 'Stalingrad of the Kursk salient'.

On the first day of the attack on Ponyri the railway embankment on the north-western edge of the village had been taken by 292nd Division. Thereafter 18th and 9th Panzer Divisions clawed their way into Ponyri where the most fiercely contested points were the tractor and railway stations, the school and the village's water tower. Panzer grenadiers captured the slopes around Hill 253.5, but failed to take the high ground stubbornly defended by 1032nd Rifle Regiment. The fighting flowed back and forth through Ponyri where the Russians held the crossroads at the centre of the village and the Germans clung to the schoolhouse.

On the night of 10–11 July, Model drew on his dwindling reserves, replacing 292nd Division (which had been reduced to a shell) with 10th Panzer Grenadier Division, commanded by Lieutenant-General August Schmidt. The Bavarian panzer grenadier division had an exceptionally powerful artillery complement: seven artillery battalions, a *Nebelwerfer* regiment, a heavy mortar battalion and an assault-gun battalion. This was sufficient to stem the series of Russian counter-attacks which began on the morning of the 11th while the panzer grenadiers were still moving into their positions. On the 12th three daylight counter-attacks were driven back by well-directed artillery fire. The forests on the slopes around Ponyri were ablaze from end to end as Stuka attacks, artillery duels and *Katyusha* and *Nebelwerfer* barrages reached a climax. A Russian cavalry charge across the front of the 110 Armoured Reconnaissance Battalion came to grief in a storm of German machine-gun fire and the kicking legs of mortally wounded horses.

The Russians failed to retake Ponyri, but Ninth Army's spear-heads were now stuck fast before Rokossovksy's last major lines of defence which they had been unable to breach by frontal assault. The downhill ride to Kursk lay agonizingly beyond the reach of Model's armour which had taken heavy punishment not only from the Russian artillery but also from the ground-attack air-craft of Sixteenth Air Army.

The Il-2m3 Shturmoviks of General V.G. Ryazanov's 1st Ground Attack Air Corps put their new 37mm cannon to good use against the armour of 18th and 9th Panzer Divisions. Roaring in line past the columns of German tanks, the Shturmoviks then swept into a huge circle overhead, diving to pour fire into the vulnerable rear of armoured vehicles where protection was at its thinnest. These high-intensity attacks could be maintained for up to twenty minutes and took a heavy toll. Soviet sources later claimed the destruction of seventy of 9th Panzer's tanks in the space of twenty minutes. However one chooses to interpret the official figures, their significance lay in the tightening grip Soviet aviation was beginning to exert over the northern sector of the salient.

On the first day of the offensive Ninth Army had advanced five miles. In the following seven days it managed only another six, and now its force was spent. The lack of armour on Model's left had prevented a breakthrough at Maloarkhangelsk and exposed Ninth Army to the full weight not only of the strategic reserve moving into the salient but also the carefully prepared counter-blow which Stavka was about to unleash.

CHAPTER 8

Prokhorovka

'The Russians manage everything, and we manage nothing at all . . . That's the last time I listen to my General Staff.' Adolf Hitler, 13 July 1943

IN THE NORTH Model's infantry and armour had been fought to a standstill. In the south the situation looked more serious for Voronezh Front. Vatutin had planned a counter-attack for dawn on the morning of the 6th. Katukov, however, had talked him out of it. The counter-attack was cancelled and, as Rokossovsky had done on Central Front, Vatutin ordered his tanks to be dug in and his anti-tank guns redeployed and camouflaged to await the onslaught of XLVIII Panzer and II SS Panzer Corps.

Over the Berezov sector on the morning of the 6th flew the Stuka ace Flight Lieutenant Hans-Ulrich Rudel. He noted: 'Below us great tank battles rage . . . a picture such as we have rarely had the chance to witness since 1941.' The sight of the Soviet armoured concentrations, dug-in T-34s and the new, long-barrelled SU-85 tank destroyers nosing their way through the sea of tall, silver-grey grass below, planted an idea in his mind. Accompanying him from the Crimea was his cannon-armed Ju87G from the Anti-Tank Experimental Unit. Rudel decided to test its effectiveness on the gallery of targets below. He discounted the risks involved:

It is true that the flak defences among the Soviet tank units are very heavy, but I say to myself that the two groups [of tanks] are facing each other at a distance of 1200 to 800 yards and unless I am brought down like a stone by a direct hit from flak* it must always be possible to crash-land the damaged aircraft in our own tank lines. The first flight therefore flies with bombs behind me in the only cannon-carrying aeroplane.

Success followed on the 7th:

In the first attack four tanks explode under the hammer blows of my cannons; by evening the total rises to twelve. We are all seized with a kind of passion for the chase from the glorious feeling of having saved much German bloodshed.

After the first day the fitters have their hands full, for the aircraft have been heavily damaged by flak. The life of such an aeroplane will always be limited. But the main thing is: the evil spell is broken, and in this aircraft we possess a weapon which can speedily be employed everywhere and is capable of dealing successfully with the formidable numbers of Soviet tanks . . . In order to secure supplies of this aircraft a signal is immediately sent to all sections of the Anti-Tank Experimental Unit, asking for all serviceable aircraft to be flown here at once with crews. So the anti-tank flight is formed. For operational purposes it is under my command.

Tactics were quickly refined. While the Ju87Gs went into the attack, some of the bomb-carrying Ju87Ds suppressed the ground defences while others circled at 'a fairly low level like a broody hen round her chickens in order to protect the anti-tank aircraft from interception by enemy fighters'.

The cannon-carrying Stukas delivered their attacks in a shallow dive which took them within fifty feet of their targets; they aimed for the most vulnerable parts of the tank, the sides and particularly the stern where the engine was protected only a by a thin layer of plating. Rudel observed, 'This is a good spot to aim at because where the engine is there is always petrol. When its

---

* In spite of losing part of one leg in February 1944, Rudel fought to the end of the war, destroying an estimated 519 tanks, eighty self-propelled guns, a battleship, a cruiser and a destroyer, seventy assault craft, 800 vehicles, four armoured trains and nine other aircraft. During a career which encompassed 2530 missions he was shot down thirty times and wounded on five occasions.

engine is running a tank is easily recognizable from the air by the blue fumes of its exhaust. On its sides the tank carries petrol and ammunition. But there the armour is stronger than at the back.'

The Russians attempted to counter this new threat by moving up anti-aircraft guns with the leading tank formations and making greater use of the smoke shells with which the T-34s were equipped to simulate tanks already on fire in the hope that the Stukas would veer off to seek new targets. This tactic did not fool their tormentors for, as Rudel points out in his autobiography, 'a tank which is really on fire will show very bright flames, and to simulate such flames is far too risky a business. In many cases the tank will blow up as the fire catches the ammunition . . .'

The Stukas spread alarm through the Russian armoured formations. Rudel noted: 'The tanks frequently carry infantry; if we are in sectors where we are already known these tank riflemen jump off, even when travelling at full speed. They all think their hour has come and that they have only a second before we are upon them. And Ivan prefers to meet the attack on *terra firma*.'

Below Rudel, on the *terra firma* to which the Russian infantry-man clung with such tenacity, XLVIII and II SS Panzer Corps were grinding their way into Sixth Guards Army's main defensive field. On the 6th, XLVIII Corps made no progress as it struggled to cross the swollen stream between Alekseyevka and Sertsev. Russian tanks and guns which had moved forward into the ruined villages on the opposite side now poured direct fire on to the Corps's armoured formations and engineers as the latter struggled under an erratic smokescreen to lay their bridging equipment.

On Hausser's front, while Leibstandarte and Das Reich blasted their way forward a yard at a time, Totenkopf, on II SS Panzer Corps's right, shook free of the Soviet flank defences and advanced twenty miles to the north. By dusk on the 6th, Totenkopf had crossed and cut the Belgorod–Oboyan highway and had halt-ed for the night astride the Belgorod–Kursk railway.

That morning Das Reich's Der Führer Regiment, wading through knee-high mud, had passed through the positions held by Deutschland Regiment to attack Hill 243. Heavy defensive fire threw back Der Führer's 1 and 2 Battalions, but late in the morning the divisional artillery and heavy weapons were concentrated on

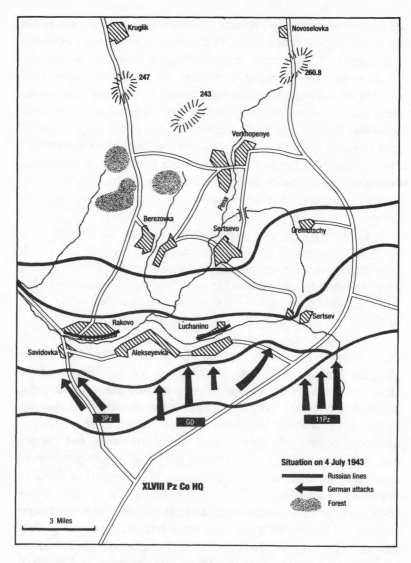

Mud and a swollen stream held up XLVIII Panzer Corps' advance between 5 and 7 July before the defenders fell back on Sertsevo the high ground and the panzer grenadiers were 'lifted' on to their objective. The capture of Hill 243 cleared the road to Luchki, and armour was brought up to move through the breach and on to Prokhorovka. The Russians threw in repeated air attacks and renewed artillery fire to hold up the advance while reinforcements were rushed forward to plug the gap beginning to open between Sixth Guards and Sixty-Ninth Armies.

German self-propelled guns attracted special attention from the Shturmoviks of Second Air Army, as Heid Ruehl, an artilleryman serving with Das Reich's assault-gun detachment, recalled:

> While a small wound was being dressed at the Regimental Aid Post, Russian aircraft attacked our battery and cost us 108 casualties, including the Company Commander . . . I had a slight collision with a Tiger which damaged my own vehicle. I went back to 'B' Echelon to collect a replacement machine and arrived there just at the start of another air raid. Once again I was slightly wounded – this time in the back. Some sort of liquid with a high alcoholic content was poured on, a sticking plaster applied and I returned to the battery to find more of my comrades had been killed in the time that I had been away.

On the evening of the 6th, Vatutin reported by telephone to Stalin who had already ordered the movement of Twenty-Seventh Army to the south of the salient. Vatutin emphasized the scale of the fighting, estimating that, 'as a result of the day's fierce engagement, 332 enemy tanks* and eighty aircraft had been destroyed, large numbers of officers and men killed. In the sector of Seventh Guards alone twelve attacks were beaten off and more than 10,000 enemy troops killed.'

Stalin agreed to Vatutin's urgent request for more reinforcements but insisted that the enemy must be held on the prepared lines 'until the moment was ripe for the launching of the counter-blows on the Western, Bryansk and other fronts'. The mounting pressure was beginning to tell on Stavka. Vasilevsky, coordinating operations on the southern front with Zhukov, proposed moving 2nd and 10th Tank Corps up to the Prokhorovka area while

---

* Between 6 and 7 July Fourth Panzer Army's tank strength declined from 865 vehicles to 621.

simultaneously placing 5th Guards and Fifth Guards Tank Armies under Stavka control. Fifth Guards Tank Army was to be ordered to move from Ostrogorzhsk to Stary Oskol, fifty miles north-east of Prokhorovka.

This produced a strong protest from Steppe Front's commander, Konev, who was alarmed at the proposed piecemeal dismemberment of the strategic reserve. But his argument that Steppe Front should retain its integrity, and be committed as a whole in the defensive battle, was rejected by Stavka. Never-the-less, two days later Steppe Front was aligned on the Belgorod–Kharkov axis.

On 6 July Konev had flown to Rotmistrov's headquarters to brief him on the combat situation and to deliver the news of Fifth Guards Tank Army's attachment to Voronezh Front. 'Concentrate here as soon as possible,' said Konev, marking an area west of Stary Oskol on the map in red pencil.

About an hour after Konev had left, Stalin telephoned Rotmistrov and asked him about his deployment plans, suggesting that his tanks might not 'survive such a long trek and would be better taken by rail'. Rotmistrov demurred, arguing that the Luftwaffe would almost certainly attack the train and the railway bridges along its route. Moreover, given the gravity of the situation rapidly developing on the southern front, it would take too long to reassemble the Army on arrival. Nor would it be practical to transport the infantry alone to the combat area, as they might immediately be confronted with enemy tank formations. Stalin then asked Rotmistrov if he planned to move only by night. 'No,' replied Rotmistrov, 'there are only six hours of darkness and we would have to hide the tanks in forests by day and bring them out at nightfall, and there are too few forests en route.'

Rotmistrov then asked Stalin for permission to move by day and night. Stalin protested that the Luftwaffe would pose too much of a threat during the day. Rotmistrov coolly conceded that this was indeed possible, and asked for air cover. Stalin agreed to his request, instructed him to inform Vatutin and Rokossovsky the moment he moved off, wished him luck and then rang off.

It was Rotmistrov's birthday, and that evening he had intended to hold a dinner party for his corps commanders. When they

arrived at his headquarters, they found dinner cancelled and
Rotmistrov awaiting them by a map, ready to give advance marching orders. After the briefing, champagne captured from the
Germans was served and Rotmistrov toasted by his corps commanders before they left for their units. Within an hour, following
further orders from Vatutin and Stavka, Rotmistrov had completed
the assignments for his corps and army units and the redeployment was about to begin.

At 1.30am on 7 July Fifth Guards Tank Army moved off on the
200-mile journey to the front line. Rotmistrov's two tank corps,
29th and 18th, made up the first echelon with 5th Mechanized
Corps in the second echelon. To control the Army on the move
and, if necessary, to deliver an armoured strike while on the
march, Rotmistrov's headquarters accompanied the first echelon.
As dawn broke fighter escorts from Second Air Army appeared
overhead. Konev later told Rotmistrov that he had been aloft early that morning, watching the Army's progress.

One of the more vivid stylists among senior commanders of the
Second World War, Rotmistrov later described the first day of the
march:

> It grew hot as early as 0800hrs and clouds of dust billowed up.
> By midday the dust rose in thick clouds, settling in a solid lay-
> er on roadside bushes, grain fields, tanks and trucks. The dark
> red disc of the sun was hardly visible through the grey shroud
> of dust. Tanks, self-propelled guns and tractors (which towed
> the artillery), armoured personnel carriers and trucks were
> advancing in an unending flow. The faces of the soldiers were
> darkened with dust and exhaust fumes. It was intolerably hot.
> Soldiers were tortured by thirst and their shirts, wet with
> sweat, stuck to their bodies. Drivers found the going particu-
> larly hard. The crew members tried in every way to make it
> easier for them by taking their place at the controls every now
> and then and letting them rest during brief halts. The hard-
> ships had to be endured as time was running short.

During the night of 6–7 July the temperature had dropped on
the Southern Front. Fighting flared in the dank mist which filled
the dips and hollows in the battlefield. With daylight came a
renewed effort from XLVIII and II SS Panzer Corps which threat-

ened to cut clean through Vatutin's defences. Having regrouped in the night, XLVIII Corps finally forced its way across the creek-bed which had held it up for two days but had now dried sufficiently to allow the passage of armour. Grossdeutschland broke through on both sides of the village of Sertsev, pushing its defenders back into Sertsevo and Gremutschy.

Retreating in disorder, the remnants of Sixth Guards Army on Krivoshein's front were caught by accurate German artillery fire and suffered heavy casualties. Grossdeutschland's armour and elements of 11th Panzer Division now wheeled north-west towards Sertsevo, the last major Soviet defensive position before Oboyan, where they were halted by strong defensive artillery fire and a determined counter-attack by 3rd Mechanized and 6th Tank Corps.

The situation seemed more promising on XLVIII Panzer Corps's right wing where some of Grossdeutschland's panzer grenadiers were reported to have fought their way five miles north to take Verkhopenye. Immediately a battle group was formed to exploit this apparent success. Consisting of the division's armoured reconnaissance and assault-gun detachments, it was ordered to advance as far as Hill 260.8, south of Novoselovka. When the battle group arrived in Gremutschy, however, it found the panzer grenadiers there, convinced that they were in Novoselovka. As von Mellenthin later dryly observed, 'Thus the report of the so-called success of the grenadiers was proved wrong; things like that happen in every war and particularly in Russia.'

As night fell on the 7th a hill north of Gremutschy was captured after a stiff fight and the panzer regiment shot Russian tanks off Hill 230.1. By the end of the day 11th Panzer Division had drawn up level with the forward elements of Grossdeutschland, securing its right flank. 3rd Panzer Division's slow progress towards Berezovka, however, meant that Grossdeutschland's left flank was dangerously exposed. Darkness fell on troops exhausted by the day's fighting. Panzer grenadiers slept where they dropped while tank crews, numbed by noise, dehydrated by heat and half-poisoned by fumes, fell into a deep sleep by their machines, undisturbed by the clatter of maintenance and servicing crews working through the night.

On Hausser's attack frontage his three SS Divisions had made deeper penetrations than had been achieved by von Knobelsdorff's corps. On 7 July Leibstandarte's immediate objective had been Teterevino. In the forefront of the fighting, once again, was Michael Wittmann who claimed seven more T-34s and nineteen guns of the Soviet 29th Anti-Tank Artillery Brigade. Racing through the gap in the Russian line punched by Wittmann's Tigers, a Leibstandarte motorcycle company captured intact a Russian brigade headquarters as the panzers and supporting grenadiers pressed on to Psyolknee. Here the Soviet 3rd Mechanized Corps launched a fierce counter-attack, the main weight of which fell on a single Tiger of 1st Panzer Regiment's 13th Company commanded by Lieutenant Staudegger who, in a two-hour battle, claimed over twenty T-34s destroyed.

While Totenkopf covered II SS Panzer Corps's right flank, Leibstandarte and Das Reich chopped their way forward against tough resistance. Each division was carving a hole in the Russian defences without being able to push the enemy back along a continuous front. Thus, although their advance left in its wake a colossal junkyard of mangled Russian armour and heavy weapons, they came under continuous enfilade fire. Nevertheless, as SS field police herded thousands of dazed Russian prisoners to the rear, it seemed as if II SS Panzer Corps was on the brink of achieving the breakthrough which would roll up the Southern Front of the Kursk salient.

Throughout the day fresh Soviet units were fed in to stem the tide of the German advance. To cover Sertsevo, now threatened by XLVIII Panzer Corps, Katukov and Chistyakov moved in tank and artillery reinforcements and 67th Guards Rifle Division. First Tank Army was holding on by its fingernails as the front covering the road to Oboyan fell apart. Vatutin was now contemplating a flank attack delivered towards Tomarovka by Colonel-General Moskalenko's Fortieth Army.

As midnight approached on the 7th orders were issued to Moskalenko but, in the small hours, he received revised instructions to transfer most of his armour and artillery to bolster Sixth Guards and First Tank Armies. On the morning of the 8th Fortieth Army was able to initiate no more than a 'demonstration attack'.

Of greater concern at the headquarters of Fourth Panzer Army was the failure of Army Detachment Kempf to make significant progress against the Russian defences east of the Donets. On Fourth Panzer Army's right flank, north of Belgorod, stretched a belt of woodland which Kempf's divisions had not cleared. It remained the object of constant aerial reconnaissance. Near Gostishchevo, in the slot north-east of Belgorod, a combat group of the Soviet 2nd Tank Corps was lagered in part of these woodlands. Vatutin now ordered it to move westward to strike II SS Panzer Corps in the flank and relieve the mounting pressure which the Corps was exerting in the Greznoye sector on the junction of 3rd Mechanized and 31st Tank Corps. If Hoth broke through here, his armour could cross the River Psel to roll up the rear of First Tank Army and seal the fate of Voronezh Front.

As the morning mist cleared, sixty T-34s and their supporting infantry emerged from the wood and moved west against Hausser's deep flank, aiming to cut the Belgorod–Oboyan highway and II SS Panzer Corps's supply route. The tanks rumbled forward in a huge wedge preceded by dense blocks of infantry, like a medieval army on the march. Their progress did not go unobserved. The sector was being reconnoitred at low level by a section of Hs129B aircraft of IV/SchG9, based at Mikoyanovka. The unit had been posted to VIII Fliegerkorps straight from a gun test in Germany, just in time for Zitadelle.

Leading the patrol was the Gruppenkommandeur, Flight Lieutenant Bruno Meyer, who immediately used his radio to alert Mikoyanovka to the danger of a Russian flank attack in brigade strength. The Gruppe's four *staffeln* – each sixteen aircraft strong – took off in rotation and the first arrived over the Russian armour within fifteen minutes. Flying on the deck, the Hs129s attacked from astern and abeam while Meyer circled overhead directing operations. Their tungsten-cored 30mm cannon shells bit into the thin armour at the rear of the Russian tanks as the wedge broke up in confusion and T-34s careered wildly over the landscape. Within a few minutes six tanks were ablaze. While the Hs129s dealt with the armour, ground-attack FW190Fs led by Major Alfred Druschel, swept in to shower the infantry and mobile anti-aircraft units with SD-1 and SD-2 fragmentation bombs. In

the space of an hour some fifty T-34s were knocked out and the
threat to Hausser's flank removed even as the first requests were
being made to VIII Fliegerkorps for air support.

To the north-west 31st Tank Corps held out. Nikita Khrushchev,
installed in an artillery observation post at the advanced headquarters of Katukov's First Tank Army, had got a grip on the situation, despatching General Popel and two commissars to rally
Lieutenant-General Cherniyenkov's Corps. Arriving in the combat
zone, Popel intervened to prevent a headlong retreat and ordered
withdrawing units back into action. Joining Cherniyenkov in the
front line, he ordered 29th Anti-Tank Brigade to cover a withdrawal to a hastily prepared defence line. The rot had been
stopped, but II SS Panzer Corps was still squeezing hard on
Katukov's jugular.

Throughout the battle Das Reich's Der Führer Regiment had
been using a special task force of six Hiwi interpreters to listen
in to Russian radio traffic. On the afternoon of the 8th they picked
up a furious row between staff officers of First Tank Army and
31st Tank Corps over the bringing up of reserves. Panic seemed
to be setting in and Der Führer seized the opportunity to send
1 Battalion's 3rd Company, under Captain Lex, through a gap in the
front to surprise and capture a Soviet rifle brigade general, his staff
and headquarters company in their well-fortified command post.

On the morning of the 8th, in scorching heat, Grossdeutschland's battle group pushed up the road to Oboyan to reach Hill
260.8 before wheeling west to cover the advance of the divisional
panzer regiment and panzer grenadiers, who were bypassing the
straggling and strongly held village of Verkhopenye on the east.

While Grossdeutschland's rifle regiment attacked Verkhopenye
from the south, the divisional panzer regiment and panzer
grenadiers assaulted Hill 243 immediately to the north of the
village. This position was held by a strong force of Russian tanks
and commanded a superb field of fire. Heavy fighting continued
throughout the day but, when night fell, Hill 243 and the western
outskirts of Verkhopenye remained in Russian hands.

Russian tanks seemed to swarm everywhere that afternoon,
allowing Grossdeutschland's battle group no respite. The assault-
gun battalion, commanded by Major Frantz, threw back seven

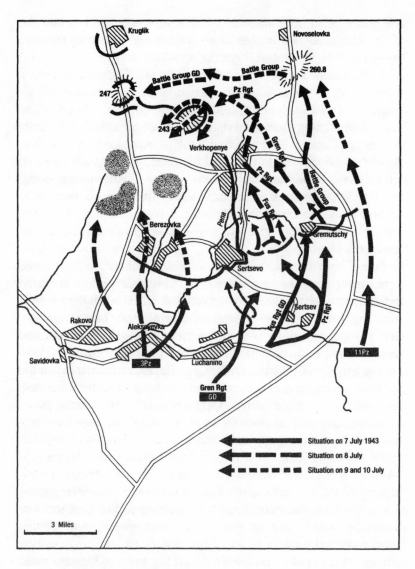

Between 5 and 10 July XLVIII Panzer Corps punched a rectangular hole in the Russian lines without breaking through successive tank attacks. Intercepted Soviet wireless traffic indicated that the T-34s had orders to breach the German front regardless of cost. At the end of the day thirty-five wrecked T-34s lay in front of the assault-gun battalion's lines.

On 8 July Totenkopf had been tied down, waiting for 167th Division to relieve it on the right flank of II SS Panzer Corps. Marching east across the German supply columns, 167th arrived on the evening of the 8th and took up positions along the Belgorod–Kursk railway line. Behind them, on the high ground north of Luchki, were observers of the 238th Artillery Regiment, directing fire on repeated 'human wave' attacks launched on a front of barely 500 yards by Soviet infantry formations. The Corps's flank defence held, enabling Hausser to push his mechanized battalions northwards towards the Psel river along the line of contact between Leibstandarte and Das Reich.

On the 9th the weary assault groups of Leibstandarte, Das Reich and Totenkopf fought their way through the maze of machine-gun nests, bunkers and trenches in the last Soviet defence line. On the 10th resistance began to crumble and during the afternoon 3 Battalion of Totenkopf's 1st Panzer Grenadier Regiment, led from the front by Colonel Karl Ullrich, cleared the last Russian strongpoints in its sector and forded the Psel, the only natural barrier standing between Fourth Panzer Army and Kursk. After an agonizing wait for heavy bridging equipment to be brought up, Ullrich's panzer grenadiers established a bridgehead on the north bank of the Psel, storming the villages of Vasilyevka, Koslovka and Krasny Oktobar which they held against strong Soviet armoured and infantry counter-attacks. Having made the northernmost penetration on the southern front, Totenkopf was well placed to wheel left and strike at the rear of First Tank Army. South of the Psel, Leibstandarte and Das Reich slogged forward, through heavy rain and clinging mud, on both sides of the railway line and road leading to Prokhorovka.

In Fourth Panzer Army's battle plan XLVIII Panzer Corps was to strike north across the Psel and then turn eastward, with II SS Panzer Corps, to occupy the land-bridge at Prokhorovka before Stavka's massive armoured reserve poured across it to slam into Hausser's right flank. But in its progress north von Knobelsdorff's

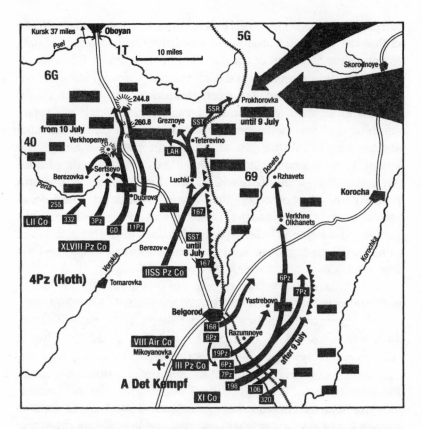

Fourth Panzer Army's drive on Prokhorovka, the speed of which was not matched by Army Detachment Kempf on its right flank

Corps had been forced to fight every inch of the way. On 9 July Soviet counter-attacks on the Corps's northern front had forced it on to the back foot in a series of bitter defensive engagements. On the Corps's left 3rd Panzer Division, attacking in the Pena bend, advanced up the Rakovo–Kruglik road towards Berezovka – cleared by its tanks on the evening of the 9th.

This success was exploited by 332nd Division, the bulk of which crossed the Pena to seize an area extending the southern edge of Melovoye, driving the main body of Russian forces in the sector northwards where it regrouped and continued to offer stiff resistance. On the 10th, while the Corps's engineers laboured to throw a 60-ton bridge across the Pena, the 'mopping-up' operations north of the river led to heavy German casualties as a large force of Russian tanks, stranded in the withdrawal by a shortage of fuel, fought to the last man.

After a week of heavy and almost continuous fighting Grossdeutschland was showing signs of exhaustion. On the 10th, far from driving north, the Division was ordered to wheel to the south and south-west to clean up the enemy on XLVIII Panzer Corps's left flank and then move south to assist 3rd Panzer which was held up by strong Russian forces in a forested area north of Berezovka. Supported by Stukas, Grossdeutschland accomplished the first part of its mission, clearing Hills 243 and 247, forcing their defenders to join the troops bottled up by 3rd Panzer in the Berezovka pocket. The war diary of the Division's reconnaissance battalion noted the effectiveness of the air support provided by VIII Fliegerkorps:

> With admiration we watch the Stukas attacking the Russian tanks uninterruptedly and with wonderful precision. Squadron after squadron of Stukas come over to drop their deadly eggs on the Russian armour. Dazzling white flames indicate that another enemy tank has 'brewed up'. This happens again and again.

Nevertheless, Grossdeutschland was stretched to the limit to complete the clearing of the Pena bend and throw back the storm of counter-attacks beating on its northern front. In his report on 10 July, von Knobelsdorff expressed doubts about his Corps's ability to accomplish its objectives with the forces he had at his disposal. Accordingly, Hoth took a calculated risk on his left flank, extending the sector of LII Corps's 52nd Division to move 225th Division over to take on the covering role performed by 332nd Division, the remainder of which was now free to cross the Pena and move up to support 3rd Panzer to the north. The relatively enfeebled state of Soviet Fortieth Army ensured that Hoth's gamble paid off, albeit only temporarily.

The Waffen-SS was now no more than twelve miles from Oboyan, the lynchpin of the Russian defences on the southern sector of the Kursk salient. By massing the tanks of his elite armoured divisions on a five-mile front to the west of Prokhorovka, Hoth

intended to smash the Soviet defences to the south and join hands
with Army Detachment Kempf which was now forcing its way
north and north-east through a corridor bounded on the west by
81st Guards Rifle, 375th Rifle and 51st Guards Rifle Divisions
(which, with 2nd Guards Tank Corps, also provided a cordon
against any eastern advance by II SS Panzer Corps) and, on the
east, by 73rd and 94th Guards Rifle Divisions and 305th Rifle
Division of Seventh Guards Army. Having switched 6th Panzer
from his left wing to his right, Kempf was now making faster northward progress. As the battle neared its climax, he was to be cast in
the role of Marshal Grouchy at Waterloo. Kempf was marching
rather more resolutely towards the sound of guns than the unfortunate Grouchy, but would he arrive in time?

Success at Prokhorovka would ensure the encirclement and
destruction of the two main Soviet groupings in the southern half
of the salient and open a new road to Kursk, bypassing the strong-
hold at Oboyan to the east. On the evening of the 10th the fresh
XXIV Panzer Corps, comprising SS Viking Panzer Grenadier and
17th Panzer Divisions, was moving up from the Donbas with
orders to strike north from Belgorod. Meanwhile, Rokossovsky
and Vatutin were submitting hourly reports to Stalin as both sides
regrouped, moving blocks of armour and artillery around the
critical sectors of the battlefield like so many giant chess pieces.

The most important Soviet piece of all, Fifth Guards Tank Army,
had arrived south-west of Stary Oskol on the morning of the 8th.
The rest of the day was spent bringing up the rearguard troops
and deploying units in their concentration areas. Only a small
number of tanks had dropped out of the strenuous march with
engine failure, and they were quickly repaired and returned to
their units. In the small hours of the 9th Rotmistrov received
orders to concentrate Fifth Guards Tank Army north-east of
Prokhorovka where it was to join General A.S. Zhadov's Fifth
Guards Army, another component of Steppe Front, under the control of Voronezh Front. Fifth Guards Army was to move up to the
Psel river, occupying a frontage of twenty miles running east from
Oboyan to Prokhorovka. It was to be at full combat readiness by
the morning of the 11th.

On Zhadov's left Rotmistrov, reinforced by 2nd Tank and 2nd

Guards Tank Corps, was deploying on a front of ten miles around Prokhorovka, facing the head of the ominous bulge which was swelling in the direction of Stary Oskol. Rotmistrov made a rapid survey of the theatre of operations:

> Since we were to join battle with a strong enemy tank group which, according to our intelligence, had about 700 tanks, including over 100 Tigers and Ferdinands and self-propelled guns, we decided to deploy all the four tank corps in the first echelon. The second echelon was made up of the 5th Guards Mechanized Corps, and troops of the leading units and anti-tank artillery regiments were left in reserve under the command of my deputy, General K. Trufanov.

As a back-stop, Stavka ordered Twenty-Fourth Army and 4th Guards Tank Corps to move to Kursk while 4th Mechanized Corps was positioned on the south-eastern approaches to the city.

Fourth Panzer Army continued to pose a threat to Oboyan but it was clear to Stavka that the main blow would fall at Prokhorovka. Hoth's command, however, had been seriously weakened by the fighting which preceded the climax to the battle. Fourth Panzer Army had begun Zitadelle with an operational armoured strength of 916 mission-capable vehicles, but Russian minefields, anti-tank guns and the mechanical failures which always accompany high-intensity operations after a period of inactivity, had bitten into its offensive power.

The Army's daily tank and assault-guns returns reveal the process of attrition. By 8 July the Army's armoured strength had fallen to 626 vehicles, most losses being caused by Russian minefields; it reached a low of 501 on the 9th, a loss of 415 vehicles. It crept up to 530 on the 11th when most of the mechanical problems had been ironed out (with the exception of those plaguing the Panthers) and the thickest belts of minefields had been traversed. Thereafter it remained relatively stable. II SS Panzer Corps's armoured strength had fallen from approximately 470 vehicles at the beginning of Zitadelle to some 300 on 11 July, a figure significantly lower than Soviet intelligence estimates of the force bearing down on Fifth Guards Tank Army at Prokhorovka.

By dawn on Sunday, 11 July, Army Group South had completed

its regrouping and the offensive ground on. East of the Donets, Kempf jumped off with 6th, 7th and 19th Panzer Divisions, supported by three infantry divisions. To the north-west XLVIII Panzer Corps renewed its drive on Oboyan and, at 9.30am, II SS Panzer Corps began to slog its way towards Prokhorovka. The weather was foul, gusting winds and lashing rain making the going extremely heavy. Huge air battles raged overhead. By late afternoon a powerful German force was approaching Prokhorovka while, at Storozhevoe to the south-west, more tanks threatened to break through into the rear of Fifth Guards Tank Army.

In the early hours of the 11th Vasilevsky who, along with Zhukov, was now coordinating operations on the southern front, arrived at Rotmistrov's command post for a briefing and a tour of the tank corps's deployment areas. Soon their jeep was lurching over rain-filled potholes as it passed through Prokhorovka, overtaking long lines of ammunition trucks and fuel bowsers moving slowly up to the front. Outside the village the road wound mazily through a sea of yellow wheatfields, beyond which stretched a forest with a village on its fringe. Rotmistrov explained to Vasilevsky that it was here, on the northern edge of the forests, that 29th and 18th Tank Corps had taken up their positions.

Vasilevksy ordered the jeep to stop and walked a little way down the road, his eyes sweeping the horizon where shell bursts and thick columns of smoke marked the front line. He pointed out to Rotmistrov lines of tanks crawling over the plain below them. Raising his binoculars to his eyes, the commander of Fifth Guards Tank Army saw at once that the armour was not his own, as Vasilevsky had surmised, but elements of II SS Panzer Corps. Another breakthrough loomed. Rotmistrov immediately radioed General Kirichenko, the commander of 29th Tank Corps, and ordered him to advance to meet this new threat.

Rotmistrov hurried back to his command post to revise his plans. The positions from which he had intended to launch his counter-attack on the 12th were now in German hands. Amid a cacophany of constantly jangling telephones, orders were revised, updated and then revised again. The original choice of gun emplacements, the schedules for artillery preparation and the provisions for troop control were torn up and reworked while

General V. Baskakov, Rotmistrov's Chief of Staff, 'his face taut with fatigue and his eyes red from lack of sleep, made regular reports on the latest developments'.

Within a few hours Rotmistrov had recast his order of battle and had signed and despatched an operational report confirming that Fifth Guards Tank Army was now in position and ready to begin the counter-offensive. Then, at 4.00am, he received orders from Vatutin to despatch his reserves to the combat zone of Sixty-Ninth Army which was struggling to stem Army Detachment Kempf's northward drive.

On the night of 11 July elements of 6th Panzer Division penetrated to Kazachye, eight miles south of the northern reaches of the Donets. If Sixty-Ninth Army's front gave way, Kempf could cross the river barrier to take Fifth Guards Tank Army in the left flank and rear, and roll up the entire left flank of Voronezh Front. Blocking Kempf's advance to the Donets was the strongly fortified town of Rzhavets with its bridge over the river. That night Rzhavets was seized in a remarkable *coup de main* devised and led by Major Franz Bäke of the reinforced 11th Panzer Regiment, 6th Panzer Division.

Divisional orders for the 12th were to force a crossing of the Donets at Rzhavets after an artillery bombardment, a conventional but potentially costly operation. After a lively discussion with his combat group leader, Colonel von Oppeln-Bronikowski, Bäke secured permission to seize the bridge over the Donets under cover of darkness, using a small task force comprising 2 Battalion 11th Panzer Regiment and 2 (Armoured) Battalion, 114th Panzer Grenadier Regiment.

At the head of Bäke's armoured column was a Trojan Horse, a captured T-34 on which a suitably small German cross had been painted. The column moved off with the panzer grenadiers' armoured personnel carriers sandwiched between tanks at the front and command vehicles at the rear. Radio silence was to be observed and fire was not to be opened on the enemy. Bäke's men were instructed to ride on top of their tanks, relaxed and smoking, to allay the suspicions of any Russian units which might cross their path. There was to be no talking in German.

The phantom column rumbled through the darkness, deep into

the Russian lines, passing thickets of artillery positions whose occupants paid them no attention. Columns of tanks had been rolling by all day. The Germans even overtook an infantry column without incident and without any of the Russian soldiers hitching a ride. Later, Bäke recalled:

> After about six miles our T-34 went on strike. Moved no doubt by national sentiment, it stopped and blocked the road. So our men had to climb out of their tanks and, in spite of the Russians standing all around them watching curiously, they had to haul the T-34 off the road and push it into the ditch in order to clear the way for the rest of the formation. In spite of the order that not a word of German was to be spoken, a few German curses were heard. Never before had I winced so much under a curse as at Rzhavets. But the Russians still did not notice anything. The crew of our T-34 was picked up, and on we moved.

On the outskirts of Rzhavets, Bäke's task force passed a Russian tank unit, their hatches open and crews stretching out on the grass. However, their luck was about to run out. Motoring towards them was a line of twenty-two T-34s. The Russian tanks clattered by, seemingly as incurious as all the other formations past which Bäke's phantom force had glided. Then Bäke, at the rear of the column in his command vehicle, saw several of the T-34s turn round and start to follow him. He halted, blocking the road, and ordered the rest of his force to drive on. Bäke was defenceless as his command vehicle boasted only a wooden dummy gun. The T-34s milled around him like large and not very bright animals unsure of how to deal with an unexpected newcomer to the herd. Behind Bäke one of his armoured personnel carriers waited, ready to open fire in what threatened to be a one-sided battle.

While the Soviet tank commanders dithered, Bäke and his orderly, Lieutenant Zumpel, jumped from the command vehicle and attached explosive charges to two of the T-34s. Only then did the infantry sitting on top of the enemy tanks show any sign of animation. Before they could open fire Bäke threw himself into the ditch by the side of the road, finding himself chest-deep in brackish water. Two muffled explosions signalled the destruction of the two T-34s to which Bäke and Zumpel had attached their 'sticky bombs'. In the confusion which followed Bäke managed to destroy a third enemy tank before all hell broke loose as one of his own tanks returned to shoot up a fourth. Flares shot into the sky and machine-gun fire opened up on all sides.

Bäke's column raced into Rzhavets, overrunning anti-tank positions and capturing a *Katyusha* battery. But a wrong turning in the village denied them the bridge. They arrived at the river moments after it had been blown by Russian engineers. Nevertheless, the panzer grenadiers were quickly across to the northern bank after finding a nearby footbridge which the Russians had neglected to destroy. The confusion which Bäke's task force had sown among the defenders of Rzhavets enabled them to form a bridgehead and, as dawn came up, German forces were firmly entrenched on the northern bank of the Donets. The divisional commander, General Walter Hünersdorff, immediately fed across 1 Battalion 114th Panzer Grenadier Regiment and, by late afternoon on 12 July, it had been joined by 19th Panzer Division's Battle Group Horst.

Success was quickly followed by self-inflicted disaster. The Luftwaffe had not been informed of the bridgehead at Rzhavets and, on the 12th, it came under attack from a formation of Heinkel He111 medium bombers which mistook the Germans on the north bank for an enemy armoured formation. When the bombs began to fall, General von Hünersdorff was holding a conference by his command vehicle with staff officers and unit commanders. Fifteen were killed and forty-nine wounded, including Colonel von Oppeln-Bronikowski and Hünersdorff himself.

Hünersdorff stayed with his division, hurrying six miles to the east where the bulk of 6th Panzer was tied down in a fight for the high ground around the village of Aleksandrovka on his right flank. While its defenders held out, they posed a threat to the expanding bridgehead at Rzhavets. It was not until the 13th that the Russian defence zone between the Donets and Korocha was overcome, leaving Army Detachment Kempf free to resume its advance to Prokhorovka.

The panzers were not accompanied by the forty-five-year-old von Hünersdorff. On 14 July, while returning to his advanced headquarters after inspecting the bridgehead, he was shot in the head by a Russian sniper. Hünersdorff was taken to the military hospital at Kharkov where surgery failed to remove the bullet fragments in his brain. He died on the 17th without regaining consciousness, tended to the end by his wife who was in charge of the forward forces' convalescent centre of the German Red Cross. Had von Hünersdorff woken from his coma he would have learnt that the offensive – about which he had so robustly expressed his doubts – had failed.

By the late afternoon of 11 July, II SS Panzer Corps's thrusts had been halted and it spent the rest of the day stabbing all around Prokhorovka, mopping up resistance and regrouping to deliver what was confidently expected to be the knockout blow to Voronezh Front on the 12th. German intelligence had not picked up the arrival of Fifth Guards Tank Army and its 850 tanks* and assault guns. That night the Chief of Staff of Fourth Panzer Army wrote in his journal that, in spite of continued enemy resistance, it appeared that only weak forces were located to the deep east flank of the Army. Strong enemy forces had been identified north-east of Prokhorovka, but he nevertheless anticipated that the attack front to the east would be widened on the morrow and the Russians thrown back over the Psel towards Oboyan.

Not everything, however, was going according to plan. On the night of the 11th, Grossdeutschland had been relieved by 3rd Panzer Division and reassembled astride the road south of Hill 260.8 with orders to stand by for a renewed offensive to the north. Von Mellenthin recalled that the panzer grenadiers 'moved off with a sense of uneasiness'. The last stages of the relief were carried out under heavy shelling and the men of Grossdeutschland left their trenches to the accompaniment of the battle noises of a Russian counter-attack. Their fears were well founded; that night 3rd Panzer was thrown out of its forward positions.

At 6.00am on 12 July Rotmistrov arrived with a group of officers at the command post of 29th Tank Corps, sited on a hill south-west of Prokhorovka. It was an excellent choice as an observation post from which to fight the day's battle, commanding a panoramic

---

* Among Fifth Guards Tank Army's tanks were thirty-five British A22 Churchills, a model universally unpopular with Soviet crews.

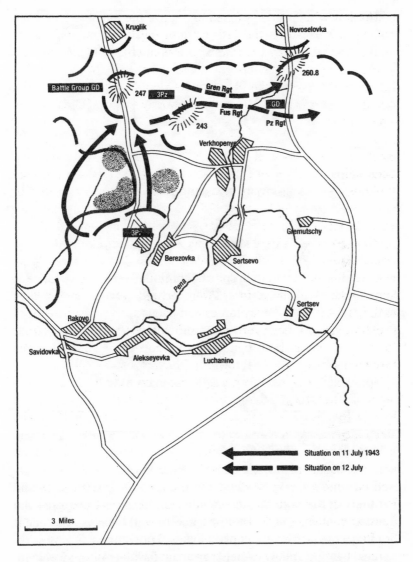

By 12 July heavy fighting had sapped Grossdeutschland Division's offensive power as it strove to contain Soviet counter-attacks

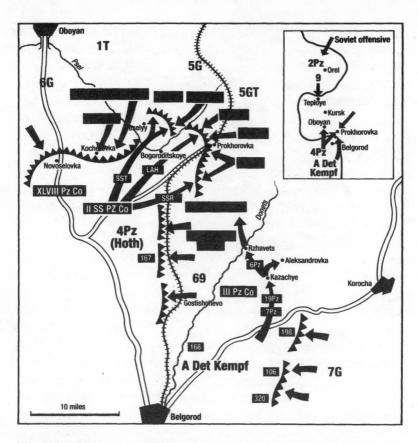

The clash at Prokhorovka, the huge 'armoured brawl' which brought II SS Panzer
Corps to a halt and sealed the fate of Zitadelle

view of the plain below. Rotmistrov settled down in a dug-out in an
orchard whose severed and scorched trees bore testimony to the
proximity of the front line. Below the command post stretched an
undulating plain, golden with wheatfields in the rays of the early
morning sun, dotted with copses and cultivated plots and cut with
ravines. Beyond the wheatfields ran the dark line of the forest in
which II SS Panzer Corps's armour was lagered. Concealed in the
corn around it were the anti-tank guns and tank destroyers of Fifth
Guards Tank Army.

The sun quickly gave way to thundery clouds and sudden
bursts of heavy rain. The tense silence which hung over
Rotmistrov's observation post was broken at intervals by the

voices of the telephone and radio operators in trenches around the dug-out and in a neighbouring ravine which sheltered the despatch riders' motorcycles.

At 6.30am the arrival of German fighters overhead indicated the imminence of an air raid. Soon Stukas were plunging down on the villages and woodlands which harboured Russian positions. Smoke and flames rose from the copses and settlements beneath Rotmistrov's command post. Fire raced through the wheatfields while Yak-9s and La-5s of Second Air Army drove off the Stukas. As they straggled back to their bases the air was filled with a steady roar as waves of Soviet bombers and their fighter escorts, maintaining rigid formation, flew over to the south-west. This was the signal for the Russian artillery to open up. The time was 8.30am. Rotmistrov later wrote: 'Most of the fire was directed at the areas where we believed the enemy's tanks and artillery were emplaced. We had no time to locate precisely where the enemy batteries and tank concentrations were and it seemed impossible to determine the effectiveness of their artillery fire.'

When the barrage reached a climax, the guns were joined by the Guards *Katyusha* regiments. With rockets screeching off their launchers in huge ripples of flame, the tanks of 29th and 18th Corps left cover and advanced to meet II SS Panzer Corps whose armour was emerging from its lagers to launch a simultaneous attack. The scene was set for a head-on collision of armour which has become one of the great myths of military history.

The battlefield below Rotmistrov was compressed into an area of roughly three square miles, bordered on the north by the Psel and on the south by the railway embankment at Belenichino. From the moment the leading elements of Soviet armour crashed through II SS Panzer Corps's first echelon, the commanders on both sides lost all control of their formations and the battle became a confused free-for-all in which every tank and its crew fought individually amid a packed mass of armour, like knights on a fifteenth-century battlefield. In this colossal melée, fought at practically point-blank range, the Tigers lost all the advantages of armour and armament which they enjoyed over the T-34s at longer range. Nor could their crews exert the greater cohesion and tactical flexibility which time and again had been made to tell against heavy odds. In the swirling, dust-shrouded maelstrom into which both sides had careered even the light Soviet T-70s had a chance to inflict damage on the enemy.

From the smoke and dust which enveloped the battlefield spurted huge flashes of flame as ammunition exploded aboard stricken tanks, sending their turrets wheeling through the air as they separated from shattered hulls. Tanks collided, rammed each other, remained locked together in tangled embrace as the battle spun around them like a vast whirlpool, flattening orchards and churning wheatfields in a confusion of blazing vehicles and charred corpses.

Unable to interfere in this extraordinary armoured brawl, the artillery on both sides held their fire. Ground-attack aircraft were also denied a role, although dogfights continued overhead and the scream of disabled aircraft plunging to earth could be heard over the constant, undifferentiated roar on the plain below Rotmistrov's observation post. Rotmistrov plotted the course of the battle as best he could from the situation reports of his corps commanders and their radio despatches. He also gleaned information from the intercepted radio orders of the German and Soviet tank commanders: 'Forward!' 'Orlov, take them from the flank!' 'Schneller!' 'Thachenko, break through into the rear!' 'Vorwarts!'

On the north bank of the Psel, on Hausser's left flank, Totenkopf fought a series of savage close-quarter tank and infantry engagements with 31st Tank and 33rd Guards Rifle Corps. No mercy was shown to men of the SS division who fell into Russian hands; their death's head insignia was a virtual death warrant. On II SS Panzer's right flank, Rotmistrov's 2nd Guards Tank Corps slammed into Das Reich across the gap which Zitadelle's timetable had required to be closed by Army Detachment Kempf, still some twelve miles distant from Prokhorovka, stalled by the forces which Rotmistrov had sent south on Vatutin's orders.

In the centre of the Russian line 18th and 29th Tank Corps – the equivalent of four German divisions – were slugging it out toe to toe with Leibstandarte, the spearhead of Hausser's attack. The impact of the Russian armour – its machines fresh, unworn and with a full complement of ammunition – thudding into Hausser's battle-weary divisions had knocked the momentum out of the

German advance. As one German witness to the battle recalled:

> We had been warned to expect resistance from *pak* [fixed anti-
> tank guns] and some tanks in static positions, also the possi-
> bility of a few independent brigades of the slower KV type. In
> fact we found ourselves taking on a seemingly inexhaustible
> mass of enemy armour – never have I received such an over-
> whelming impression of Russian strength and numbers as on
> that day. The clouds of dust made it difficult to get help from
> the Luftwaffe, and soon many of the T-34s had broken past our
> screen and were streaming like rats all over the battlefield . . .

By the early afternoon 2nd Guards and 2nd Tank Corps had
broken into the woods west of Belenichino and the farms east of
the village of Kalinin. The battle for the railway embankment
at Belenichino was particularly intense, and not without those
surreal moments which punctuate heavy fighting. A company
report from Das Reich's Der Führer Regiment records that
Second-Lieutenant Krueger, who had been wounded twice in the
previous day's fighting, was struck by a rifle bullet which set one
of his incendiary grenades on fire. Tearing off his trousers and
underpants, Krueger* continued to fight, naked from the waist
down, at the head of 10th Company until its objectives were taken.

In mid-afternoon a crisis flared up on Rotmistrov's right flank, at
the junction of Fifth Guards and Fifth Guards Tank Armies, where
18th Tank Corps was coming under increasingly heavy pressure.
Fifth Guards Army, which had no tanks and was weak in artillery,
was also threatening to cave in as German tanks broke through
two of its infantry divisions. Rotmistrov now committed the
remainder of his Army – 10th Guards Mechanized and 24th Guards
Tank Brigades – to the battle to secure his right flank and rear.

Colonel Karpov's 24th Guards Tank Brigade was despatched
towards the Voroshilov state farm to join the right-flank forces of
18th Tank Corps and the infantry of Fifth Guards Army in the
Polezhayev sector. Simultaneously, Colonel Mikhailov's 10th
Guards Mechanized Brigade raced five miles to the north-east of
Prokhorovka to block Hausser's north-east drive. The situation

---

* Krueger was killed in action on the 14th.

was stabilized and Hausser's divisions forced on to the defensive.

A celebrated incident which took place in the 18th Tank Corps's combat zone involved Captain Skripkin, commander of 2 Battalion of the Corps's 181st Brigade. Skripkin had ploughed directly into a Tiger formation, knocking out two enemy tanks before an 88mm shell hit his turret and another smashed into his side armour. The T-34 caught fire and the wounded Skripkin was dragged from the blazing wreck by his driver, Sergeant Nikolayev, and wireless operator Zyranov. They took shelter in a shell hole, but one of the Tigers spotted them and moved forward to finish them off. Nikolayev and loader Chernov jumped back into the disabled T-34, restarted it and drove it straight at the Tiger. Both tanks exploded in a ball of flame.

By 9.00pm, after a series of jabbing German counter-attacks, both sides were assuming defensive positions. With the coming of darkness, the gunfire fell away and the armour ground to a halt. Rotmistrov secured Vasilevsky's permission to order his tank corps and anti-tank artillery to hold their positions. Corps were to refuel their machines, replenish their ammunition and feed their men in preparation for a renewed offensive at dawn on the 13th. Disabled tanks were recovered from the battlefield and towed to the rear for repairs.

Lightning flickered over the plain and rain spattered on the hulls of gutted vehicles. Flames licked through burning woods and villages. Across the entire front the fighting had died away, leaving the air rank with the smell of smoke and soot. From no-man's-land came a series of dull thumps as Hausser's engineers destroyed disabled vehicles which were too badly damaged to be towed away. Stretching his legs near his dug-out, Rotmistrov watched 'the night workers of the war . . . on the job; engineers making their way to the front line to lay mines where enemy tanks were expected to attack, medical personnel . . . taking away the wounded and logistic troops . . . bringing up ammunition, fuel and lubricants'.

At Hoth's headquarters Fourth Panzer Army's Chief of Staff, Major-General Fangohr, taking a seemingly sanguine view of the day's fighting, recorded merely that the enemy had attacked the entire front of the Panzer Army in a coordinated manner and with a minimum of nine tank and mechanized corps, identifying the main Russian efforts as having been directed against the Army's flanks.

Before snatching two hours of fitful sleep, Rotmistrov had pondered the prospects for the 13th, concluding that the enemy still had substantial reserves which he had begun to commit by nightfall. Perhaps the Germans would revise the tactics and formations which so far had failed to secure a breakthrough in eight days of fighting: 'In general, I expected the enemy to hit us with a strong tank strike, to try to capture the initiative and to impose his will on us.'

But the time for the imposing of German will – Adolf Hitler's entire raison d'être, which had cost so much in blood and treasure – was slipping away, influenced by events on the northern shoulder of the salient and on the other side of Europe in Sicily.

CHAPTER 9

Retreat to the Dnieper

'We were now in the position of a man who has seized a wolf by the ears and dare not let him go.' Major-General von Mellenthin

'The depressing thing is that we haven't the faintest idea what Stalin has left in the way of reserves.' Josef Goebbels's diary for 10 September 1943

'Do you think I am enjoying this damned business?' Hermann Göring to Baldur von Schirach, Gauleiter of Vienna

ON 1 JULY FIELD Marshal Erwin Rommel flew to the Wolf's Lair where he attended the Führer's daily conference, a stocky, silent figure among the generals gathered around the map table. It was rumoured that Hitler was planning a reshuffle of his high command, with Rommel taking over as acting Commander-in-Chief of the Army. In fact, Hitler had chosen Rommel to command an armed occupation of Italy, codenamed Alarich, in the event of an Allied invasion or the overthrow of Mussolini.*

During the first days of July, Rommel shared the excitement

---

* Rommel had hoped to succeed Field Marshal Albert Kesselring as Commander in Chief South but, in December 1943, he returned to France as commander of Army Group B.

which gripped Rastenburg as Zitadelle was finally launched. On the afternoon of the 9th, following the midday Führer conference, he had written in his diary, 'Attack operations in the East are going well.' The entry for the 10th, however, rang alarm bells for the Third Reich: 'War conference with the Führer. The British and Americans have invaded Sicily with paratroops and landing craft.' That day the greatest armada of the war, more than 3000 ships, had arrived off the beaches of southern Sicily. The landing force, consisting of eight divisions (three more than were used at Normandy in June 1944), were greatly superior to the Axis garrison on the island. The Allied airborne forces, drawn from the US 82nd and 1st British Airborne divisions, suffered severe casualties when inexperienced pilots dropped them into the sea and nervous Allied anti-aircraft gunners shot down their aircraft. But the seaborne landings against Italian coastal defence units, who were uniformly reluctant to put up a fight, went smoothly. Some of Sicily's Fascist defenders even helped to unload the invaders' landing craft. By 12 July the Allies had landed 160,000 men and 600 tanks. Three days later General Sir Harold Alexander, Commander in Chief North Africa, issued orders for the elimination of the Axis forces on the island.

The invasion of Sicily took the German high command completely by surprise. So, too, did Stavka's counter-offensive, code-named Kutuzov, which was launched on 12 July against the north and east faces of the Orel salient held by General Rudolf Schmidt's* weak Second Panzer Army; the counter-offensive aimed to take Model's Ninth Army in the rear. Stavka's planning for the Orel counter-stroke was part and parcel of the strategic defence at Kursk and had begun in late April 1943. Kutuzov called for three converging attacks on Army Group Centre's forces in the Orel salient, Second Panzer and Ninth Armies. From the north, on the left flank of Marshal Sokolovsky's Western Front, the attack

---

* Schmidt did not survive the opening of the Russian counter-offensive. His brother had been arrested for treason and the Gestapo had discovered among his correspondence letters from General Schmidt critical of Hitler. Schmidt was removed from his command and from 13 July to 5 August it was exercised by Model.

was to be made by Bagramyan's Eleventh Guards Army (previously Sixteenth Army). Popov's Bryansk Front was to attack from the east with Sixty-First, Third and Sixty-Third Armies, while Central Front's Thirteenth and Seventieth Armies would drive up from the south. The timing of the counter-attack, which was critical, was wholly contingent on the course of the fighting on the northern shoulder of the Kursk salient; it was to be launched at the moment the German attack had been brought to a halt. Western and Bryansk Fronts' shock groups were to go into action first, followed by other forces held in reserve on Western Front and, finally, by Central Front. The offensive plans were finalized, and the concentration of forces undertaken, at the beginning of July after Lucy revealed that Zitadelle would be launched between 3 and 6 July.

Using a range of *maskirovka* measures, including the continuation of defensive work begun in April, Bagramyan concentrated his attacking force (three rifle corps and two tank corps) on a ten-mile section of his left flank, leaving a single division to defend the remaining fifteen miles of his sector. Perhaps his greatest *maskirovka* asset was the grim battle on the northern shoulder of the Kursk salient which distracted German attention from the growing danger to their flank. As a result, German intelligence had formed only a hazy picture of the Soviet concentrations in the Orel sector. It identified the arrival of a new army (Sixteenth) but did not anticipate its role or know its new designation. The Germans also failed to pick up the forward deployment of 5th Tank, 1st Tank and 1st Guards Tank Corps.

On 11 July, as II SS Panzer Corps closed on Prokhorovka, reinforced reconnaissance battalions from Western and Bryansk Fronts began to probe the defences in the Orel sector under the cover of a smoke screen laid by Pe-2 dive-bombers. Their attacks continued throughout the day, drawing off forces from Ninth Army which Model had been preparing to commit in a last effort to break through at Olkhovatka. During the night Seventeenth Air Army's 213th Night Bomber Air Division and AFLRO units,* reinforced by 313th Night Bomber Air Division, flew 362 sorties against

---

* Stavka's strategic reserve.

German positions, dropping over 200 tons of bombs. With the dawn, seventy Pe-2s and forty-eight Shturmoviks from General M.M. Gromov's fresh First Air Army struck at Ninth Army as a preliminary to Eleventh Guards Army's attack on Model's rear.

Bagramyan's reconnaissance battalions withdrew at 3.00am on the 12th. Twenty minutes later 3000 Soviet guns and mortars began a two-hour barrage while Bagramyan's assault troops huddled barely 100 yards from the forward German positions, preparing to attack under cover of the artillery's 'fire zones'. To the south-east, Bryansk Front's artillery was hammering the head of the Orel bulge as the moment arrived to slice into the salient from the north and east.

Conceived primarily as a relieving attack prior to the unleashing of counter-offensives along the entire Eastern Front, Kutuzov nevertheless achieved a rapid initial success. By the evening of 14 July Eleventh Guards Army had advanced over ten miles. To maintain Bagramyan's momentum Stavka fed in Eleventh Army, commanded by General I.I. Fedyuninsky, and rushed up Lieutenant-General V.M. Badanov's Fourth Tank Army. Simultaneously, Rokossovsky was on the point of mounting his own counter-attack which would launch Thirteenth Army from the northern shoulder of the Kursk salient into the soft underbelly of the German-held Orel bulge.

On 13 July Kluge and Manstein were summoned to Rastenburg. According to Manstein's account, Hitler

> opened the conference by announcing that the Western Allies had landed in Sicily that day and that the situation there had taken an extremely serious turn. The Italians were not even attempting to fight, and the island was likely to be lost. Since the next step might well be a landing in the Balkans or Lower Italy, it was necessary to form new armies in Italy and the western Balkans. These forces must be found from the Eastern Front, so Zitadelle would have to be discontinued.

Manstein, displaying an enthusiasm for Zitadelle which had been notably absent since the rejection of his 'backhand' option, argued that the Russian tank reserves were fast running out and that the battle should be continued to the point of their destruction. Failure to do so would bring powerful Soviet forces crashing down on Army Group South's long salient to the Donets basin and the Black Sea in a re-run of the crisis which followed Stalingrad.

Kluge, however, reported that Ninth Army was making no headway and was being forced to transfer all its mobile forces north to check the Soviet penetration into the Orel salient. He believed that there 'could be no question of continuing with Zitadelle or of resuming the operation at a later date'.

Manstein was doubtless using the advantage of hindsight when he wrote his account of this critical meeting after the war. Zitadelle was to continue for several days before it was cancelled. The Allied invasion of Sicily did not pose a fatal threat to 'Fortress Europe', nor would the immediate withdrawal of formations like II SS Panzer Corps and their movement west have an immediate impact on the situation in the Mediterranean. It is more than likely that, on 13 July, Hitler talked in general terms, warning Manstein of the probability that troops would have to be transferred from the East to meet the new threat in the West. For the undeniable fact was that the landings in Sicily had ushered in a new phase of the war in which Germany would now have to fight on two fronts rather than stand guard over one. Hitler hoped to contain the situation in Sicily while continuing to prepare for the main blow in the West to fall in northern Europe – which he had good reason to believe was some months away. His principal fear, however, remained the overthrow of Mussolini.

Although Zitadelle had not fulfilled OKH's expectations, about which the Führer had always harboured doubts, he nevertheless derived some comfort from the damage it appeared to be inflicting on the Russian reserves. A few days more punishment might ensure that these reserves would be burned away, leaving the Red Army in no shape to mount another winter offensive. This qualified optimism, however, failed to take into account the attrition suffered by the Ostheer at Kursk. The oversight was to draw this observation from the OKW war diarist:

> After the bloody struggle for the city of Stalingrad there followed another struggle for strongly fortified field positions, a second 'Verdun', followed by a third, which was supposed to make the enemy exhaust his 'last forces' at a strategically

important point. However, this 'Verdun' swallowed up even
more of our divisions in an ever more horrifying whirlpool.

The fighting continued in the Kursk salient although it was now
shifting in favour of the Red Army. For Hoth 13 July was not
an encouraging day. II SS Panzer Corps's thrusts were halted
and the SS divisions struggled even to hold their ground. Heavy
rain turned the Psel crossings into quagmires, seriously hamper-
ing the resupply of Totenkopf's shallow bridgehead on the northern bank.

Hoth then secured from Manstein permission to switch his
attack from north to east along the axis Ivanovka–Vinogrodovka, a
line which the commander of Army Group South had originally
favoured. The new attack jumped off at 2.00pm but by nightfall
had failed to reach Ivanovka. From General Kirichenko's command
post Zhukov and Rotmistrov watched as the day's fighting wound
down. Both sides were exhausted, reduced to exchanging fire:
'Shells exploded sporadically, bullets whistled by and enemy
tanks, armoured personnel carriers and trucks were seen to be
moving in the distance.'

There were tactical successes. Das Reich fielded a formation of
T-34s captured from a factory east of Kharkov. These were used in
a flank attack on a column of enemy tanks rolling along the floor of
one of the many small valleys in Das Reich's sector. Of the Russian
tanks only the commanders' were equipped with radio receivers
and transmitters and these were invariably the first to be knocked
out by experienced German tank crews. The next target was the
full petrol container often carried on the rear of the T-34 which
could be set ablaze with a well-aimed shot. The Russian tank scol-
umn was destroyed before its commanders realized it was being
fired on by enemy-crewed T-34s.

For the Red Army, the price of halting the German drive on Prokhorovka had been high. In a detailed report sent to Stalin in the
small hours of 14 July, Vatutin stated that, in two days of fighting,
29th Tank Corps had lost totally or on a temporary basis 60 per
cent of its armour and 18th Tank Corps 30 per cent – in all, over
400 tanks. By the 14th, 112 vehicles had been repaired and
returned to action, most of them patched up with spare parts can-
nibalized from tanks beyond repair. Rotmistrov's engineers were

hampered not only by a shortage of spare parts but also by a lack of machine-tools,* welding equipment and cranes. A week after Prokhorovka, Fifth Guards Tank Army still had approximately 180 tanks which required medium and running repairs, while most of the tanks which remained in action were operating with worn-out engines and gears in desperate need of overhaul.

Hoth had his problems, too. The situation was deteriorating on his left flank where the extended LII Corps, which had no tanks, was inviting a counter-attack on the entire Fourth Panzer Army. On the afternoon of the 13th, von Knobelsdorff appeared at Grossdeutschland's battle headquarters to give orders which 'left no hope for any advance to the north'. The division was to attack westward on the 14th – much as it had on the 10th and 11th – to reach the Rakovo–Kruglik road from which 3rd Panzer had been driven earlier in the day. The Russians had also ejected 3rd Panzer from Hill 247 and had retaken Berezovka, five miles to the south.

On the 14th German progress was slow. Under mounting pressure, Totenkopf was forced to relinquish its bridgehead on the north bank of the Psel. At 4.00am Das Reich attacked again with an artillery and *Nebelwerfer* barrage, followed by an infantry assault led by 1 and 3 Battalions of Der Führer Regiment. Taking heavy casualties from the dense minefields in their path, the panzer grenadiers reached the outskirts of Belenichino by midday and began a bitter house-to-house battle for the village. Twelve counter-attacking T-34s were destroyed with hollow-charge anti-tank grenades while Stukas drove off their infantry support. Having cleared Belenichino, the panzer grenadiers regrouped and, supported by the panzer regiment, threw back several Russian attempts to retake the village. As darkness fell, they moved forward, but heavy rain washed away the road surfaces and once again the advance was bogged down.

On Hoth's sagging left flank, Grossdeutschland pushed westward for the second time. On its right wing a battle group, consisting of the reconnaissance and assault-gun battalions, a rifle and a tank company, was charged with retaking Hill 247. In the

---

*The shortage of machine-tools was remedied by Lend-Lease.

centre Grossdeutschland's panzer regiment, supported by
infantry, was to recapture Hill 243. On the left the panzer
grenadiers were to attack to the south-west to clear the wood
north of Berezovka.

By the afternoon, after heavy fighting, contact was made with
3rd Panzer at Berezovka. The forest to the north of the village was
cleared but it proved impossible to dislodge the enemy from Hill
247 from which they launched counter-attacks as the day's fighting drew to a close. When night came Grossdeutschland could
congratulate itself on regaining vital ground and inflicting severe
losses on the enemy. As von Mellenthin observed:

> All this was certainly a success of some sort; the dangerous sit-
> uation on the left wing had been rectified, and the 3rd Panzer
> Division had been given support. But Grossdeutschland was
> dangerously weak after heavy fighting lasting for ten days,
> while the Russian striking power had not appreciably dimin-
> ished. In fact, it seemed to have increased.

On the 15th Das Reich's panzer regiment finally made contact
with Kempf's III Panzer Corps when it joined hands with elements
of 7th Panzer Division. Their junction accomplished the encirclement and destruction of substantial enemy forces in the
Gostishchevo–Liski area, but these tactical successes could not
salvage the strategic failure of Zitadelle. Events outside the Kursk
salient were now moving faster, and assuming greater importance,
than the continuing effort to destroy Vatutin's reserves. Two days
after meeting Hitler at Rastenburg, Manstein told Hoth and Kempf
what was rapidly becoming obvious, that Zitadelle, as it had originally been planned, was no longer possible, principally due to the
lack of progress made by Model's Ninth Army and the counter-
offensive now beating on its rear. Far from ordering a withdrawal,
however, Manstein announced his intention of bringing Fourth
Panzer Army up to the line of the Psel. It was noted that Hoth
seemed pleased that the southern half of the operation was to be
carried forward, albeit in a restricted form, rather then being completely abandoned.

Two days later the game was up. On 17 July a powerful Soviet
attack on the German defences in the south, along the Mius line,

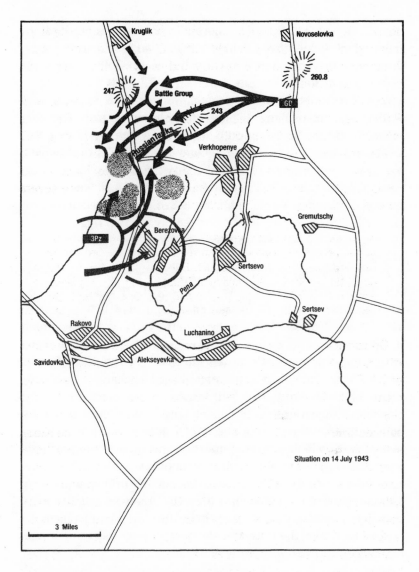

The labels in the map, from top to bottom and left to right, are:

Kruglik

Novoselovka

260.8

247

Battle Group

GD

243

Russian Tanks

Verkhopenye

Gremutschy

3Pz

Berezovka

Sertsevo

Pena

Sertsev

Rakovo

Luchanino

Savidovka

Alekseyevka

Situation on 14 July 1943

3 Miles

As the battle wound down, Grossdeutschland continued to make local gains but made no headway towards its target of Oboyan

was launched by Colonel-General Tolbukhin's South-Western Front which fielded five infantry armies, two mechanized corps, three tank brigades and a cavalry corps. On Tolbukhin's right Malinovsky's South-Western Front attacked First Panzer Army across the Donets south of Izyum. North of the Kursk salient Model was undertaking a 'planned withdrawal' from the Orel salient to escape being cut off by Kutuzov, which, by 19 July, had smashed through his first and second defence belts to achieve a penetration forty miles deep and eighty miles wide. Model, with about 600,000 men, 492,300 of them combat troops, was facing a second Stalingrad. By 18 August he had avoided encirclement and withdrawn to the temporary safety of the Hagen line, a system of field fortifications running across the neck of the Orel salient.

On 17 July Hitler directed that II SS Panzer Corps be withdrawn from the front line; within twenty-four hours Hoth was also obliged to relinquish control of Grossdeutschland, which was sent to assist Army Group Centre. On the 19th the OKW war diarist noted that 'operation Zitadelle is no longer possible on account of the violence of the enemy's counter-offensive'. By then II SS Panzer Corps's headquarters had been established in Kharkov; by 23 July Fourth Panzer Army had withdrawn to its start line. Over Manstein's objections, XXIV Panzer Corps, which had moved up behind Hoth in the closing stages of Zitadelle and was the only reserve with which to exploit success, was moved south to reinforce First Panzer Division against Malinovsky's counter-offensive.

In spite of the collapse of Zitadelle, Hitler's principal preoccupation remained the situation in Italy. On 19 July he met Mussolini near Feltre, talking uninterruptedly for two hours until a message arrived informing the Duce that Rome was under heavy air attack. Later that day Mussolini wrote in his diary:

> He [Hitler] told me that the Italian crisis was a leadership crisis, and hence a human one. He would send reinforcements for the air force and new divisions to defend the peninsula. He declared that the defence of Italy is also in Germany's highest interests. His choice of words was friendly at all times, and we parted on the best of terms. The Führer's aircraft took off soon afterwards.

A more realistic view of the strategic dilemma confronting the Axis was taken by Marshal Vittorio Ambrosio, Chief of the Italian General Staff, who took the opportunity at Feltre to ask Keitel about the situation on the Eastern Front. Keitel would say no more than that the Russians were being worn down. 'This', replied Ambrosio, 'is not an active programme, but the renunciation of the initiative in operations. In substance the Axis is besieged; it is in a closed ring; it is necessary to get out. What prospects have you got for doing this?' Keitel gave no reply.

On 25 July Mussolini was deposed by the Fascist Grand Council. Convinced that Italy was about to drop out of the war,* Hitler ordered Zeitzler to withdraw II SS Panzer Corps for transfer to the West. The extraction of the Corps, however, did not follow immediately nor, when all the moves were completed, did the whole Corps travel to Italy. At the end of July II SS Panzer Corps was still needed in the East to stem the Russian offensive on the Mius, now threatening to engulf Hollidt's Sixth Army which had been reformed after the débâcle at Stalingrad.

On the night of 13 July Rotmistrov drove Zhukov to the headquarters of 29th Tank Corps. On the way Zhukov stopped the car several times to view the sites of recent tank battles. Rotmistrov wrote: 'It was an awesome scene, with battered and burned-out tanks, wrecked guns, armoured personnel carriers and trucks, heaps of artillery rounds and pieces of tracks lying everywhere. Not a single blade of grass was left standing on the darkened soil.' At one point Zhukov left the car to peer at a burned-out Panther which had been rammed by a T-70. A few yards away a Tiger and a T-34 were locked in a crazy embrace. 'This is what a head-on clash is like,' murmured Zhukov, doffing his cap in tribute to the Soviet tank crews who had died in the fighting on the 12th.

In the years after the war Prokhorovka achieved almost mythic status as a dramatic symbol of Russian armoured renaissance and as a convenient rationalization of German defeat by overwhelming

---

* Hitler's fears were confirmed when, on 29 July, he received the transcript of an intercepted radio-telephone conversation between Roosevelt and Stalin in which the Allied war leaders discussed the 'imminent armistice' with Italy.

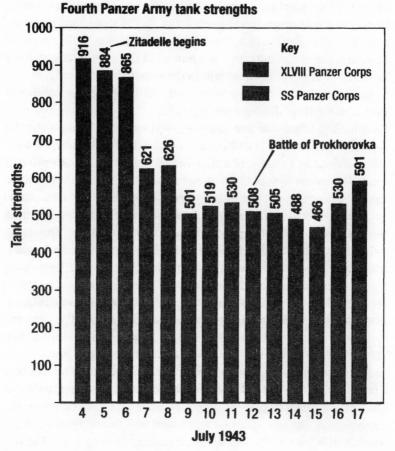

Operation Zitadelle
Fourth Panzer Army tank strengths

Fourth Panzer Army's daily returns which indicate that its armour sustained its heaviest losses before Prokhorovka

numbers – the 'steamroller' of Russian military legend. An examination of Fourth Panzer Army's daily tank returns, however, suggests that, for all the violence of the encounter, German armoured losses at Prokhorovka were relatively slight. If, as the Russians claimed, over 400 tanks were dug up from the fields around Prokhorovka after the war, the great majority of them must have been the T-34s of 29th and 18th Tank Corps.

At Kursk Fourth Panzer Army suffered its worst losses in the first six days of the fighting before the climactic encounter at Prokhorovka. Tank figures are hard to pin down because of the regular replenishment of front-line units as damaged vehicles were repaired and brought back into action. On the 13th Vasilevsky was informed by a German prisoner-of-war that, after two replenishments in the first week of fighting, the strength of Das Reich stood at 100 tanks. Fourth Panzer Army's daily returns show that, between 11 and 13 July, its armoured strength fell from 530 vehicles (on the 11th) to 505 (on the 13th), a loss of only twenty-five tanks after the clash at Prokhorovka. Many more tanks may have been lost at Prokhorovka, to be replaced by a surge of repaired vehicles on the evening of the 12th; this seems unlikely, however, given that, after the 13th, Fourth Panzer Army's strength remained relatively stable, dropping to 466 on the 15th and then recovering to 530 on the 16th and 591 on the 17th.

Perhaps the real significance of Prokhorovka lay in the fact that – heavy losses or not – Fifth Guards Tank Army stopped II SS Panzer Corps in its tracks. The effect of this was felt not so much on the aggregate of German armour as on the morale of Fourth Panzer Army's elite troops for whom this must have seemed like the last straw. The fact that, in the subsequent fighting at Kursk, German losses remained relatively low suggests that the terrible slog through Vatutin's echeloned defences had sapped morale to the point where the will to press home attacks against continuing strong Russian resistance was ebbing away. After 12 July even elite units had had the stuffing knocked out of them. Significantly, on the 15th Rotmistrov noted a change of German tactics in the Prokhorovka sector. Rather than commit forces in dense combat formations, the SS divisions sent out small reconnaissance groups of three to five heavy tanks, supported by motorized infantry, in the hope of drawing anti-tank fire and locating the weak points in the Russian defences. These probing attacks were followed by artillery and mortar preparation for more frontal attacks, all of which were repulsed. By the evening of the 15th the fighting had died down around Prokhorovka. According to Rotmistrov, 'the enemy gave up their attacks and did not even harass our troops with artillery fire'.

Even as Zhukov was muttering his tribute to the Soviet soldier on the battlefield at Prokhorovka, Central and Voronezh Fronts' tank losses at Kursk had reached 1500 vehicles, nearly half the tank fleet with which they had begun the battle. Fourth Panzer Army claimed to have destroyed 185 in the fighting on 8 July alone. These losses, however, were rapidly made good by the almost super-human efforts of the Russian field-repair shops. By 3 August Soviet tank strength in the Kursk sector had risen to 2750. The immediate problem for Zhukov and Vasilevsky was not the number of mission-capable tanks but the replacement of crews killed in the battle.

German losses had also been high. Fourth Panzer Army's twenty-five-mile advance had cost it some 330 tanks and assault guns; 3rd Panzer Division was down to thirty vehicles by 17 July. Fourth Panzer Army's losses assume a grim significance when one considers that this was almost the exact figure for Germany's monthly tank production, which had not achieved the 1000 a month scheduled for 1943. By the end of July 1943 total German tank losses on the Eastern Front would reach 645 tanks and 207 assault guns. As a result the central armoured reserve on which the Ostheer had previously been able to draw in a crisis was now dissipated and could not be built out of current production which was committed to the replacement of normal losses. The panzer arm would continue to inflict heavy punishment on clumsily led Russian tank masses, but Soviet tank production, which would reach 2500 a month in 1944, kept steadily ahead of losses, enabling the Red Army remorselessly to increase its net complement of armoured formations.* Henceforth the Ostheer would be

---

* By October 1943 the Red Army fielded five tank armies, eighty tank brigades and 106 independent tank regiments. Additionally, there were thirteen mecha-nized corps, 126 rifle corps, seventy-two independent rifle divisions, six artillery corps, twenty-six artillery divisions, forty-three regiments of self-propelled guns, twenty artillery brigades and seven divisions of *Katyusha* rocket-launchers.

deprived of the means of seizing the initiative which, as General Ambrosio observed, had passed to the Soviet Union.

Nor had Zitadelle netted a huge haul of Russian prisoners to be marched back to the Reich and there worked to death as slave labour. Army Group South took approximately 24,000 prisoners, a fraction of the millions who had fallen into German hands in 1941–2. In the immediate aftermath of Kursk the Soviet formations which had borne the brunt of the onslaught were seriously weakened. But the power of the Red Army continued to grow, drawing on a total force of 6.5 million men with another half million in reserve.

In contrast, the Ostheer was a shrinking asset. At the end of August Manstein was complaining that, for the 133,000 casualties sustained by Army Group South in July and August, there had only been 33,000 replacements. Even in an elite division like Grossdeutschland which usually received favoured treatment when it came to replacements, the manpower shortage was becoming acute and the rate at which junior officers were killed or wounded very high. Between 26 July and 5 September 1943 the division's 6th Grenadier Company went through ten commanders, of whom two were NCOs. Two months after Zitadelle the average size of a Grossdeutschland company was about twenty men while the division's 2 Grenadier Battalion consisted of just three officers and twenty-two men. The assault infantry divisions which had laboriously been brought up to strength in the weeks preceding Zitadelle had been smashed up: in Army Detachment Kempf 106 Division had lost 3224 officers and men, 320 Division 2839 and 168 Division 2671. John Ellis has pointed out that, in terms of the combat infantry in each division, these losses represented casualty rates of, respectively, 38, 29 and 27 per cent, each suffered within a fortnight. In 1944 the worst-hit British divisions in north-west Europe took six months to match such casualty rates.

Conceived, planned and executed by the heirs of the Great General Staff, Zitadelle had been a complete failure on the part of the professional military class which Hitler so despised. Mussolini's overthrow by his generals only increased the Führer's isolation and paranoia. A *Materialschlacht* – clash of machines – had been sought at Kursk in the full knowledge that the attacking forces were inferior to the enemy and that there were insufficient reserves to exploit any success to the hilt. The operation seems to have been planned on the assumption that, as had invariably happened before, the Russians would collapse at the first impact. Little thought was given to what might happen if they did not, although Model had a pretty clear idea of the consequences. Dash, and the dismissal of the enemy as Slavic *Untermenschen*, was no longer enough. When the enemy stubbornly refused to disintegrate, and then began to pick apart both Hoth's and Model's weakly held left flanks, the folly of the exercise was starkly revealed. Poor German intelligence at every stage of the operation and the masterly placing and handling of the Russian strategic reserve had ensured the failure of Zitadelle.

The failure of Zitadelle was compounded by Manstein's schizophrenic approach to the likelihood of a Russian counter-blow following a German withdrawal. On the one hand he had warned Hitler of the danger to his Army Group's southern flank. On the other he had informed Hoth that Zitadelle would be concluded by moving up to the Psel, a course of action which suggests that Fourth Panzer Army had not suffered the grievous losses which characterize the received view of Prokhorovka. The rest of the summer would be spent straightening the line and transferring the weight of German armour southward, 'to iron out things in the Donets area', in preparation for a Russian counter-offensive in the winter.

Thus the rhythms of the Eastern Front would be preserved: German gains in the summer followed by a Russian riposte after the autumnal *rasputitsa*. Further evidence of the German belief that the blow dealt to Russian armour would not be repaired until the winter is provided by the insistence on a rigorous tank inspection programme which took in all vehicles in need of repair and sent them back to maintenance depots in Kharkov and Bogodukhov. This created such a logjam that, after 1 August, tanks and assault guns were being sent as far west as Kiev, even for minor repairs to the running gear and gunnery-control equipment. In this way much of Manstein's armoured strength was dissipated.

Stalin had originally ceded to his Stavka representatives the right to decide when the moment was ripe to move on to the offen-

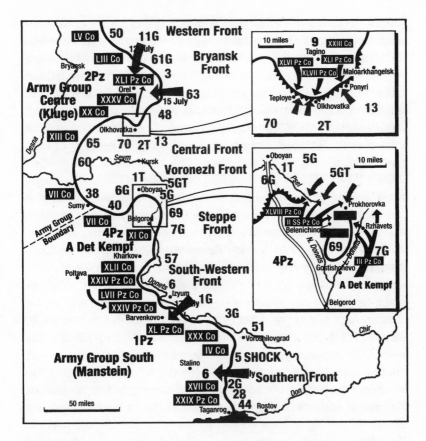

The Red Army goes on to the offensive north and south of the Kursk salient, the preliminary to the recapture of Kharkov

sive after Zitadelle had been fought to a halt. Ever a man of impulse, however, he seized back the reins even while the battle was still raging, determined to dictate every move. By 15 July Stalin was reverting to strategic type, urging an immediate counter-offensive which was postponed only after much argument from Zhukov and Vasilevsky convinced the dictator of the need to pause for resupply and preparation.

The initial operations – Kutuzov in the Orel salient and the recapture of Kharkov, codenamed Rumiantsev – were just two of a series of offensives planned to unroll along the entire Eastern Front. South of the Sea of Azov, General I.E. Petrov's North

Caucasus Front was ordered to maintain the pressure on Kleist's Army Group A in the Taman bridgehead and the Crimea while Tolbukhin's Southern Front attacked Manstein's right flank along the Black Sea littoral. To Malinovsky's South-Western Front fell the task of liberating the area of the Donets basin in the centre; Vatutin and Konev were to attack out of Kharkov on Manstein's left wing. Simultaneously, Rokossovsky's Central, Popov's Bryansk and Sokolovsky's Western Fronts were to combine against Kluge's Army Group Centre. To the north Colonel-General Eremenko's Kalinin Front was to be readied for an offensive against Army Group Centre in the Smolensk sector, to be launched before the end of August. Behind Army Group Centre a full-scale partisan offensive was to be mounted against German communications with the aim of pinning Second Panzer and Ninth Armies well forward in the Orel bulge by destroying their rearward rail links.

Stalin was still wedded to the old-style 'broad front' strategy which he had favoured since the winter of 1941. On several occasions in August Zhukov attempted to persuade him to substitute encirclements for this unsubtle western drive, but Stalin dismissed his arguments with the observation that the enemy was still too strong for such operations. He might have added that the Red Army still lacked the necessary skill and scope for initiative at the middle and lower levels of command. Stalin's overriding aim was to drive the Ostheer off Russian soil as quickly as possible. Ground regained in the Donbas, with its industrial and agricultural assets, was as important as inflicting heavy losses on the enemy who was to be rolled back by the weight of repeated blows rather than by being annihilated in a single battle. Above all, Stalin wanted to retake Kiev at the earliest opportunity.

The initial Soviet exploitation of the victory at Kursk was the essential preliminary to the main counter-blow, the recapture of Belgorod and Kharkov. Heavy losses were incurred in both the Orel salient and in the attack on the German-held Mius line. In both sectors the Germans had plenty of time in which to prepare a strong system of field fortifications; the Ostheer had first built defences on the Mius in October 1941 and had been strengthening them ever since. Nevertheless, they served their purpose in drawing off Manstein's operational reserve in 'fire-fighting' operations to the north and south. In the drive on Orel the tanks of Rybalko's Third Guards Tank Army were chewed up as they attempted to batter their way through a fortified line south-east of the city. Their orders had come directly from Stalin and the commander of Bryansk Front, Popov, was too old a hand to protest at such waste.

The partisan operations against Army Group Centre's communications were unprecedented in scale but relatively ineffective. Huge quantities of explosives had been flown in to the partisans before they renewed the 'war of the rails' but, for all the damage they caused – the Russians recorded 10,000 reported demolitions in the last days of July – the Ostheer kept its lines of communication open. Too much valuable explosive had been squandered on branch lines rather than being concentrated to deliver a smaller number of crippling blows at key points on the main lines.

Now it was the turn of the Germans to dig in their tanks and prepare *pakfronts* in the high wheatfields of the Orel bulge. On 26 July Badanov's Fourth Tank Army, equipped with over 500 new tanks and, on Stavka's orders, swinging south-east to eliminate the German pocket around Bolkhov, took a terrible pounding from concealed German tanks and assault guns. Badanov's tank crews lacked the training for rapid breakthrough operations against an experienced enemy and paid the price. Nevertheless, the Germans pulled out of the Bolkhov pocket and then Orel, itself,* which was entered by the Soviet Third and Sixty-Third Armies on 5 August.

Tolbukhin had attacked on the Mius line on 17 July, crossing the river and establishing a bridgehead before committing his two mechanized corps. His advance was quickly checked, however, by well-prepared German defences and then thrown back after a counter-attack by forces shifted from the north – 23rd Panzer Division, II SS Panzer Corps and XXIV Panzer Corps. After one engagement Heid Ruehl counted thirteen blazing T-34s 'lined up like beads on a necklace'. But the centre of gravity of the Russian counter-stroke was Rumiantsev, the Belgorod–Kharkov operation,

---

* Hitler had ordered the immediate withdrawal of Kluge's troops in the area of Orel on 1 August, after learning of the trans-Atlantic telephone conversation between Churchill and Roosevelt.

to the success of which all the other Soviet counter-offensives were subordinated.

Surprise was the key to the retaking of Belgorod and Kharkov, and once again great emphasis was placed on *maskirovka* during the preparation of the offensive. The Germans were to be successfully misled over the timing, strength, shape and location of Rumiantsev. The decision to proceed with the Belgorod–Kharkov operation had been taken by Stalin on 22 June, but it was not until 24 July that Stavka instructed Voronezh and Steppe Fronts to prepare detailed plans for the liberation of the two cities.

Zhukov presided over the planning which bore his unmistakable stamp: attack on a narrow front after massive artillery preparation (370 guns and mortars for every mile) to achieve a rapid and deep penetration with powerful assault groupings. Voronezh Front and Steppe Front, the latter now deployed on Vatutin's left flank east and south of Belgorod, were to attack positions around Belgorod and advance towards Bogodukhov and Valki, driving a wedge between Fourth Panzer Army and Army Detachment Kempf before enveloping and destroying the enemy forces in the Kharkov area. As the operation unfolded and Soviet forces closed on Kharkov, South-Western Front's Fifty-Seventh and First Guards Armies were to join the assault. Subordinate headquarters were given ten days to prepare the offensive which was to begin on 3 August.

After detailed discussion with Zhukov, Vatutin and Konev decided to launch the main attack north and north-west of Belgorod with joined flanks. In the opening stage four armies, Fifth and Sixth Guards, Fifty-Third and Sixty-Ninth (plus elements of Seventh Army) would be used. In the exploitation phase they would be joined by First and Fifth Guards Tank Armies, introduced through the breach made by Fifth and Sixth Armies to drive south-west from the Tomarovka area towards Akhtyrka. Along the flanks of the main attack other armies would launch a series of phased attacks designed to add to the weight of the main blow.

Although Manstein had indicated on 1 August that he considered Kharkov to be Stavka's next target, he was convinced that the Soviets would need several weeks at least to replenish and regroup. Given the scale of Soviet losses in the fighting at Kursk, his calculations did not stray from orthodoxy. But he had failed to anticipate that the Soviet intention was to make the best use of timing to achieve surprise with an attack launched by under-strength forces and patched-up tank armies against a sector now bereft of its own operational reserve. Nevertheless, even taking into account the heavy losses they had incurred in the defensive fighting at Kursk, Voronezh and Steppe Fronts enjoyed an overall superiority of 3:1 in manpower over Army Group South, 4:1 in guns and tanks and 3:2 in aircraft. Manstein, meanwhile, waited for 'more definite signs of an impending offensive'.

Stavka made extensive use of *maskirovka* to increase German uncertainty as to its intentions and to conceal where the main blow was to fall. On the northern Donets, Steppe Front engineers built twenty-two secret underwater bridges complete with camou-flaged approaches and false bridges. Overall *maskirovka* plans called for the rifle corps employed in the offensive to create three dummy tank company or battalion concentration areas and each rifle division to create ten false artillery positions. A movement plan was devised to mask the regrouping and resupply of the assault forces while signals units created phantom radio nets to conceal Soviet command and control.

On the right flank of Voronezh Front *maskirovka* conjured up in the Sudzha region a simulated assembly of two rifle corps, a tank army (which German intelligence suspected might be Fifth Guards) and several tank corps. In the rear another simulated deep con-centration was created by elements of Moskalenko's Thirty-Eighth Army. Engineers assigned to 340th Rifle Division built 215 dummy artillery pieces and 250 dummy tanks to 'animate' the sector around the railhead at Lokinskaya. Smoke screens laid over the station, daylight movements through the area by two regiments of 340th Division and a daily shuttle train service completed the illusion of a large concentration, attracting considerable attention from the Luftwaffe which flew 244 sorties over the area, dropping a large tonnage of bombs.

German intelligence also noted the activity around Lokinskaya and, while failing positively to identify a tank army in the area, nevertheless detected sufficient signs of an imminent offensive in this sector to shift 7th Panzer and 7th (Infantry) Divisions west-ward to cover Soviet Thirty-Eighth Army shortly before the Soviet blow fell to the east. This left only two panzer divisions, 19th* and 6th, to support the infantry north-west of Belgorod where, on 3 August, they were engulfed by a tidal wave of Soviet armour.

At 5.00am on 3 August the Soviet counter-blow began with a five-minute artillery barrage. Silence then fell across the front for thirty-five minutes, after which the guns started to fire at selected targets. At 6.35am the artillery opened up with a sustained bombardment which was joined an hour later by a torrent of *Katyusha* salvoes while successive waves of Soviet bombers pounded the German front line. Rotmistrov watched the artillery preparation from General Zhadov's command post:

> Red and yellow flashes appeared along the entire front and, farther to the south, purple flashes flared up with stones and earth shooting into the air in a thick dark wall. Smoke and dust rose up, enveloping the enemy positions which were shaken by the storm of artillery fire. It was the first time I had witnessed such devastating artillery preparation.

At 8.00am a deep, rolling 'Hurrah' reverberated across the battlefield as the assault units of Fifth and Sixth Guards Armies went into action, moving through the gaps between the artillery's 'fire lanes'. By 2.00pm Zhadov's infantry, supported by First and Fifth Guards Tank Armies, had broken through the main line of German defences. Rotmistrov's 18th and 29th Corps were pushing on at speed down a corridor bounded on one side by a deep ravine and on the other by a swampy depression. A series of ridges, minefields and other obstacles failed to slow the tanks which were now overtaking Zhadov's infantry, passing though a shambles of wrecked German trenches, gun emplacements and armour. The ground was littered with German corpses. A shell-shocked officer of the 328th Motorcycle Regiment of the German 167th Division, a battleworthy formation at the beginning of the day but no longer, was brought to Rotmistrov's observation post. As his hands shook, the words spilled out: 'We do not understand what has happened. We were told just yesterday that our

---

* In the immediate aftermath of Kursk 19th Panzer was left with just seventeen mission-capable tanks.

division would advance . . . and look what has happened to us.'

By nightfall First and Fifth Guards Tank Armies had broken through the second line of German defences to a depth of about fifteen miles, cutting the Tomarovka–Belgorod railway. On the morning of the 5th, while Soviet forces cleared Orel, Steppe Front advanced on Belgorod which was encircled by noon as 1st Mechanized Corps drove past the city to the west, severing its road and rail links with Kharkov. Belgorod was cleared by 89th Guards and 305th Rifle Divisions after heavy street fighting which left 3000 German dead in the ruins of the city.

That night Stalin ordered twelve 124-gun salutes to be fired in Moscow to celebrate the retaking of Belgorod. He proclaimed: 'Eternal glory to the heroes who fell in the struggle for freedom for our country . . . Death to the German invaders.' These last words were to become familiar to citizens of the Soviet Union as they were used by Stalin every time he announced a Russian victory – more than 300 times before the end of the war.

On 25 July, at a meeting with Kluge, Hitler told the commander of Army Group Centre that he was no longer master of his own decisions. No longer could he dictate the course of events. As Steppe Front stormed Belgorod, First and Fifth Tank Armies were driving south-west, opening up a twenty-five mile gap between Fourth Panzer Army and Army Detachment Kempf before fanning out to the west and south to overrun the field workshops in which Manstein's tanks were being repaired. Fifth Guards Tank Army had advanced sixty-two miles in five days, threatening to encircle 19th Panzer Division and the remnants of 57th, 255th and 332nd Divisions. These battered units were withdrawing to the south-west to form a new line between Akhtyrka and Gravyoron, unaware that Tromifenko's Twenty-Seventh Army was racing ahead of them on a parallel course.

On the morning of 7 August, above the roads running south of Belgorod, FW190s swooped over the withdrawing German columns, carrying out mock dive-bombing attacks in an attempt to convince Russian forward observers that Soviet units were under attack from the Luftwaffe. This did not fool Voronezh Front's artillery commander, Lieutenant-General Varentsov, who ordered Twenty-Seventh Army to bring all its guns to bear on the retreating

Germans. Ground-attack aircraft and the Russian guns left the road littered with gutted vehicles while Tromifenko's infantry swept the woods on either side of the highway to pick up prisoners. They found the body of 19th Panzer's commander, Lieutenant-General Gustav Schmidt, behind a tree.

By 8 August a forty-mile gap yawned between Fourth Panzer Army and Army Detachment Kempf. That day Zeitzler flew out to meet Manstein at Army Group South headquarters. Manstein was adamant that 'from now on we could no longer confine ourselves to such isolated problems as whether such and such a division could be spared, or whether the Kuban bridgehead should be evacuated or not.' Manstein then outlined alternative courses of action: the immediate despatch to the south of ten divisions from other sectors on the Eastern Front or the evacuation of the entire Donets region. Zeitzler was unable to commit himself and Manstein's proposals produced nothing more than a formal acknowledgment from OKH.

On the evening of the 9th, Rotmistrov and Zhukov met in more congenial circumstances. Rotmistrov found Zhukov installed in a railway car hidden in the heart of a dense pine forest. When he was ushered in he was confronted with the Deputy Commissar for Defence dressed in an embroidered white shirt 'sitting in a chair and slowly stretching the bellows of a Russian accordion'. Rotmistrov observed, 'You play well.' 'It's nothing,' replied Zhukov, 'You should have heard Mangarov [commander of Fifty-Third Army and a noted accordionist]. When I go out to his army, I could listen to him for hours on end.'

Moving over to the map table, Zhukov voiced his concern that, in spite of the initial success of Rumiantsev, he might yet be caught by a German counter-stroke similar to that which Manstein had delivered in the previous February. Zhukov told Rotmistrov '. . . the enemy may try to duplicate that manoeuvre to cut off and divide our troops which encircle Kharkov from the west. We must not allow this to happen . . .' Indicating an area south-west of Bogodukhov, Zhukov informed Rotmistrov that his task was to concentrate Fifth Guards Tank Army in formation under the cover of General Rodmitsev's 32nd Infantry Corps and, 'as soon as the artillery preparation is over and the infantry has gone into attack to deliver a strong tank strike on a narrow front, encircling the German concentration at Kharkov from the south'. Rotmistrov was given three days to redeploy.

Meanwhile the pressure was mounting on Kharkov. Vatutin's right wing continued to drive south-west, denying Manstein the opportunity to form a stable front, while Steppe Front began to probe the city's outer defences. On 10 August South-Western Front committed Fifty-Seventh Army. By the evening of the 11th it had crossed the northern Donets, captured Chuguyev and begun to advance on Kharkov from the south and south-east while Sixty-Ninth and Seventh Guards Armies prepared to strike at Kharkov's outer defences from the east. Outflanking Kharkov from the north-west were Fifty-Third and Fifth Guards Tank Armies.

On 12–13 August, while Vatutin responded to a counter-attack on his right wing by German armour concentrated at Akhtyra and a thrust mounted against Valki from south of the Poltava–Kharkov railway by Das Reich and Totenkopf Divisions,* the final battle for Kharkov began. Manstein had no desire to condemn Army Detachment Kempf to the fate suffered by Paulus's Sixth Army at Stalingrad. Hitler, true to type, demanded that the city be held at all costs, claiming that its fall would have 'an unfavourable effect on the attitude of Turkey and Bulgaria'. It was, as Manstein recognized, an impossible task. On 12 August Russian tanks broke through the sector held by the weak and inexperienced 282nd Division and occupied the industrial suburbs to the east of Kharkov. For a fleeting moment Manstein considered the drastic expedient of inflicting decimation on 282nd Division to prevent further panic. The Russian tanks were dislodged by 6th Panzer Division and the breach in the German line sealed, but now only a narrow corridor stood between Kempf and encirclement.

Soviet aircraft were dropping leaflets on Kharkov's defenders. In the sector held by 3rd Panzer Division, around the village of Polevoye, north-west of the city, the leaflets read: 'Comrades of

---

* Leibstandarte had been withdrawn on 3 August and posted to Italy, handing over its armoured fighting vehicles to Das Reich. The departure of Leibstandarte meant the end of II SS Panzer Corps. A third corps was created with Das Reich, Totenkopf and 3rd Panzer Division.

3rd Panzer Division, we know that you are brave soldiers. Every other man in your division has the Iron Cross. But every other man on our side has a mortar. Surrender!'

On 19 August, Konev used Fifth Guards Tank Army to smash its way into Kharkov from the north-west along the main road to Akhtyrha. In forty-eight hours of frenzied fighting with General Raus's XI Corps, culminating in a nocturnal repeat of Prokhorovka on the night of the 20th, Rotmistrov lost over 300 tanks to well-sited *pakfronts* and Panther, Tiger and Elefant units.

Raus's corps also suffered heavy casualties. The 394th Panzer Grenadier Regiment of 3rd Panzer Division had been reduced to little more than two rifle companies; the 331st Grenadier Regiment of 167th Division, moved up as a reserve, arrived with only 200 men. There were only fifteen mission-capable tanks in 6th Panzer Division, and Heavy Panzer Battalion 503 could field only nine Tigers. Ammunition was running low. Manstein was prepared to lose a city but not an army. On 22 August he ordered the evacuation of Kharkov. By dawn on the 23rd two Soviet divisions, 183rd and 89th Guards, had reached the city centre and at noon the city was officially liberated.

General Kempf became the scapegoat for the loss of Kharkov. His command was redesignated Eighth Army and on 14 August he was replaced by General Wöhler, who had been Chief of Staff when Manstein commanded Eleventh Army. Manstein later wrote: 'Although I got on well with General Kempf, I did not oppose the change.'

On 13 August Malinovsky had renewed the offensive on the eastern bank of the Donets. And even as German troops were setting Kharkov's huge supply dumps ablaze, Tolbukhin was once again hammering on the Mius line and bursting through the front of Hollidt's Sixth Army. A breakthrough here would give the Red Army a clear run through the southern Ukraine to the Dnieper. On 26 August, after being delayed for a week by a shortage of fuel and ammunition,* Rokossovsky's Central Front opened an attack which quickly tore a fifty-mile gap between Army Group Centre and

---

* In July and August the Soviet Fronts received 26.6 million shells and mines but expended no less than 42.1 million rounds, and the dumps were running low.

Army Group South, threatening the approaches to Kiev and an envelopment of the deep northern flank of Manstein's command.

On 27 August Hitler met Manstein in the stifling heat of Vinnitsa, the Führer headquarters in the Ukraine. Among Manstein's party was General Hollidt who presented some alarming figures:

> My XXIX Corps has 8706 men left. Facing it are 69,000 Russians. My XVII corps has 9284 men; facing it are 49,500 Russians. My IV Corps is relatively best off – it has 13,143 men, faced by 18,000 Russians. Altogether, 31,133 Germans against 136,500 Russians. The relative strength in armour is similar: Tolbukhin yesterday had 165 tanks in operation; we had seven tanks and thirty-eight assault guns.

At the meeting Manstein pressed Hitler for more freedom to make his own decisions and requested either immediate reinforcement or permission to evacuate the Donets basin. Hitler who, according to Manstein, was preoccupied with the situation in the Mediterranean and the gathering threat to Western Europe, ordered that the Donbas, with its industrial and mineral assets, was to be held. He made vague promises to provide Manstein with reinforcements drawn from Army Group Centre and Field Marshal von Küchler's Army Group North. They were not forthcoming. On 28 August Kluge hastened to Rastenburg to protest against the transfer of any of his troops. As Albert Seaton has observed:

> This was to become the pattern throughout the German Army, for not only did the bickering Jodl and Zeitzler compete in trying to draw off formations from each other's theatres, but the army group commanders in the East themselves vied against each other, and against Zeitzler, when the OKH passed on Hitler's orders to give up divisions to assist their neighbours. Their usual reaction was a visit or a telephone call direct to the tired Hitler who, by now, when faced with the necessity of making a decision between competing demands, having no reserves of his own to offer, often gave in to the last caller.

At the end of August the futility of standing on the Mius line was underlined when XXIX Panzer Corps, on the coast of the Sea of Azov, was encircled by two Soviet mechanized corps. XXIX Corps was extracted, with some difficulty, by 13th Panzer Division and Rudel's Stukageschwader. In a telephone call to the Führer,

Manstein demanded that Sixth Army be allowed to pull back some forty miles to a hastily erected barrier covering Stalino, the so-called 'Tortoise line'. At every turn crisis loomed.

Manstein and Kluge paid another call on Hitler at Rastenburg on 3 September. They found the Führer as reluctant as ever to make any hard decisions. He ignored a plea from the two field marshals to establish an integrated Supreme Command for all theatres of war under a single Chief of General Staff and to hand over his own control of the war in the East to a commander-in-chief who would exercise complete and independent command of operations in Russia. That Hitler would reject any abridgement of his personal authority was a foregone conclusion. To deal with the immediate situation, Manstein and Kluge were offered only crumbs of comfort. Kluge managed to secure Hitler's agreement to the withdrawal of the southern wing of Army Group Centre behind the Desna. Hitler also agreed to allow Manstein to pull back Sixth Army from the Mius line to the 'Tortoise line' if there was no alternative. On the same day General Sir Bernard Montgomery launched British Eighth Army across the Straits of Messina to land at Reggio di Calabria on the toe of Italy.

For Manstein there was no alternative but to withdraw. On 6 September a new assault by South-Western Front's Third Guards Army ripped open the newly established 'Tortoise line' at the junction of First Panzer Army and Sixth Army. After a supreme effort the thirty-mile gap was closed on 11–12 September by 23rd and 9th Panzer Divisions, but Red Army tanks merely found another gap in the line farther to the west and plunged on towards Dnepropetrovsk. Simultaneously, to the north, Rokossovsky's continuing offensive cut clean through the front of Second Army, threatening to engulf the northern wing of Army Group South.

On 7 September Manstein sent an urgent teleprinter message to Hitler:

> Fifty-five Soviet divisions and two tank corps are now facing the Army Group. Further forces from other Soviet fronts are being brought up. The Russians have concentrated their main effort here on the southern front. I need reinforcements or a free hand for a further withdrawal to shortened, more favourable sectors.

This terse message sent Hitler hurrying to his Condor for a flight to Zaporozhye where, on the 8th, he met Zeitzler at his head-quarters.

The mood at the meeting was sombre. Soviet 1st Mechanized Corps and 23rd Tank Corps had broken through north of the boundary between First Panzer and Sixth Armies and their recon-naissance detachments were nearing Pavlograd, thirty miles east of the Dnieper and 100 miles behind the German front. That day Krasnoarmyskoye had fallen to the Red Army. Flanked by Field Marshal von Kleist and the newly appointed commander of Seventeenth Army, General Jaenecke, Manstein briefed the Führer on the last few days' fighting, emphasizing the danger to the northern wing of Army Group South. If the Soviet envelopment was carried off, 'then two armies will be lost, my Führer, and nothing can ever bring them back again'. Nor could the situation on Manstein's southern flank be restored east of the Dnieper. In order to scrape together sufficient forces to save his northern flank, he urged a similar withdrawal to the Dnieper by Army Group Centre.

Later, Manstein wrote:

> Hitler now accepted in principle the need to take the right wing of the army group [South] back on the Melitopol–Dnieper line, though he still hoped to avoid doing so by bringing up new assault-gun battalions. As usual, he thought the use of techni-cal resources was sufficient to halt a development which, in fact, could have been averted only by throwing in several divisions. As for acquiring forces from Army Group Centre by taking it back to the upper Dnieper, Hitler maintained that it was impossible to withdraw that distance at such short notice. The muddy season would be upon us before a movement of those dimensions . . . could be completed, and, as had already happened in the evacuation of the Orel salient, too much equipment would be lost in the process. The best one could hope for was to withdraw to some intermediate line. This, of course, would not have achieved the manpower economy we were after.

Hitler made some concessions to reality. He agreed that it was necessary to strengthen Army Group South and directed Kluge to assemble a strong force in front of Kiev. He agreed to the liquidation of the Kuban bridgehead where Seventeenth Army was maintaining a tenuous toehold in the Caucasus. This last, however, was the only promise Hitler kept. On 14 September Manstein informed OKH that, in twenty-four hours, he would be forced to issue orders for a withdrawal behind the Dnieper, 100 miles to the rear. On the 15th he continued to press for reinforcements from Army Group Centre to avert not only the collapse of the southern sector but also that of the entire Eastern Front. This dire warning stirred Hitler into promising Manstein four of Kluge's divisions and further reinforcements from the West, but he had prevaricated too long. The withdrawal to the Dnieper had begun.

At the outset it was delayed by more of Hitler's meddling. The Führer insisted that First Panzer Army strengthen the bridgehead east of Zaporozhye to protect the nearby manganese mines at Nicopol; this was a complete waste of Manstein's scant reserves which were needed to shore up Army Group South's buckling left flank rather than retain a bridgehead which was tactically worthless.

At every stage the withdrawal threatened to dissolve into chaos. The fatal delay imposed by the Führer meant that there had been no time to prepare roads, river crossings, demolition charges or minefields. Manstein's task was to get four armies – plus refugees and prisoners – over five major river crossings – at Dnepropetrovsk, Kremenchug, Cherkassy, Kanev and Kiev – and then turn to defend a front of 450 miles.

The west bank of the Dnieper was supposed to have become an integral part of the East Wall, or Panther line, a fortifications system running from Lake Narva to the Sea of Azov. This might have held the Red Army in check until winter, when the Dnieper froze over, had it been built. But the Führer had refused requests to begin work, partly because of his pathological fear of withdrawal and partly because the Atlantic Wall was consuming all the available materials. After the failure at Kursk some effort had been made to build earthworks on the western bank of the Dnieper, but it was not until 12 August that the army groups were given the go-ahead to develop the defences. The order did not give them permission to withdraw to the East Wall which, in any case, was an illusion. Josef Goebbels reflected, 'The troops are naturally indignant that no eastern wall has been built along the Dnieper. That is the question officers as well as men keep repeating. No convincing answer can be given.'

Real enough, however, was the scorched-earth policy under-taken by the withdrawing Germans to 'sterilize' the rich farmlands and coalfields between the Donets and Dnieper. As von Mellenthin later wrote:

> As is well known the Russians make very limited use of supply columns, and their troops live mainly on the country . . . The only method of slowing armies of this kind is totally to destroy everything that can be used to feed and house them . . . We cer-tainly did not relish the idea of destroying all food supplies and putting a zone of scorched earth between us and the pursuing Russians. But the existence of an entire army group was at stake.*

But even here the Ostheer fell short of its objectives, lacking the equipment, available manpower and time to remove much heavy equipment or destroy what they abandoned. Behind it Army Group South also left 1.6 million tons of grain, most of it standing ready to be harvested, and 2.9 million horses and cattle. The south Ukraine also yielded an equally important human harvest for the Red Army: 80,000 men who were immediately given a gun and a uniform and sent to the front line. Those who survived would become good soldiers.

Survival was uppermost in the minds of the German troops slog-ging their way westwards in scattered regimental groups, harried all the way by Russian mobile columns, fighting by day and march-ing by night along main roads and railway lines. The race to the Dnieper ended in a virtual dead heat. On 21 September the first Red Army units arrived on the east bank of the river opposite Kanev as the Germans blew the last bridge and dug in on the west bank. Much heavy equipment had been lost in the withdrawal

---

* Manstein's scorched earth policy formed the basis of war crimes' charges brought against him by the British in 1949. On 24 February 1950 he was sen-tenced to eighteen years' imprisonment, commuted to twelve years. He did not serve the full term and was released on 6 May 1953.

and ammunition was in short supply. A report on the morale of Eighth Army submitted by General Wöhler on 2 September stated:

> While we are forced to conduct the most difficult ammunition tactics, the enemy has unlimited artillery and mortar ammunition available to him. With these weapons he creates focal points and thins out our ranks to such an extent that the manning of the main defensive lines can no longer be ensured and local defence groups, linked by patrols, have been formed. Whenever the enemy has broken in he can then only be dislodged by locally scraped-up reserves. Casualties are extremely high. This morning the combat strength of 39th Infantry Division was down to six officers and roughly 300 men ... Apart from their dwindling strength, the men's state of fatigue gives rise to great anxiety. I am informed by unit commanders that, owing to excessive fatigue, such a state of apathy has arisen among the troops that draconian measures do not at this moment produce the desired results, but only the good example of officers and 'kindly persuasion'. Both these, however, depend very greatly on the dwindling number of officers.

Ominous Russian bridgeheads had appeared on the Dnieper even as Army Group South established itself on the heights of the river's west bank. On the night of 22 September at Bukrin, forty-eight miles south-east of Kiev, four men of a sub-machine gun company crossed the Dnieper in a rowing boat and climbed several hundred feet up the bank, drawing heavy fire from German outposts. Others followed and, by daylight, a company had gained a foothold on the west bank. Then, like a swarm of ants, the whole of Third Guards Tank Army began to cross, the infantry using anything that would float – planks, doors, oil drums, even straw wrapped around ponchos – while the engineers built causeways for heavy equipment and artillery provided covering fire. The four sub-machine gunners were made Heroes of the Soviet Union,* the first of 2000 soldiers who won this honour during the battle for the Dnieper.

On the night of 25 September forward elements of Steppe

---

* A Hero of the Soviet Union was granted a pension for life and a life-size bust of him was put on display in his home town.

Front's Seventh Guards Army crossed the Dnieper south-west of Kremenchug. South-Western Front reached the Dnieper on 26 September when detachments of Sixth Army secured two small bridgeheads south of Dnepropetrovsk. Within a week, twenty-three bridgeheads, ranging in depth from 1000 yards to twenty miles, dotted the western bank of the Dnieper.

For a while it proved impossible to reinforce the bridgeheads. An attempt by the long-range bombers of the ADD on the night of 26 September to parachute in three airborne brigades to hold and expand the bridgehead at Bukrin ended in disaster. In early October Fifth Guards Tank Army reached the Dnieper near Zaporozhye where its engineers found two large barges abandoned by the Germans. They repaired them and, on the night of 5–6 October, ferried sixty tanks across. Two weeks later the Russians succeeded in reinforcing another bridgehead at Lyutezh, twenty miles north of Kiev. On 4 November tanks of Third Guards Tank Army broke out of the Lyutezh bridgehead, headlights blazing and sirens howling. Two days later they were in Kiev.

As the *rasputitsa* took its slimy grip on the steppe, Gerd Schmückle reflected on Kursk: 'What was it that the Führer had prophesied? . . . The battle will decide the war.' By the time Stavka was regrouping its forces for the battle of the Dnieper line the war had been lost. Less than twelve months earlier the Red Army had turned the tide at Stalingrad; it had seized the psychological advantage for the first time. But it was in the terrible killing grounds near Kursk that Hitler's panzers, and his ambitions, were dealt a blow from which they never recovered. Victory was a thing of the past. The premonition of defeat, which had stirred at Stalingrad, was now a daily reality for the officers and men of the Ostheer.

Hitler had intended Zitadelle to be a 'beacon' to the world and a reaffirmation of German power to his increasingly apprehensive allies. Instead, it had tripped a series of convulsions in the East which, in two and a half months, had thrown the Ostheer back 150 miles on a front of 650 miles.

Failure at Kursk had dealt the Ostheer heavier psychological and material blows than it had suffered at Stalingrad. After Stalingrad, Manstein had retrieved the situation, stabilized the front and retaken Kharkov. Now the Ostheer faced the prospect of permanent retreat and a growing manpower crisis. German manpower losses during the period of Kursk and the Russian counter-offensive were far greater than at Stalingrad where the Ostheer estimated that it had sustained 209,000 'irreplaceable' losses (dead, missing and one third of the wounded). In July–October 1943 'irreplaceable' losses on the Eastern Front, the greater part inflicted at Kursk and during the retreat to the Dnieper, were 365,000.

At Stalingrad the Red Army had fought on the basis of an approximate parity: one million Russians against the same number of Germans, Italians, Hungarians and Romanians. At Kursk it had gained a superiority of about 1.5:1 (1.3 million to 900,000 men). On the Dnieper in October 1943 the Red Army enjoyed a superiority in men of 2.2:1 (2.6 million troops against 1.2 million) and a superiority in both tanks and guns of 4:1. For the bombardment which preceded Kutuzov, 3000 guns and mortars and over 300 Katyusha launchers had been assembled, three times larger than the artillery which had supported the Moscow counter-offensive in December 1941 and a concentration one third more powerful than that at Stalingrad.

There were to be no more major German offensives in the East until the abortive attempt to relieve Budapest in January 1945. The story was one of Russian advance and German retreat. After the war Guderian reflected sadly on the fate of the panzers committed to Zitadelle:

> The armoured formations, reformed and re-equipped with much effort, had lost heavily in both men and equipment and would now be unemployable for a long time to come. It was problematical whether they could be rehabilitated in time to defend the Eastern Front; as for being able to use them in defence of the Western Front against the Allied landings that threatened next spring, this was even more questionable. Needless to say, the Russians exploited their victory to the full. There were to be no more periods of quiet on the Eastern Front. From now on the enemy was in undisputed possession of the initiative.

APPENDICES

Key to Map Symbols

GERMAN UNITS AND ALLIES

4Pz	Fourth Panzer Army
9	Ninth Army
XLVIII Pz Co	XLVIII Panzer Corps
A Det Kempf	Army Detachment Kempf
11Pz	11th Panzer Division
168	168th Infantry Division
10PzGr	10th Panzer Grenadier Division
GD	Grossdeutschland Division
LAH	SS Division Leibstandarte Adolf Hitler
SSR	SS Division Das Reich
SST	SS Division Totenkopf
Fus Rgt GD	Fusilier Regiment, Grossdeutschland Division
Gren Rgt GD	Grenadier Regiment, Grossdeutschland Division
3 Hungarian	Third Hungarian Army
✈	Airfield

SOVIET UNITS

40	Fortieth Army
5G	Fifth Guards Army
5GT	Fifth Guards Tank Army
5 SHOCK	Fifth Shock Army
31 T CO	31st Tank Corps
3 Mech Co	3rd Mechanized Corps
35 GR Co	35th Guard Rifle Corps
81 GR	81st Guards Rifle Division
107 R	107th Rifle Division
Popov	Popov's 'Front mobile group'

Notes on Personalities

Antonov, General A.I.

Chief of Operations, Soviet General Staff, from December 1942. From April 1943 he served simultaneously as First Deputy Chief of Staff. Chief of General Staff February 1945–March 1946

Bagramyan, Marshal I.Kh.

Commander of Eleventh Guards Army (formerly Sixteenth Army) at Kursk. Subsequently commander First Baltic Front 1943–45

Batov, General P.I.

Commander of Sixty-Fifth Army at Stalingrad and Kursk subsequently in Dnieper crossing and Belorussian offensive, in assault on East Pomerania and crossing of Oder estuary. Commander of Army in Germany 1945–49

Belov, Colonel-General P.A.

Commander of Sixty-First Army at Kursk, Dnieper crossing, advance into Poland and assault on Berlin. Commander Southern Ural Military District 1945–55

Guderian, Colonel-General Heinz

Appointed Inspector-General Armoured Troops, March 1943. Replaced Zeitzler as Chief of Army General Staff, July 1944. Dismissed by Hitler, after a blazing row, 28 March 1945

Hoth, General Hermann

Commander of Fourth Panzer Army at Kursk on southern side of salient. Dismissed by Hitler in November 1943, after the fall of Kiev, and retired from active service

Jodl, Colonel-General Alfried

Chief of Staff of the High Command of the German Armed Forces (OKW) 1939–45. Signed the German surrender at Rheims, 7 May 1945. Tried for war crimes at Nuremberg and hanged 16 October 1946

Keitel, Field Marshal Wilhelm

Chief of the High Command of the German Armed Forces (OKW) February 1938–May 1945. Tried for war crimes at Nuremberg and hanged 16 October 1946

Kleist, Field Marshal Ewald von

Commander Army Group A November 1942–April 1944. Died in Soviet prison camp in October 1954 after extradition from Yugoslavia in 1949

Kluge, Field Marshal Gunther von

Commander Army Group Centre 1942–43. Injured in air crash. Appointed C-in-C West July 1944 but relieved of his command on 15 August. His tenuous links with the conspirators in the bomb plot against Hitler on 20 July 1944 led him to commit suicide rather than face arrest

Konev, Marshal I.S.

Commander of Steppe Front at Kursk. Subsequently commanded Second and First Ukrainian Fronts in Soviet offensive in the Ukraine, Poland and the battle for Berlin. C-in-C Soviet forces of occupation in Austria and Hungary 1945–46

Malinovsky, Marshal R.Ia.

Commander of Southern, South-Western, Third and Second Ukrainian Fronts in offensive operations in Ukraine, Romania, Hungary, Austria and Czechoslovakia 1943–45. Commander Transbaikal Front in war with Japan 1945. Commander Far Eastern Military District, C-in-C Soviet Forces in Far East 1945–46

Manstein, Field Marshal Erich von

Commander Army Group Don 28 November 1942–14 February 1943. Commander Army Group South 12 February 1943–30 March 1944 when he was dismissed by Hitler after a series of disagreements

Mellenthin, Major-General F.W. von

Chief of Staff XLVIII Panzer Corps from 1 November 1942. Subsequently Chief of Staff Fourth Panzer Army August-September 1944. Thereafter Chief of Staff Army Group G until 5 December 1944. Attached to 9th Panzer Division January-February 1945 before appointment as Chief of Staff Fifth Panzer Army

Model, Field Marshal Walter

Commander of Ninth Army at Kursk. From October 1943 to August 1944 he was, successively, commander Army Groups North, South and Centre. Appointed C-in-C West August 1944. Replaced by Field Marshal von Rundstedt 5 September but remained in command of Army Group B. Committed suicide in the Ruhr pocket 21 April 1945

Novikov, Marshal Aleksandr

C-in-C Soviet Air Force from 1942 and responsible for air operations during the battles of Stalingrad, Kursk, Belorussia and Königsberg. In charge of Soviet air operations in Manchuria August 1945. Imprisoned by Stalin in 1946

Popov, General M.M.

Commander of 'Front mobile group' February 1943 during advance on Kharkov. Appointed commander Bryansk Front in May 1943. Subsequently commanded Second Baltic Front. Relieved of his command February 1944

Rokossovsky, Marshal K.K.

Commander of Don Front at Stalingrad and Central Front at Kursk. Subsequently commander First and Second Belorussian Fronts. C-in-C Soviet Forces in Poland 1945–49

Rotmistrov, Marshal Pavel

Commander of Fifth Guards Tank Army at Kursk and subsequently in the drive through the Baltic states with Third Belorussian Front in the autumn of 1944. Later Deputy Commander of Armoured Forces

Sokolovsky, Marshal V.

Commander of Western Front in the Soviet counter-offensive following Kursk. In 1944 transferred to First Ukrainian Front as Chief of Staff. Later Deputy Front commander with First Belorussian Front for the assault on Berlin. Identified Hitler's charred corpse from the Führer's dental records. Subsequently C-in-C Soviet Forces in Germany

Vasilevsky, Marshal A.M.

Appointed Chief of Soviet General Staff June 1942, in which capacity he served almost to the end of the war. Of 34 months in the post he spent 22 at various fronts. In February 1945 he took over command of Third Belorussian Front after the death of General Chernyakhovsky. C-in-C Soviet armies in the Far East August 1945

Vatutin, General N.F.

Commander of Voronezh Front at Kursk. On 6 November 1943 his command, renamed First Ukrainian Front, took Kiev. Killed by anti-Soviet partisans near Rovno 29 February 1944

Zeitzler, Colonel-General Kurt

Replaced Colonel-General Franz Halder as Chief of Army General Staff in September 1942. Responsible for planning of Zitadelle. Replaced by Guderian in July 1944 after the collapse of the German armies on the Upper Dnieper

Zhukov, Marshal G.K.

Appointed First Deputy Supreme Commander-in-Chief Soviet Armed Forces August 1942, in which capacity he served until the end of the war. Exercised key responsibility for the planning of the Stalingrad and Kursk battles. Co-ordinated First and Second Ukrainian Fronts in winter offensive of 1943–44. Commanded First Ukrainian Front, spring 1944, and co-ordinated First and Second Belorussian Fronts, summer offensive 1944. Commanded First Belorussian Front in final assault on Germany in 1945. C-in-C Soviet occupation forces in Germany 1945–46

Select Bibliography

Allen, W.E.D. and Muratoff, P. *The Russian Campaigns of 1941–43* (1944)

Batov, Omer *The Eastern Front 1941–45: German Troops and the Barbarisation of Warfare* (1985)

Bekker, Caius *The Luftwaff War Diaries* (1967)

Bialer, S. *Stalin and His Generals* (1970)

Bullock, Alan *Hitler, a Study in Tyranny* (1952)

Carell, Paul *Scorched Earth* (1970)

Clark, Alan *Barbarossa: Russian–German Conflict 1941–45* (1965)

Cooper, Matthew *The German Army 1933–1945* (1978)

—— *The Phantom War: The German Struggle Against Soviet Partisans 1941–44* (1979)

Dallin, Alexander *German Rule in Russia 1939–45* (1981)

Ellis, John *Brute Force* (1990)

Erickson, John *The Soviet High Command: A Military–Political History* (1962)

—— *The Road to Stalingrad* (1975)

—— *The Road to Berlin* (1983)

Fest, Joachim *Hitler* (1973)

Foote, A. *A Handbook for Spies* (1967)

Gallagher *The Soviet History of World War II: Myth, Memories and Realities* (1963)

Garthoff, Raymond *Soviet Military Doctrine* (1953)

Glantz, David M. *Soviet Military Deception in World War II* (1989)

Goebbels, J. *The Goebbels Diaries* (1948)

Görlitz, W. *Der Zweit Weltkrieg* (2 Vols) (1951/2)

—— *The German General Staff 1657–1945* (1953)

Guderian, Heinz *Panzer Leader* (1952)

Halder, F. *Hitler as War Lord* (1950)

Irving, David *Hitler's War* (1977)

Jukes, Geoffrey *Kursk: The clash of Armour* (1968)

Keegan, John *The Second World War* (1989)

Kleine, Egon and Kühn Volkmar *Tiger: The History of a Legendary Weapon* (1989)

Klink, E. *Das Gesetz des Handelns 'Zitadelle' 1943* (1966)

Larson, Kent A. *The Battle of Prokhorovka: Death Ride of the Panzers?* (unpublished ms)

Lucas, James *War on the Eastern Front 1941–45* (1978)

—— *Das Reich* (1991)

Manstein, Erich von *Lost Victories* (1958)

Mellenthin, F.W. von *Panzer Battles* (1955)

Morozov, V.P. *Zapadnee Voronezha* (1956)

Orgill, Douglas *T–34: Russian Armour* (1970)

Overy, Richard *The Air War 1939–45* (1980)

Parotkin, Ivan (ed.) *Kursk* (1974)

Paul, W. *Geschichte der 18 Panzer Division 1940–43* (n.d.)

Popel, N.K. *Geroi Kurskoibituy* (1971)

—— *Tanki povernuli na zapad* (1960)

Quarrie, Bruce *Panzer Grenadier Division 'Grossdeutschland'*

Read, Anthony and Fisher, David *Operation Lucy* (1980)

Rokossovsky, KK. *A Soldier's Duty*

Rotmistrov, Pavel *'Tanks Against Tanks'* (in *Main Front*, 1987)

Rudel, Hans-Ulrich *Stuka Pilot* (1952)

Schmückle, Gerd *Ohne Pauken und Trompeten Erinner ungen an Krieg und Frieden* (1982)

Schramm, P. (ed.) *Kriegstagebuch des OKW der Wehrmacht* (8 vols, 1963)

Schwabedissen, Walter *The Russian Air Force in the Eyes of German Commanders* (1960)

Seaton, Albert *The Fall of Fortress Europe* (1981)

—— *Stalin as Warlord* (1976)

Shtemenko, S.M. *The Soviet General Staff at War* (1941–45)

Shores, Christopher *Duel for the Sky* (1985)

Spaeter, H. and Schramm, W. *Die Geschichte des Panzerkorps Grossdeutschland* (1958)

Speer, Albert *Inside the Third Reich* (1979)

Stadler, Sylvester *Die Offensive gegen Kursk 11 SS Panzerkorps* (1980)

Stein, G.H. *The Waffen SS 1939–45* (1977)

Trevor-Roper, Hugh *Hitler's Table Talk* (1973)

Warlimont, Walter *Inside Hitler's Headquarters* (1964)

Weidinger, O. *Division Das Reich, vol. 4* (1979)

Wheeler-Bennett, John W. *The Nemesis of Power: The German Army in Politics 1918–1945* (1954)

Zhukov, G.K. *Marshal Zhukov's Greatest Battles* (1969)

Picture Acknowledgments

The publishers would like to thank the following sources:

Fotokhronika Tass 1 *(top right and bottom)*, 5 *(top)*, 7 *(bottom)*, 12 *(full)*, 13 *(top and bottom*, 14 *(full)*, 15 *(full)*, 16 *(top and bottom)*; Mary Evans Picture Library 1*(middle)*, 8/9 *(full)*, 11*(bottom)*; Robert Hunt Library 5 *(bottom)*; Suddeutscher Verlag 1(top left), 2*(top and bottom)*, 3*(top and bottom)*, 6 *(top and bottom)*, 7*(top)*, 10*(top and bottom)*, 11*(top)*

INDEX